TIRED

OF

WINNING

ALSO BY JONATHAN KARL

Betrayal

Front Row at the Trump Show

The Right to Bear Arms:
The Rise of America's New Militias

TIRED

OF

WINNING

DONALD TRUMP
AND
THE END OF
THE GRAND OLD PARTY

JONATHAN KARL

DUTTON

DUTTON

An imprint of Penguin Random House LLC
penguinrandomhouse.com

LIBRARY OF CONGRESS CATALOGING-IN-PUBLICATION DATA
has been applied for.

ISBN 9780593473986 (hardcover)
ISBN 9780593473993 (ebook)

Printed in the United States of America
1st Printing

For my family

CONTENTS

TIRED
OF
WINNING

INTRODUCTION

On the roadway outside the Mar-a-Lago Club in Palm Beach, Florida, a few dozen Trump diehards showed up to herald the big announcement. Decked out in gear emblazoned with the former president's name, they came armed with flags—not American flags, but Trump flags, hailing his last campaign rather than the one he was set to announce. The biggest banner of all loudly proclaimed, TRUMP WON.

The atmosphere was festive but the crowd was small. There had been about as many people waiting in line at Howley's diner across the lagoon earlier in the day. But the limited turnout wasn't for lack of hype. Trump had promoted the impending launch of his third presidential campaign as perhaps the "most important speech given in the history of the United States of America" and a day—November 15, 2022—that "will be remembered FOREVER."*

---

*This line echoed the way Donald Trump described January 6. "These are the things and events that happen when a sacred landslide election victory is so unceremoniously &

1

The setting was fittingly opulent for such a grand occasion. Lincoln delivered the Gettysburg Address on a scarred battlefield in southern Pennsylvania; Trump's play for history would come under the grandiose crystal chandeliers, gold-adorned mirrors, and gilded Corinthian columns of the Mar-a-Lago ballroom.

Two days earlier, Trump's preparation had included a round of golf with Senator Lindsey Graham of South Carolina, who used the time on the links to encourage Trump to hold off on launching another presidential campaign. The effort to delay continued into the afternoon, with Senator Graham later meeting Chris Ruddy, a Mar-a-Lago member and longtime Trump friend, for lunch and asking him to help convince the former president to pull the plug on the planned announcement. As they spoke, Graham got a call from Fox News host Sean Hannity, who was on the same page: There needed to be an all-out effort to talk Trump out of kicking off his third campaign—at least for now.

Many of Trump's most longtime supporters and advisors wanted nothing to do with his supposed rendezvous with history, and neither did most of his own family. Trump's children were all together at Mar-a-Lago for his daughter Tiffany's wedding the weekend before his planned announcement, but they quickly dispersed before their father jumped into the 2024 fray. Tiffany was off on her honeymoon. Don Jr. had embarked on a hunting trip, and claimed bad weather prevented him from making it back in time. Even daughter Ivanka—who was front and center for Trump's first campaign launch in 2015

---

viciously stripped away from great patriots who have been badly & unfairly treated for so long," Trump wrote a few hours after the attack on the Capitol, in a message that was later deleted by Twitter. He added, "Go home with love & in peace. Remember this day forever!"

and served as his senior advisor in the White House—opted to stay away, releasing a statement wishing her father well but making clear she would have nothing to do with a campaign this time around. Trump's wife, Melania, agreed to be there, but only after what was described to me by a Trump family friend as some fairly intense negotiations—and the former first lady remained mostly out of sight of the cameras, spending less than thirty seconds onstage at the very end of her husband's speech.

I arrived at Mar-a-Lago a few hours before the main event, returning to the place Trump called the "Southern White House" for the first time since I'd spoken with him there weeks after he left the actual White House as a defeated and disgraced president. In my March 2021 interview, which took place in the middle of the club's lobby, Trump lashed out at many of the Republicans who had served him. He said Attorney General Bill Barr had betrayed him by debunking his stolen-election claims, and he accused former United Nations ambassador Nikki Haley of being disloyal—pronouncing her political career over—because she had condemned his behavior on January 6. He mocked Senator Graham for crawling back to him "maybe a few hours" after trying to distance himself following the attack on the Capitol, and he slammed the Republicans who had voted to impeach him, including "stupid Liz Cheney." He took shots at Senate Republican leader Mitch McConnell and House Republican leader Kevin McCarthy. "If McConnell and McCarthy fought harder," Trump told me, "you could have a Republican president right now. And now they don't have anything."[1]

I could tell Trump was relishing the opportunity to trash his fellow Republicans—he seemed to enjoy it more than going after his real political opponents in the Democratic Party. "You know what?" he said. "I find this stuff so exhilarating and so interesting. You see, Biden couldn't have this conversation with you."

Trump harbored no such resentment, however, for those who stormed the Capitol on January 6 and threatened his vice president, chanting, "Hang Mike Pence!" "Well, they were angry," he told me. "It's common sense, Jon."

I didn't try to debate with Trump in that interview or to argue with him. I was trying to draw out his true thoughts about the destructive end of his presidency, and I couldn't believe what I had just heard: Trump was not only refusing to condemn calls for his own vice president's execution; he was justifying them! I figured these words would surely be the last straw, driving top Republicans to finally disavow the leader of their party once and for all. But when the audio was published, GOP officials greeted the former president's comments with a shrug—or ignored them altogether.

I was reminded of those "Hang Mike Pence!" chants as I walked by the Trump diehards on my way back into Mar-a-Lago. The flags they were waving were like the two enormous TRUMP 2020 banners that had been draped over the inaugural platform on the west side of the Capitol on January 6 as the rioters made their way inside. But the atmosphere was entirely different. The people standing outside the resort where Trump would be making his announcement didn't look like a threat to the Republic; they looked like aging hippies hanging outside a Woodstock anniversary concert because they couldn't get tickets to see the show.

Once I was inside, the first familiar face I saw was that of Mike Lindell, the mustachioed businessman who peddles pillows and conspiracy theories about voting machines. He was loitering near the television cameras in the back of the room, eager to be interviewed but not generating much interest. His reputation as a loudmouth preceded him: When you try to talk to Lindell about politics, he shouts at you just as he does in his MyPillow infomercials, but with less credibility.

A few other Trump-list celebrities were in attendance. Convicted felon Roger Stone was milling about, as was Sebastian Gorka, who served briefly in the Trump White House and is known best for hawking Relief Factor pills on Fox News. And sitting prominently in the second row was a guy dressed in a suit designed to look like a brick wall. Back in the 2020 campaign, the man had developed a modest social media following by wearing his brick suit to Trump rallies. Now he had a prime seat for the 2024 launch.

The list of who *wasn't* there is much more telling, as nearly every high-profile figure from Trump's White House and previous campaigns decided they had better places to be. Kellyanne Conway was missing in action, as were the other key players in his 2016 campaign—Steve Bannon, Hope Hicks, and Dan Scavino. Trump's Treasury secretary, Steven Mnuchin, didn't show, and neither did his secretary of state Mike Pompeo. In fact, not a single confirmed cabinet secretary from the Trump administration made the trek to Mar-a-Lago. Trump had four press secretaries and four chiefs of staff over the course of his four-year presidency, and went zero for eight in getting any of them to be there for his big day.

This wasn't a coincidence—the people who knew Trump best actively decided to steer clear of his launch. The former president had hoped to showcase his sustained political strength by parading a number of supportive Republican lawmakers through the hall, but only two members of Congress were spotted: Representative Troy Nehls of Texas and Representative Madison Cawthorn, the scandal-plagued twenty-seven-year-old who had managed to lose a Republican primary in North Carolina with Trump's endorsement months earlier and would be leaving public office in a matter of weeks. Representative Matt Gaetz of Florida—who was among those who'd urged Trump to delay the campaign announcement—said that he wanted to go but that he had to stay in Washington for votes. The last House vote that day was at 1:17 P.M., and Trump's speech at Mar-a-Lago began at 9 P.M.

Some of the no-shows offered strikingly lame excuses. Sean Spicer, the longtime Republican flack who sacrificed his dignity to serve as Trump's first press secretary, was spotted at the West Palm Beach airport the day after his former boss's announcement. What kept him away? He hadn't "adjusted to daylight savings time yet," he said. It had been nine days at that point since clocks had been set back an hour.

Media outlets couldn't skip the event entirely, like Spicer did, but many of them ducked out early. CNN cut away from Trump's speech after about thirty minutes, and even Fox News didn't air the diatribe in full. Trump's favorite newspaper, the *New York Post*, mocked the former president in the following morning's edition, confining the news to a single line at the bottom of the front page: FLORIDA MAN MAKES ANNOUNCEMENT. On page 26, the *Post* also noted Trump was famous "for gold-plated lobbies and for firing people on reality television," and would be seventy-eight on Election Day.

The distinct lack of enthusiasm didn't seem to bother Trump as he entered the ballroom to the soundtrack from *Les Misérables*. The words blaring from the ballroom speakers while Trump walked to the stage set the tone Trump wanted set:

Do you hear the people sing?
Singing a song of angry men?

But once Trump started speaking, the men and women in the ballroom seemed more bored than riled up. About thirty-five minutes into the speech, I noticed a few attendees were getting up to leave. Before too long, what had started as a trickle became a steady stream of people working their way to the exit near the back of the room. Once people heard Trump announce he was running for president again and snapped some selfies with the former president speaking in the background, they didn't want to sit through his ramblings about past glories and why he was now a victim. As the exodus grew, the staff blocked the exit, citing security. Visitors were told they could not leave until the event was over. They were now captive at Mar-a-Lago.

Watching from afar, Steve Bannon, Trump's former chief strategist, found the speech devoid of the kind of disruptive, controversial, and counterrevolutionary ideas that ignited Trump's first run for the White House. In this speech, Trump offered a series of stale and unoriginal ideas, like imposing term limits on members of Congress in order "to further drain the swamp." To Bannon, that was a joke. "We had a chance to drain the swamp," Bannon told me after the speech. Of Trump, he added, "You chose sides. You ain't draining, you're filling."

The world had changed dramatically since 2015, but Trump's third campaign announcement did bear some resemblance to his first, when he descended a Trump Tower escalator next to Melania. In each instance, he didn't bother leaving home to let the world know he was running for president—the first announcement taking place down the elevator from his Trump Tower apartment, and this one down the stairs from his Mar-a-Lago residence. And at the start of both campaigns, he had virtually no support from prominent Republican officials or party donors. In 2015, Trump had so few political followers at the start of his campaign that he put out a casting call offering aspiring actors fifty dollars to enthusiastically cheer him on through his opening speech; in 2022, his team barred the exits to ensure people stuck around for the entire address.[2]

But the Donald Trump who spoke at Mar-a-Lago in November 2022 was not the same person who had come down the escalator seven years earlier. In 2015, the self-described billionaire and reality-TV star—with his own private jet and a supermodel wife—could present himself to Republican primary voters as the ultimate winner. He can't anymore.

Against most of his own allies' wishes, Trump chose to announce his third presidential campaign exactly one week after the GOP suffered crushingly disappointing results in the midterm elections—results that arguably did more damage to the former president's standing in the party than his role in the January 6 attack on the Capitol.

Apparently to some, inciting an insurrection is bad, but losing clearly winnable Senate races—that's inexcusable.

After two years of out-of-control inflation, rising crime, and chaos along the southern border, Republicans—and just about everyone else—expected voters to punish President Joe Biden and incumbent Democrats with a red wave rivaling the GOP's Tea Party gains in 2010. It didn't happen.

Instead, Republicans lost dozens of seats they believed they would win, barely gaining control of the House of Representatives and losing ground in the Senate. And as the disappointing results came in, no factor loomed larger than Donald Trump. Many of the candidates the party put up were hand selected by the former president in the primaries, and he picked some real crackpots. And the more electable nominees were forced to defend Trump's lies about the 2020 election or else face withering attacks from the leader of their party. American voters had clearly had enough—and the dismal election results finally woke some top Republicans, at least for a moment, from their yearslong stupor: *We can't win with this guy anymore.*

Tracking the returns on ABC News's election night broadcast, I relayed to viewers what was quickly becoming the key takeaway in Washington: "The biggest loser of the night is Donald Trump." That may have been obvious on November 8, 2022, but the truth is, Trump wasn't just the biggest loser of the midterm cycle. He's the biggest loser in the history of American politics—and he'd earned that title well before the first votes had been counted in 2022.

Six years earlier, Trump had shocked the world and won an election almost nobody thought he could win. It was arguably the biggest electoral upset the United States had ever seen—a genuinely impressive feat for someone with no political experience. He survived controversies that would have destroyed just about anybody else, and he vanquished enemies—Democratic and Republican alike. He presided over a legitimately strong economy until the pandemic hit in 2020, and despite his belligerence and ignorance of global affairs, his four years in office coincided with relative peace around the world. You don't become the biggest loser without having a hell of a lot to lose.

And Trump did have a hell of a lot to lose. He entered office in January 2017 not only with an opportunity to redefine the Republican Party for decades to come, but also having built a brand as one of the most successful businessmen in America. Sure, he wasn't *actually* as prosperous as he claimed—his empire was built on a mountain of debt, and he found a way to go bankrupt six times in the hotel and casino business—but he managed to define himself as a symbol of wealth in the American psyche.[3] There's a reason hip-hop artists reference Trump in their songs about becoming rap moguls and not, say, Stephen Schwarzman or Sam Walton.

Winning—and winning bigly—was key to crafting and maintaining this image, and a hallmark of Trump's first presidential bid in 2015. "We are going to win so much, you may even get tired of winning," Trump famously boasted in April 2016. "And you'll say, 'Please, please, it's too much winning, we can't take it anymore, we can't take it anymore, Mr. President—it's too much.' And I'll say, 'No, it isn't. We have to keep winning. We have to win more. We're going to win more.'"[4]

There was a certain logic to this obsession. "If you have a record of winning, people are going to follow you," he told biographer Michael D'Antonio before launching his first campaign. "You can be tough and ruthless and all that stuff and if you lose a lot, nobody's going to follow you, because you're looked at as a loser."[5]

Those ten words—"if you lose a lot, nobody's going to follow you"—explain Trump's behavior after the 2020 election better than just about anything that's been written in the years since. He was so terrified of his winning being exposed as a facade that he was willing to tear down American democracy. He knew that if his devotees accepted the truth—that he lost to Biden by seventy-four electoral votes and more than seven million individual votes—Trump's time as a force within Republican politics would come to an end. If his image as a winner was Trump's superpower with Republicans, losing is his kryptonite.

American history is filled with stories of men and women who suffered great defeats, faced adversity, learned from their mistakes, and bounced back to reach even greater heights. That's Abraham Lincoln's story. That's Martin Luther King Jr.'s story. In some ways, that's the story of the United States itself, beginning with the Continental Army's crushing defeat at Fort Washington in November 1776. The comeback kid is a quintessentially American story, but it's not Donald Trump's.

Trump's story—the story this book will attempt to tell—is one of failure. His most visible defeat may have come in November 2020, but Donald Trump was losing long before he entered politics and he's continued losing after he left the White House. His losses are so big and so thorough, they have infected just about everything and everyone he's touched. Donald Trump is the biggest loser, yes, but so are many of the people who crossed his path as he ascended to the presidency: the people who remained loyal to him and the people who betrayed him; the people who enabled him and the people who confronted him. Humiliation. Unemployment. Jail. Few who come in contact with Trump walk away better off for having done so.

But there is one area where Trump has been an undisputed winner. Over and over again, he has vanquished once-prominent Republicans who have tried to take him down, and in the process, he has remade the party in his own image. His luck may run out in 2024. Some of the most powerful people in the party are certainly tired of winning, or, more precisely, tired of Trump winning. Once again, they are determined to stop him. But whether Trump wins the GOP nomination again or loses it—or whether the prosecutors finally catch up to him and he goes to prison, for that matter—the party has changed. This is no longer the party of Reagan and Bush, Romney and McCain. It's the party of Donald Trump.

CHAPTER ONE

"COME RETRIBUTION"

Twenty-five years before my first book about Donald Trump was published, I wrote a paperback entitled *The Right to Bear Arms: The Rise of America's New Militias.* My first book, written in the wake of Timothy McVeigh's 1995 bombing of the Oklahoma City federal building, tracks the emerging anti-government movement that inspired McVeigh to make war on federal law enforcement agencies that he, and many other far-right activists, believed posed a threat both to America and to themselves.

On the cover of the book is a photograph of a building engulfed in flames—the Branch Davidians' Waco, Texas, compound called Mount Carmel. Federal law enforcement learned the group was stockpiling weapons and explosives and, after a disastrous fifty-one-day siege in early 1993, attempted to storm the compound. With agents closing in, several Branch Davidians set fire to the building, apparently preferring to die rather than be captured by authorities. The body of the cult's leader, David Koresh, was found with a gunshot to the head. Investigators concluded he was killed by one of his deputies.

The episode was widely considered a colossal failure by the FBI and the Bureau of Alcohol, Tobacco, and Firearms (ATF), which coordinated the assault. To some, though, the debacle represented something far more sinister than a federal raid gone horribly wrong—they saw it as a deliberate plot by the FBI and the ATF to trap and murder the Branch Davidians.

The Right to Bear Arms tracks how the Waco siege became a rallying cry for a national movement of mostly right-wing activists who believed Washington, DC, was dangerously corrupt and out to get them. Forming what they called "citizens' militias," they stockpiled arms and ammunition as well as food and survival gear. Some of them played weekend war games, practicing makeshift military maneuvers in vacant parking lots, on farmland, or in remote woodlands. I interviewed members of these groups. I read their writings, listened to their talk shows on shortwave radio, and attended some of their meetings.

"The ranks of the militias are made up of factory workers, veterans, computer programmers, farmers, housewives, small-business owners," I wrote in the book's introduction. "The most shocking thing about these 'paramilitary extremists' is how normal they are. They are your neighbors. But in another sense, many members of America's new militias live in a parallel universe, where civil war is already being waged by tyrants within the federal government."

On the furthest fringes of this movement were individuals who wanted to take revenge on the federal agencies responsible for not only the siege in Waco but a host of other transgressions—both real and imagined. McVeigh, for example, cited the government's "increasingly militaristic and violent" actions as his rationale in a letter to Fox News correspondent Rita Cosby weeks before he was executed under the federal death penalty. In the letter, he argued that his bombing of the federal building in Oklahoma City—at the time the deadliest domestic terrorist attack in American history—was "morally and strategically equivalent" to the US military striking government buildings in countries around the world.[1]

But McVeigh was an exception that proved the rule. For the most part, the members of these citizens' militias I encountered condemned the Oklahoma City bombing. They weren't terrorists; they were ordinary Americans who had grown increasingly paranoid. "Their mantra is self-defense," I wrote in 1995. "They have formed not to wage a campaign of terror but to defend themselves from a terror campaign they believe is already being waged by their own federal government."[2]

In the run-up to my book's publication, I planned a small party for friends and family at the Heartland Brewery in Manhattan and decided to spruce up the party invitation with some over-the-top words of praise from my friends and colleagues. A couple of my fellow reporters at the *New York Post* offered up some choice words, and on a whim, I decided to call a famous New Yorker who was both a reliable source and known for making hyperbolic statements to see if he would give me a quote as well. He readily agreed to provide a glowing endorsement of the book—provided I wrote it up myself. So I did:

> *"What a book! Karl is one of the best in the business— tough, fair and brutally honest."*
>
> —DONALD J. TRUMP

Trump signed off on the quote. To this day, I don't know whether he actually read the advance copy of *The Right to Bear Arms* I sent him—but more than a quarter of a century later, he announced that the first rally of his 2024 presidential campaign would be held in a familiar location: Waco, Texas.

Largely irrelevant in both the Republican primary and the general election, Texas was an odd choice for the campaign kickoff. A Trump spokesman would later deny the venue selection was at all related to the massacre that took place there almost exactly thirty years earlier—he claimed Waco was chosen solely because it was "centrally located" and "close" to big cities like Dallas and Houston[3]—but plenty of rally attendees drew the connection between the setting and Trump's central campaign message.

"[Trump's] making a statement, I believe, by coming to these stomping grounds where the government, the FBI, laid siege on this community just like they laid siege on Mar-a-Lago and went in and took his stuff," Charles Pace, a Branch Davidian pastor who knew Koresh but left the Mount Carmel compound several years before the deadly fire, told *The Texas Tribune*'s Robert Downen. "He's not coming right out and saying, 'Well, I'm doing it because I want you to know what happened there was wrong.' But he implies it."[4]

Shortly after the rally was announced, I asked Steve Bannon, who had served as the CEO of Trump's 2016 campaign and had once again emerged as one of Trump's most important advisors, why the former president would go to Waco for his big campaign reboot. He wasn't particularly coy.

"We're the Trump Davidians," he told me with a laugh.

Even less subtle than the rally's venue was how Trump kicked it off, standing silently onstage with his hand on his heart while he waited for the playing of "The Star-Spangled Banner." But this wasn't a traditional version of the national anthem. Trump's campaign had queued up "Justice for All," a rendition of the song recorded over a jailhouse phone by a group of about twenty inmates serving time in a Washington, DC, jail for taking part in the assault on the US Capitol.* In the song, the so-called J6 Prison Choir makes its way through Francis Scott Key's lyrics while Trump's voice interjects with stray lines from the Pledge of Allegiance, which he recorded at Mar-a-Lago.†

As the recording blared over the loudspeakers, video footage from the January 6 riot played on the massive screens flanking the stage. It was a bizarre display, but also pitch-perfect in setting the tone for what was to come over the next ninety minutes: a defiant Trump at his most inflammatory, telling his followers to prepare for one final standoff with the shadowy enemies out to get him—and them. "For seven years, you and I have been taking on the corrupt, rotten, and sinister forces trying to destroy America," he said. "They've been trying to destroy it. They're not going to do it, but they do get closer and closer with rigged elections."

"2024," Trump declared, "is the final battle."

This wasn't a campaign speech in any traditional sense. Trump echoed the themes of paranoia and foreboding embraced by David

---

* The Trump associates who helped produce the song have declined to identify exactly which inmates participated in its final recording, but *The Washington Post* was able to identify five prisoners who appeared in an earlier video recording. Four of the five had been charged with violently assaulting police officers. (Isaac Arnsdorf, Meg Kelly, Rachel Weiner, and Tom Jackman, "Behind Trump's Musical Tribute to Some of the Most Violent Jan. 6 Rioters," *Washington Post*, May 4, 2023.)

† "Justice for All" would go on to reach the top of the iTunes and Billboard charts, and Trump would later tell Fox News's Sean Hannity that the song's success made him "feel like Elvis."

Koresh and the anti-government movement that grew out of the Waco massacre. "As far as the eye can see, the abuses of power that we're currently witnessing at all levels of government will go down as among the most shameful, corrupt, and depraved chapters in all of American history," he said.

The substance of Trump's grievances paled in comparison to the resentments harbored by the people I wrote about in *The Right to Bear Arms*. Twenty-five years ago, members of those citizens' militias had some legitimate reasons to distrust the federal government. Their behavior was extreme, but they were responding to tangible government actions that had resulted in death and destruction. More than eighty Branch Davidians died in the Waco siege. Three other people had been killed in the Ruby Ridge standoff one year earlier, when federal law enforcement officials tried to arrest a survivalist and self-described white separatist named Randy Weaver—who lived in a plywood cabin with no electricity or running water in northern Idaho—on weapons violations. Weaver was eventually acquitted of the original firearms charges, but his life was never the same: His wife, son, and dog were killed during the standoff—his wife shot by an FBI sniper while she was holding their ten-month-old daughter. The episode left an indelible stain on the FBI's reputation, with several agents censured and suspended after a lengthy investigation. "Don't call Randy Weaver paranoid," I wrote in the book. "His worst fears about the government have already come true."

As Bannon made clear in my conversation with him, Trump's presence in Waco that day was designed to evoke similar feelings of injustice and persecution among the former president's followers. "They're not coming after me," he told the crowd. "They're coming after you—and I'm just standing in their way, and I'm going to be standing in their way for a long time."

Trump had used variations of the line before. "It was not just my home that was raided last month," he said at a September 2022 rally in Pennsylvania, referencing the search warrant the FBI had executed at Mar-a-Lago. "It was the hopes and dreams of every citizen who I've been fighting for since the moment I came down the golden escalator in 2015."

The message certainly seemed to resonate with his supporters, but its brazenness was staggering. Whatever you think about the investigations Trump was facing at the time, he certainly invited the scrutiny. Special Counsel Jack Smith was probing Trump's role in the January 6 attack and his failure to turn over classified material the FBI found at Mar-a-Lago. Fulton County district attorney Fani Willis was investigating his efforts to overturn the 2020 presidential election results in Georgia. And Manhattan district attorney Alvin Bragg was nearing an indictment on charges related to hush-money payments Trump made weeks before the 2016 election to a porn star, Stormy Daniels, with whom he'd allegedly had an affair.

The folks cheering Trump at his rallies had not taken boxes stuffed with classified documents out of the White House—and it's safe to assume none of them spent tens of thousands of dollars to cover up an affair with an adult-film star. Several hundred Trump supporters were being prosecuted for assaulting police officers and storming the Capitol on January 6, but Trump—the man responsible for whipping those rioters into a frenzy—couldn't do anything to stand in the way of those prosecutions. As president, he could have issued preemptive pardons for all of them. He didn't. Now he was just cheering on the defendants and lashing out at the prosecutors on social media. "The DOJ and FBI are destroying the lives of so many Great American Patriots, right before our very eyes," he posted on Truth Social the day after four members of the far-right Proud Boys militia were convicted of seditious conspiracy. "GET SMART AMERICA, THEY ARE COMING AFTER YOU!!!"[5]

But in reality, "they" weren't coming after Trump's law-abiding supporters—they were coming after Trump. Decades earlier, presidential candidate Bill Clinton told voters he felt their pain. Trump was now doing the reverse, trying to convince his supporters to feel his pain as if it were their own. "Our enemies are desperate to stop us because they know that we are the only ones who can stop them," Trump told the crowd in Waco. "Our opponents have done everything they can to crush our spirit and to break our will, but they failed. They've only made us stronger."

Trump's Waco speech was too grim for even some of his closest allies in the media. "[Trump] opened up with January 6 video, which is *insane*," Brian Kilmeade said on *Fox & Friends* days later. "He should be running from that, period. I don't care his point of view, that is *not* a good thing for him. I thought that was absolutely awful."[6]

The source of the criticism was notable. During Trump's presidency, one of the most surefire ways to get his attention was to appear on *Fox & Friends* in the morning. The show's hosts—Kilmeade, Steve Doocy, and Ainsley Earhardt—were prominent members of what was often referred to as Trump's "Cable News Cabinet." Advice they provided from the studio couch in midtown Manhattan frequently carried as much weight in Trump's mind as his actual advisors in the White House or at Mar-a-Lago. But not this time.

Trump was in a dark place in early 2023. Still reeling politically from the Republican Party's disappointing midterm performance the previous November, he'd launched his third presidential campaign but barely seemed to be trying. A close confidant of the former president told me he was trying to get Trump to do more to jump-start his effort to win back the White House, encouraging him, for example, to go on the attack against President Biden and the Democrats over the federal bailout of Silicon Valley Bank, which failed in March 2023. This advisor was urging Trump to tie the bank's failure to various Democratic policies, and contrast the effort to protect the bank's wealthy tech-industry depositors with the neglect of working-class people struggling after a train carrying toxic chemicals derailed in East Palestine, Ohio.

Trump, however, was too distracted. "I've been working non-fucking-stop on this Silicon Valley Bank thing with him, and I've got nothing," the advisor told me in mid-March. "He's just *obsessed* with this New York thing."

The "New York thing," of course, was Alvin Bragg's grand jury investigation into a hush-money payment Trump had made to adult-film star Stormy Daniels seven years earlier. The case was long believed to be dead—two investigators in Bragg's office had resigned in early 2022 in protest of his decision not to move forward with their inquiry—but on January 30, 2023, the Manhattan DA's office had impaneled a new grand jury and begun presenting evidence of Trump's involvement in the catch-and-kill scheme intended to suppress unflattering stories prior to the 2016 presidential election.[7] Over the next few weeks, it became clear the first presidential indictment in history was imminent—but nobody knew exactly when Bragg would pull the trigger.

Except, apparently, Donald Trump.

"THE FAR & AWAY LEADING REPUBLICAN CANDIDATE & FORMER PRESIDENT OF THE UNITED STATES OF AMER-ICA, WILL BE ARRESTED ON TUESDAY OF NEXT WEEK," he posted, in all caps, on Truth Social at 7:25 A.M. on March 18. "PRO-TEST, TAKE OUR NATION BACK!"[8]

Political journalists scrambled to find out what Trump was talking about. Why hadn't anybody tipped them off that such momentous news was coming? Had Bragg officially communicated to the former president's legal team what to expect? How else could Trump have been so confident about the exact date of his arrest?

One of Trump's lawyers, Joe Tacopina, would later tell reporters the former president's legal team had not been informed of any impending indictment—and he was right. So where did Trump get the idea he was about to be arrested? A source close to Trump told me the former president learned of his pending indictment from a cable news show called *Morning Joe: Weekend*. The 6 A.M. Saturday show on MSNBC didn't have many viewers, but Trump was watching, taking particular interest in a segment—a rerun from two days earlier—featuring legal analyst Andrew Weissmann on the Manhattan DA's investigation. Discussing Bragg's recent interactions with Trump's legal team and the grand jury, Weissmann said he couldn't see the DA *not* indicting the former president, telling the show's cohost Joe Scarborough that he believed such a move was imminent. "We should be very conscious that this is likely to come down soon," he said.

Trump, according to my source, interpreted Weissmann's speculation about the timing of an indictment as fact. "IT'S TIME!!!"

Trump wrote on his Truth Social platform. "THEY'RE KILLING OUR NATION AS WE SIT BACK & WATCH. WE MUST SAVE AMERICA! PROTEST, PROTEST, PROTEST!!!"[9]

Trump's rhetoric was reckless—recall what happened the last time he encouraged his supporters to protest—and it prompted a flurry of news coverage and political commentary on his alleged criminality. That might seem problematic for somebody trying to get a presidential campaign off the ground. But everyone seemed to be talking about him again, and Republicans—even his potential 2024 rivals—felt obligated to jump to his defense, or at least condemn the Manhattan DA. To Trump, that was a win.

The former president's definition of success had been forged decades earlier by his first lawyer and fixer, Roy Cohn. Known for his work with Senator Joseph McCarthy, Yankees owner George Steinbrenner, and several New York Mafia figures, Cohn taught a young Trump the key to avoiding legal trouble was to never give an inch and to immediately go after any critics—hard. If the threats and personal attacks are intimidating enough, Cohn counseled, you might get them to back down entirely.

Trump certainly tried to deploy the strategy with Manhattan DA Bragg. In the days following his prediction of a Tuesday arrest, he attacked Bragg, who is Black, as a "racist in reverse" and "degenerate psychopath" who was pursuing him while letting "MURDERERS, RAPISTS, AND DRUG DEALERS WALK FREE."[10] In a particularly provocative post—which he eventually deleted—Trump shared an article from a right-wing publication called *National File* that featured a picture of him holding a wooden bat and appearing to look at Bragg's head as if it were a baseball.

Trump's most inflammatory comments were about what would

happen to the country if Bragg went through with what he was planning. "What kind of person can charge another person," he wrote on March 24, "when it is known by all that NO Crime has been committed, & also known that potential death & destruction in such a false charge could be catastrophic for our Country?"

The implication seemed clear: Drop the case against me, or my supporters will get violent.* That same day, the Manhattan DA's office received an envelope—allegedly mailed from Florida—that contained a trace amount of white powder and a letter that read, "ALVIN: I AM GOING TO KILL YOU!!!!!!!!!!!!!!"[11]

For a few days at least, Trump believed his threats had had their intended effect. Tuesday came and went, and he remained a free man. So did Wednesday, Thursday, and Friday. By Saturday, Trump was talking as though he had successfully outmaneuvered Bragg. "I think they've already dropped the case," he told reporters on the plane ride back from his campaign rally in Waco. "It's a fake case—some fake cases. They have absolutely nothing."[12]

His confidence only grew as the week wore on and some of his lawyers became increasingly comfortable telling him what he wanted to hear. When multiple news outlets reported on March 29 that the grand jury would be taking a monthlong hiatus,[13] Trump was ecstatic. "I HAVE GAINED SUCH RESPECT FOR THIS GRAND

---

*According to an audio recording of the exchange obtained by *Vanity Fair*, Trump was repeatedly pressed on his "potential death & destruction" remark by NBC News's Vaughn Hillyard on the flight back from the Waco rally. The former president can be heard losing his temper, telling Hillyard, "I don't want to talk to you," and, "You're not a nice guy." When Hillyard, who is both a good reporter and a nice guy, wouldn't drop it, Trump instructed his aides to "get him out of here" and grabbed Hillyard's two cell phones, tossing them onto a nearby seat. (Charlotte Klein, "'Get Him Out of Here': Donald Trump Tossed NBC Reporter's Phones During Tirade Aboard Campaign Plane," *Vanity Fair*, May 1, 2023.)

JURY, & PERHAPS EVEN THE GRAND JURY SYSTEM AS A WHOLE," he posted on Truth Social. "THE EVIDENCE IS SO OVERWHELMING IN MY FAVOR, & SO RIDICULOUSLY BAD FOR THE HIGHLY PARTISAN & HATEFUL DISTRICT ATTOR- NEY, THAT THE GRAND JURY IS SAYING, HOLD ON, WE ARE NOT A RUBBER STAMP."[14]

The grand jury voted to indict him the next day.

As Trump prepared to fly to New York the following week, rumors swirled that he was planning to turn his arraignment into a spectacle. One story claimed his advisors were ready to use his mugshot for campaign merchandise,[15] while another reported he wanted to be handcuffed behind his back as he walked into the courtroom.[16] Not- ing the upcoming Christian holidays, a close Trump confidant told me he'd hoped the former president would lean into the comparisons some of his fans were making online. "Go to church on Palm Sunday, then we can make the whole Christ analogy," the Trump confidant mused. "I thought he should have done some showmanship here. I thought he should come down the escalator and have a rally right in the Trump Tower lobby and then get in the car and go downtown."

Trump didn't do any of it, opting instead to get in and out of New York as quickly and quietly as possible.

Politically speaking, the former president's advisors may have been right. His campaign received millions of dollars in donations in the days after the indictment was announced. Arriving in Manhattan with dozens of supportive lawmakers in tow and holding a combative press conference in the gold-plated lobby of his skyscraper would have been a show of strength at a time he could have really used one.

It could have reminded the world he was still the frontrunner for the Republican presidential nomination—and sent the message Bragg hadn't rattled him.

The problem was that the indictment *had* rattled him. For all his bluster, Trump desperately wanted to stave off an arrest, and he was embarrassed he hadn't been able to. Cohn, his longtime lawyer, had been indicted multiple times in the 1960s and 1970s and told his friend Donald it was something to be avoided at all costs. Once you're under arrest, he'd said, you lose control of your own situation.

Trump was many things on that fateful afternoon in New York—despondent, scared, seething with rage—but "in control" was not one of them. When it came time to turn himself in, he slipped out of Trump Tower without saying a word publicly and got into a black SUV for the fourteen-minute ride to the courthouse at 100 Centre Street in lower Manhattan. Aside from the driver and his lead Secret Service agent, Trump took that ride alone.

It wasn't supposed to be that way; the two lawyers taking the lead on the case—Susan Necheles and Todd Blanche—had planned to ride with him. At a meeting in Trump Tower the night before, however, two other Trump lawyers—Joe Tacopina and Boris Epshteyn—insisted on coming along, too, according to a source at the meeting. But all four of them couldn't fit in Trump's car. Instead of arguing on the sidewalk about who would ride with the boss, the lawyers agreed to jump in another SUV, leaving the soon-to-be indicted former president to make the journey by himself. As the motorcade made its way through Manhattan, news helicopters tracked every turn of its journey, which was broadcast live on network and cable television.

"Heading to Lower Manhattan, the Courthouse," Trump said in a message posted to social media as he sat in the back seat of his SUV.

"Seems so SURREAL—WOW, they are going to ARREST ME. Can't believe this is happening in America. MAGA!"[17]

Upon arrival at the courthouse, Trump's lawyers were brought to a holding room as he was taken to another floor to be fingerprinted and processed, just like anybody else facing criminal charges in New York. After several minutes, he was escorted to the room where his lawyers were waiting. Across the hallway from this holding room were several empty jail cells.

"They stood up and saluted," Trump told his lawyers when he returned from processing, according to a source who witnessed his comments. He was referring to the court employees who booked him and took his fingerprints. Trump may or may not have been telling the truth to his lawyers, but his story would soon change. One week later, he'd tell then–Fox News host Tucker Carlson the court employees' eyes were welling up as they processed him.

"They were actually crying," he claimed. "They said, 'I'm sorry.' They said, 'Twenty twenty-four, sir. Twenty twenty-four.' And tears were pouring down their eyes."[18]

The court employees at 100 Centre Street have seen it all. It's a place packed with defendants of all kinds—petty criminals, alleged killers, mobsters, celebrity defendants, and, yes, disgraced politicians. They aren't known for saluting people as they take their fingerprints, and they certainly aren't known for crying on the job. Shortly after the Carlson interview aired, "a law enforcement source" familiar with the proceedings told journalist Michael Isikoff of Yahoo! News that Trump's claims were "absolute BS."

"There were zero people crying," the source added. "There were zero people saying, 'I'm sorry.'"[19]

In their holding room at the courthouse, Trump and his lawyers were given copies of the thirty-four-count felony indictment that would soon be presented formally upstairs in the fifteenth-floor courtroom. Trump, however, took more interest in the placement of the television camera he would walk by on his way there. He knew the image of him walking by that camera—his "perp walk"—would be played over and over again on television and social media. So Boris Epshteyn pulled out his phone and showed Trump the video feed that was already being broadcast on TV, according to a source who was with them.

He was not happy with what he saw. The camera would be way down the hallway—separated from the courthouse door by two barricades—making it difficult, if not impossible, to be heard if he wanted to say anything as he walked by. But there was nothing Trump could do about that. This wasn't his show. He was just another criminal defendant.

When it came time to go to the courtroom, Trump and his lawyers were taken out of the holding room, past the empty jail cells, and to the elevator. Once on the fifteenth floor, he was visible on camera for less than ten seconds—too far away to say anything but close enough to lock his gaze on the camera, glaring at the world as he walked by.

Inside the courtroom, Trump sat at the defendant's table, flanked by his lawyers, with four police officers standing immediately behind him. When they first walked into the room, there was no seat at the table for Epshteyn, who had insisted on being there despite not formally being part of the legal defense team. Epshteyn stood there awkwardly for a few moments before a Secret Service agent brought a chair over to him.

Once Trump and his lawyers took their seats, the former president had to wait a full five minutes before the judge came into the room. He had been spared the indignity of handcuffs and a mugshot, but he was not a free man, and couldn't leave until his arraignment was over. When the judge arrived—"All rise!"—everybody in court, including Trump, had to stand for him.

DA Bragg and Juan Merchan, the presiding judge, were met by a version of Donald Trump that was much quieter, more somber—more timid—than the man he appeared to be on television and social media. Trump had attacked Judge Merchan on Truth Social as "highly partisan" and an "unfair disaster" just hours earlier. And the night before he had said that Bragg should "INDICT HIMSELF." But finally given a chance to confront them face-to-face, Trump was mostly silent. During the fifty-seven-minute proceeding, Trump said just ten words—"not guilty," "yes," "okay, thank you," "yes," "I do," "yes"—and spoke so quietly that reporters had to strain to hear him.

The few journalists in the room said Trump seemed nervous. "He crossed and uncrossed his arms," one of them wrote. "He knocked his knuckles on the hardwood table. Once, he puffed out his cheeks in a sigh."[20]

For the first time in years, Donald Trump was not the most powerful person in the room—he wasn't in control.

As soon as the arraignment was over, Trump raced back to Florida, responding to his first indictment with a speech in the same Mar-a-Lago ballroom where he had announced his 2024 presidential campaign almost five months earlier. His remarks were relatively short, but they were focused, aimed squarely at the prosecutors closing in on him. Not just Alvin Bragg, but also Fulton County DA Fani Willis, who is also Black (Trump called her the "local racist Democrat district attorney in Atlanta"), and the special counsel leading the

Department of Justice's investigations into January 6 and his handling of classified documents (a "lunatic special prosecutor named Jack Smith"). More than any potential Republican rival for the party's presidential nomination—more than Joe Biden, even—*these* were the people he was now running against.

"REPUBLICANS IN CONGRESS SHOULD DEFUND THE DOJ AND FBI UNTIL THEY COME TO THEIR SENSES," he posted on Truth Social the following day.[21] His campaign was selling T-shirts (for $36) featuring a fake "mug shot" of Trump made to look as if it were a booking photo taken in New York. Later in the week, his campaign posted a video advertisement featuring dramatic footage from Trump's arraignment. Apparently, being indicted for paying off your porn-star mistress was not something to be ashamed of in a Republican primary—it was a badge of honor. "If they can do it to him they can do it to you," Donald Trump Jr. tweeted. "And that's clearly been their plan all along."[22]

Noticeably absent from Trump's obsession with his own victimization was any real focus on helping Americans who *weren't* under criminal investigation, but his advisors were convinced the ploy would work. "This week, Trump could lock down the nomination if he played his cards right," Bannon told me as rumors began to swirl of Bragg's indictment. "'They're crucifying me,' you know, 'I'm a martyr.' All that. You get everybody so riled up that they just say, 'Fuck it. I hate Trump, but we've got to stand up against this.'"

The trial date for the hush-money case was later set during a hearing with Judge Merchan where Trump appeared via video from a room in Mar-a-Lago. Once again, the former president had to wait for the judge to get things started. Here's how *New York Times* reporter Jonah Bromwich, who was in the Manhattan courtroom where Trump could be seen on a video screen, described the scene:

> Before the appearance started, Mr. Trump waited on camera, visible in high-definition to the entire courtroom—a remarkable way to encounter the former president. Wearing a navy suit and a red, white and blue tie, he squinted and glowered at the camera, clasping and unclasping his hands, never keeping them in the same position for very long. He looked like a man unaccustomed to waiting.

For most of the appearance, Trump silently listened, his microphone on mute. When the judge announced the court date—March 25, 2024—he reacted angrily, his microphone still on mute, but his rage visible to those watching in the courtroom. Bromwich described a clearly agitated Trump angrily waving his hands and shaking his head, noting, "His microphone was muted and it was unclear what he was saying to the lawyer seated next to him."[23]

Trump's rage, however, was clearly audible to those in the room with Trump at Mar-a-Lago—especially to Todd Blanche, the lawyer sitting next to him. According to a source there with Trump, the former president erupted at Blanche because the March 2024 trial would be during a critical point in the presidential campaign.

"That's in the middle of the primaries!" Trump yelled, according to the source. "If I lose the presidency, you are going to be the reason!"

Trump's tantrum, according to the source, continued for nearly thirty minutes after the court appearance ended and the camera was turned off—a withering attack on perhaps the most highly regarded lawyer on Trump's troubled legal team.

"You little fucker!" Trump yelled at Blanche. "You are going to cost me the presidency!"

As the rant continued, Trump started complaining about his other lawyers and how they were handling Special Counsel Jack Smith's investigations into January 6 and Trump's handling of classified documents. He complained about his lawyers, yelling, "They want me to be indicted!"

They almost certainly did not want him to be indicted, but Trump's legal team had some bizarrely unconventional lawyers. The day of his video appearance before Judge Merchan, two other Trump lawyers, John Rowley and Jim Trusty, who would resign as Trump's lawyers within weeks, fired off a one-paragraph letter to Attorney General Merrick Garland. The letter was short and angry, complaining bitterly that Trump was being treated unfairly and asking for a meeting.

"No President of the United States has ever, in the history of our country, been baselessly investigated in such an outrageous and unlawful fashion," the letter said. "We request a meeting at your earliest convenience to discuss the ongoing injustice that is being perpetrated by your Special Counsel and his prosecutors."

The letter was signed by Rowley and Trusty, but, according to a source on the Trump legal team, it was dictated by Trump. Lawyer Todd Blanche believed the angry tone would only serve to antagonize an attorney general and a special counsel who would soon be making decisions on whether to seek indictments of Trump. He refused to sign the letter, but Trump insisted that Blanche's name be included, figuring that, as a former prosecutor, it would carry some weight. As a compromise, the name "Todd Blanche, Esq." appeared at the bottom of the page, next to the letters "cc"—signifying nothing more than he had received a copy. Also cc'd on the letter: "Representatives of Congress." Trusty then forwarded the letter in an email to a Justice Department prosecutor working in the special counsel's office named J. P. Cooney.

"Can you please forward the attached to Jack, and if possible, to the Attorney General?" Trusty wrote. "A hard copy will come to DOJ in the morning for the Attorney General, but perhaps Jack can forward to him tonight."

Amazingly, Trump's lawyer was sending an email to one of the prosecutors investigating him asking him to pass on a letter to Special Counsel Jack Smith complaining to the attorney general about the "ongoing injustice" he was perpetrating on the former president.

Prosecutor J. P. Cooney responded to the email with a single word: "Received."*

Exactly one month before his first indictment, Trump was about ten miles south of the White House in Maryland at the Gaylord National Harbor Resort and Convention Center, addressing attendees at the Conservative Political Action Conference (CPAC).

CPAC had long been a rather eccentric affair, but ever since Ronald Reagan attended the conference as president, the event regularly brought together the power players of the Republican Party and a wide

---

*The lawyers never got their meeting with Attorney General Garland, but two weeks after sending the letter, they did meet with Special Counsel Jack Smith. The meeting was attended by Trusty and Rowley and a third lawyer named Lindsey Halligan. Halligan's Florida-based legal practice, according to her bio, "focuses on defending multiple carriers in first-party insurance claims." She had no known federal court experience.

range of its affiliated advocacy groups. In 2014, the conference—billed as the "largest and most influential gathering of conservatives in the world"—featured dozens of high-profile lawmakers and commentators. Senators Mitch McConnell, Pat Toomey, Marco Rubio, and Mike Lee all spoke, as did 2012 vice presidential candidate and soon-to-be Speaker of the House Paul Ryan, and Governors Chris Christie, Rick Perry, and Bobby Jindal. Panels were led by well-respected conservative columnists like George Will and Rich Lowry. Trump got a speaking slot, but it was just twenty minutes, and came on Thursday afternoon.

Nine years later, CPAC looked like a full-blown Trump convention. Devotees of the former president like Representatives Matt Gaetz and Marjorie Taylor Greene were two of its highest-billed attendees; and Kari Lake, the conspiratorial local news anchor who ran for governor in Arizona and lost, was chosen as the featured guest for the conference's annual Ronald Reagan Dinner. Mike Lindell, the pillow salesman who claimed foreign powers used voting machines to steal the 2020 election from Donald Trump, could be seen wandering around the hotel lobby, as could longtime Trump advisors Steve Bannon and Sebastian Gorka—all of them featured speakers at the conference.

Although CPAC doesn't formally take sides in Republican primary elections, Trump was, predictably, given the keynote time slot on Saturday night. After a voice over the public-address system introduced him as the "next president of the United States," he ambled onto the stage and spoke for nearly two hours. "The sinister forces trying to kill America have done everything they can to stop me, to silence you, and to turn this nation into a socialist dumping ground for criminals, junkies, Marxists, thugs, radicals, and dangerous refugees that no other country wants," he began. "If those opposing us succeed, our once beautiful USA will be a failed country that no one will even recognize."

The speech was ominous, but one rhetorical flourish stood out. "In 2016, I declared I am your voice. Today, I add I am your warrior, I am your justice," Trump said. "And for those who have been wronged and betrayed, I am your retribution." He repeated the last phrase—"*I am your retribution*"—and stepped back from the podium as the crowd started chanting: "USA! USA! USA!"

When I spoke with Bannon a few days later, he wouldn't stop touting Trump's performance, referring to it as his "Come Retribution" speech. What I didn't realize at the time was that "Come Retribution," according to some Civil War historians, served as the code words for the Confederate Secret Service's plot to take hostage—and eventually assassinate—President Abraham Lincoln. "The use of the key phrase 'Come Retribution' suggests that the Confederate government had made a bitter decision to repay some of the misery that had been inflicted on the South," William A. Tidwell, James O. Hall, and David Winfred Gaddy wrote in the 1988 book *Come Retribution: The Confederate Secret Service and the Assassination of Lincoln*. "Bitterness may well have been directed toward persons held to be particularly responsible for that misery, and Abraham Lincoln certainly headed the list."[24] Bannon actually recommended that I read that book, erasing any doubt that he was intentionally using the Confederate code words to describe Trump's speech.

Bannon's repeated use of the phrase caught my attention. Trump's speech was not an overt call for the assassination of his political opponents, but it did advocate their destruction by other means. "All of this [success] is within our reach, but only if we have the courage to complete the job, gut the deep state, reclaim our democracy, and banish the tyrants and Marxists into political exile forever," Trump said. "This is the turning point."

The 2024 election may or may not be the turning point for the country, but the "Come Retribution" speech was a turning point for Trump's campaign. As he faced a multitude of criminal indictments in the coming months, he would be waging a campaign of vengeance and martyrdom. He would talk about what is at stake in the election in apocalyptic terms—*the final battle*—knowing how high the stakes were for him personally. He could win and retake the White House. Or he could lose and go to prison.

"Trump's on offense and talking about real things," Bannon told me. "The 'Come Retribution' speech had ten or twelve major policies." But Bannon knew the speech wasn't about policies in a traditional sense. Trump spoke about who he would target once he returned to power. "We will demolish the deep state. We will expel the warmongers," Trump said. "We will drive out the globalists, we will cast out the communists. We will throw off the political class that hates our country. . . . We will beat the Democrats. We will rout the fake news media. We will expose and appropriately deal with the RINOs. We will evict Joe Biden from the White House. And we will liberate America from these villains and scoundrels once and for all."

As Trump's legal jeopardy increased, the people prosecuting him—and the witnesses, almost all of them Republicans, expected to testify against him—rose to the top of Trump's list of villains and scoundrels to be eliminated. The day after Special Counsel Jack Smith finally indicted him for his actions leading up to January 6, Trump made his threat explicit: "IF YOU GO AFTER ME, I'M COMING AFTER YOU!"[25]

That, more than anything else, is the beating heart of Trump's 2024 campaign: Vote for me, and I will punish the people who have wronged you—by wronging me. *I am your retribution.*

CHAPTER TWO

DARK DAYS AT MAR-A-LAGO

When Donald Trump left the White House for the last time early in the morning on January 20, 2021, he didn't look like a man about to mount a political comeback. Defeated and disgraced, he had grown so isolated that few of the people still serving in his administration bothered to stick around for his final send-off. But the anger and bitterness that would define his "Come Retribution" campaign of 2024 were sown in those final days and hours of his presidency.

"This is a great, great country," he told the meager crowd of two hundred or so that had assembled at Joint Base Andrews to hear his final public remarks as president, just two weeks after his supporters stormed the US Capitol. "I want to thank all of the great people of Washington, DC, all of the people that we worked with to put this miracle together. So have a good life. We will see you soon."

And with that, the opening guitar chord of the Village People's "Y.M.C.A." rang out over the speaker system, and the forty-fifth president of the United States—pausing a handful of times to pump his fists to the beat—began to make his way down the red carpet toward Air Force One, which would whisk him and the First Lady off to their new lives in Palm Beach. Sean Spicer, Trump's first press secretary, later wrote that although the scene "defied every notion of presidential and military protocol," it was a "fitting end to President Trump's disruptive, turbulent, and nontraditional administration."[1]

Spicer didn't exactly build a reputation for telling the truth during his brief stint at the White House, but he was spot-on there. Trump's presidency was never going to end like his predecessors' presidencies had ended. There would be no generous words of unity or well-wishes directed at his successor, no final farewell surrounded by the people who had worked in his White House and made his presidency possible. In fact, Spicer—who had resigned from his post after just seven months and had been out of government for more than three years—was one of only a handful of current or former Trump administration officials to make it to Trump's farewell ceremony.

Of the two hundred people in attendance that day, the vast majority were random supporters let onto the tarmac so that Trump would have an audience for his final speech as president. It wasn't supposed to be that way. Current and former White House staffers were invited—each allowed to bring up to five guests—but most declined the invitation. Trump's final chief of staff, Mark Meadows, showed up, as did longtime policy advisor Stephen Miller, but very few others were there. It's not that Trump's team didn't try to get a crowd for the big send-off. Even former chief of staff John Kelly received a call from the White House about attending the event despite having dubbed Trump "the most flawed person" he'd ever met after leaving the administration.[2] Not surprisingly, Kelly was a no-show.

"I got out of the crowd-estimating business a long time ago," Spicer wrote of the farewell. "But it was smaller than any Trump rally I've attended."[3]

Trump's own vice president, Mike Pence, decided to stay away. He did, however, attend Joe Biden's inauguration later that morning.

The outgoing president traditionally attends his successor's inauguration, too, of course. Prior to 2021, the last time a commander in chief decided to skip out on the formal transfer of power from one administration to the next was in 1869, when Andrew Johnson remained at the White House until Ulysses S. Grant was sworn in. According to diary entries from Johnson's Navy secretary, Gideon Welles, President Johnson—who reached the Oval Office after Abraham Lincoln was assassinated—told cabinet members he "could not, with proper self-respect, witness the inauguration of a man whom we knew to be untruthful, faithless and false."[4]

Fast-forward 152 years, and Trump made a similar pronouncement—but he did so on Twitter. "To all of those who have asked," he tweeted on January 8, "I will not be going to the Inauguration on January 20th."[5] It'd be his final tweet before Twitter executives decided that night to "permanently suspend" the president's account due to the risk of "further incitement of violence." They believed Trump's post about skipping the inauguration could serve as "further confirmation" for his supporters that "the election was not legitimate."[6]

In fact, Trump's choice not to attend the inauguration wasn't entirely his own. He pretended the decision was his, but Trump's hand was forced. Congressional leaders were moving to formally disinvite him. The discussions were secret, but Trump was aware of them.[7]

According to three people with direct knowledge of the talks, the push to effectively ban Trump from Biden's inauguration was spear-headed by Mitch McConnell. "We can't have something like [January 6] happen at the inauguration," the Republican Senate leader told one of his top aides the day after Trump supporters stormed the Capitol. McConnell didn't want the spectacle of a president who refused to accept defeat sitting there on the inaugural platform. The outgoing president evidently could not be trusted to sit quietly and respectfully onstage for an hour while his successor was sworn in.

McConnell's aide reached out to Meadows to inform him of the plan to disinvite Trump, and once House Minority Leader Kevin Mc-Carthy caught word of what was happening, he called the White House to let Trump know as well. McCarthy disagreed with McCon-nell's decision—he was urging Trump to finally call Biden to concede and thought it was important for the outgoing president to show up at the inauguration in a display of unity. But the wheels were already in motion. Andrew Johnson and Trump would be the only two pres-idents to both be impeached and skip their successors' inaugurations.

Although Trump departed Washington on January 20 about three hours before the end of his term, there was at least one person in his administration working right up to the buzzer. After giving the president a final handshake and pat on the back, Mark Meadows raced back to Washington with one last important job to do: Trump had issued an eleventh-hour pardon from Air Force One—of Albert Pirro, the ex-husband of Fox News host Jeanine Pirro—and Meadows was tasked with making sure the Department of Justice had all the relevant paperwork.

The last-minute flurry of activity threw a wrench in Meadows's plans. He had invited Biden's incoming chief of staff, Ron Klain, to meet him at the White House at 10 A.M. so that Klain could get a

two-hour head start before Biden officially became president—a gesture of graciousness at the end of a transition that was anything but
gracious. But now Meadows was late. With the chief of staff's office
locked, Klain waited around in the West Wing for nearly ninety minutes before a flustered-looking Meadows finally arrived at 11:30 A.M.

Apologizing for his tardiness, Meadows rushed to open the door
to his office and explained why he needed to bring the folder in his
hand over to the Justice Department. Instead of the full meeting they
had discussed, Meadows quickly showed Klain around the office and
wished him luck. Before the two men bid farewell, however, Klain
had a quick question.

"Where's the desk?" he asked, looking around an office that included a large conference table, a fireplace, and two couches, but no
desk.

"I don't have a desk," Meadows replied. "I'm not that kind of chief
of staff."

As a puzzled Klain pondered what the heck Meadows meant by
that—*what kind of chief of staff doesn't have a desk?*—Meadows
rushed off to finalize what may very well have been the last piece of
Trump administration business.

Around the same time, aboard Air Force One, Trump was already
plotting the next stage of his political career. "I'm done," he told Republican National Committee chairwoman Ronna McDaniel on the
phone. "I'm starting my own party."

As I reported in *Betrayal*, McDaniel was aghast. She had called
Trump simply to wish him the best as he ended his presidency, but
now had a dilemma on her hands that could destroy the GOP. She
told Trump as much.

"You cannot do that," she said. "If you do, we will lose forever."

"Exactly. You lose forever without me," Trump responded, making clear he didn't care. "This is what Republicans deserve for not sticking up for me."[8]

As Trump saw it, if he lost, everybody around him should lose, too.

McDaniel pleaded with Trump, reminding him of all the people who had worked so hard on his campaigns and in his administration. She futilely tried to appeal to his sense of decency and loyalty. When that failed miserably, she and her top aides changed their approach, reminding the former president that leaving the party would cost him millions of dollars. If he went through with his plan, the RNC would not only stop paying his legal bills, but it would also prevent him from raising money off the database of Trump supporters that he and the party owned jointly. Within a week, Trump backed down.

The former president was furious when I reported the details of these conversations in *Betrayal*. To soothe his ego, McDaniel issued a statement denying my report. "I have never threatened President Trump with anything," she said. "He and I have a great relationship." Trump took some personal shots for good measure, blasting me as a "3rd rate reporter" (a recycled insult he had used on me previously) for "ABC Non News."[9] Notably, however, Trump didn't deny any of my reporting.

But McDaniel did, explicitly saying what I'd written was "false." The statement prompted me to call RNC leadership and remind them I record interviews with my sources, who often speak to me on the condition that I do not reveal their identity. That conversation seemed to have its intended effect, leading a top party official to assure me that RNC leadership would not be making any further statements denying what they knew was the truth—that Trump backed down from his plan to leave the GOP only after being told the move would cost him millions of dollars.

Trump had built his entire career on the premise he was the ultimate winner—in business, in politics, and in life. The image he crafted of himself earned him tabloid fame, a hit reality-TV show, and, arguably, the presidency. But sitting aboard Air Force One on January 20, 2021—the first president to be blackballed from his successor's inauguration—Donald Trump was the biggest loser in the country. Not just because he lost the election—someone always loses the election—but because his inability to accept that loss resulted in him losing over and over and over again.

The initial defeat was bad enough. Prior to 2020, only nine incumbent US presidents had lost their reelection bids, and none of those nine had lost by more than seven million votes to a seventy-eight-year-old opponent who, because of a pandemic, chose to remain in his Delaware home for almost the entirety of the campaign. But that brutal election loss was just the beginning of his losing in 2020.

First, there were the legal challenges. Trump and his allies filed dozens of separate lawsuits in the aftermath of the election, and they lost all but one of them.* The lone legal victory came in Pennsylvania, where Trump's lawyers successfully excluded some uncounted mail-in ballots over a technical issue that did nothing to alter the

---

* While there's a general agreement on how many postelection legal challenges Trump and his allies *won* (one), there's less of a consensus on how many they *lost*. Democratic election lawyer Marc Elias's count of sixty-three is widely cited, but that tallies each individual motion within a case separately. In any case, Trump's winning percentage was laughably low. (William Cummings, Joey Garrison, and Jim Sergent, "By the numbers: President Donald Trump's failed efforts to overturn the election," *USA Today*, January 6, 2021.)

state's results. Some lawsuits were dismissed for lack of standing—essentially because the people filing the lawsuits lacked the legal authority to bring those claims—while others lost on the merits. Several of the cases were knocked down by judges Trump himself appointed. "Calling an election unfair does not make it so," one such judge, Stephanos Bibas, wrote in a unanimous ruling for the US Court of Appeals for the Third Circuit. "Charges require specific allegations and then proof. We have neither here."[10]

After failing in the court system, Trump dispatched the lawyer leading his legal efforts, the once-reputable Rudy Giuliani, on an outlandish mission to pressure Republican lawmakers in swing states Trump had lost to block the certification of Biden's victory. In two of these states—Georgia and Arizona—the GOP controlled the governor's mansion and both houses of the state legislature. It didn't matter: Even Republicans who previously had supported Trump refused to do what he was asking because they believed he was demanding they break the law. "Any attempt by the legislature to retroactively change that process for the Nov. 3rd election would be unconstitutional and immediately enjoined by the courts," Georgia's Republican governor Brian Kemp and lieutenant governor Geoff Duncan said in an early-December statement.[11]

This defiance was even more embarrassing for Trump in Arizona. Sitting at his desk on December 1, 2020, Republican governor Doug Ducey was set to sign paperwork certifying his state's election results—on live TV—when "Hail to the Chief" began to play. It was his cell phone, blaring the personalized ringtone he had set for calls from Trump. With the cameras rolling, Ducey took the phone out of his pocket, sent the call to voicemail, and certified Trump's loss in Arizona.

Even after all fifty states certified their results and sent their electoral votes to Washington, Trump continued to flounder. His demand that Attorney General Bill Barr somehow use the power of the Justice Department to undo the election results prompted Barr to publicly declare he saw no evidence of widespread fraud. When Barr's successor, acting attorney general Jeffrey Rosen, also refused to follow Trump's orders, the president initially decided to fire him and install yet another acting attorney general—one who would follow his unlawful orders. He backed off that plan only after the entire senior leadership team of the Justice Department, all of them Trump appointees, threatened to resign.

Failure after failure. Loss after loss. Each more humiliating and debasing than the last.

Nevertheless, Trump persisted. He tried to secure enough votes in Congress to toss out Biden's electoral votes, and when it became clear that effort was doomed, he tried to convince Vice President Pence to do it on his own. We all know what happened after that.

So, it was with the stench of a loser that Donald Trump landed at Palm Beach International Airport on January 20, 2021, and walked off Air Force One for the last time. At the bottom of the stairs, he paused, waved, and mouthed the words "thank you." He was addressing the small group of White House pool reporters who had flown along with him from Washington, because there was nobody else to greet the soon-to-be ex-president at the airport—no supporters, no local officials, not even Republican governor Ron DeSantis, who would not have been elected without Trump's support.

There were, however, some Trump supporters along the motorcade route to Mar-a-Lago. They wore red MAKE AMERICA GREAT AGAIN hats and waved Trump–Pence flags. Some of them held homemade signs adorned with things like WE LOVE YOU, 45! The presidential limo drove slower than usual, allowing Trump to bask in the glow of the modest crowd—while also ensuring he caught a glimpse of the protesters and hecklers who turned out. One group carried a banner touting their support for Biden, while another held up a sign with ODOR OF MENDACITY printed on it. Another protester's poster got straight to the point: LOSER![12]

By all accounts, Trump had a very difficult time transitioning back to life as a private citizen. People who interacted with him at Mar-a-Lago during those first few weeks universally described him as being in a dark and foul mood, and most of his friends and advisors simply avoided him. Mar-a-Lago members would give the dejected former president a round of applause when he showed up for dinner on the patio, but on at least one occasion, he got up from the table in the middle of his meal and left without explanation. The man who'd played hundreds of rounds of golf as president found it difficult all of a sudden to make it through eighteen holes, picking up his ball in the middle of one round and going home.

After a while, Trump found solace in an unusual activity for a former commander-in-chief: DJing on the Mar-a-Lago patio. He wasn't standing at a turntable spinning records, but he had an iPad and would pick his favorite songs. "You know what gets [people] rockin'?" Trump said when asked about his newfound hobby on the *Full Send Podcast*.* "'Y.M.C.A.,' the gay national anthem. Did you ever hear that? They call it the gay national anthem. But 'Y.M.C.A.'

---

* If you haven't heard of the *Full Send Podcast*, don't worry—you're not alone. It is hosted by a group of Canadian American YouTubers known as the Nelk Boys, and its previously featured guests include O. J. Simpson, Alex Jones, Pauly D from *Jersey Shore*, and a bodybuilder/lifestyle guru known as the Liver King. How they booked the former president of the United States is anyone's guess.

gets people up, and it gets them moving. We have a lot of good selections, and people love it when I do it."[13]

While Trump was getting senior citizens dancing down in Florida, Republicans in Washington were coming to grips with the scope of the problem they had on their hands. While many party *leaders* were itching to finally put the last four years behind them once and for all, a lot of GOP *voters* weren't ready to move on.

"What's real crazy is back in our district there are tons of people who are ready to storm the Capitol again," McCarthy told me just three days after the Capitol was attacked. "I just don't know about these people."

Before long, McCarthy's gut feeling had been translated into data. In a battle between Trump and Republicans who opposed him, Trump won. "Liz Cheney's decision to vote to impeach President Trump makes her extremely vulnerable," pollster John McLaughlin wrote in a January 27 memo summarizing results of a survey commissioned by Trump advisor Jason Miller just days after Trump left the White House. "The strong voter sentiment in this survey suggests there could be similar results for other Republicans who voted for impeachment."

The results were overwhelming. Nearly seven in ten Wyoming voters disagreed with Cheney's impeachment vote, as did 85 percent of Republicans and 96 percent of Trump supporters. The former president was elated. The polling began to lift him out of his funk, and it gave him a newfound sense of purpose and a new goal: defeating Cheney and all ten of the House Republicans who'd betrayed him weeks earlier. He would now be on a mission to turn *them* into losers.

The day after McLaughlin delivered his memo, McCarthy became the first high-profile Republican leader to visit Trump since he'd left the White House. The former president had been almost entirely out of sight for those eight days, banned from the social media platforms he'd used to communicate with his supporters and effectively banished from cable news, too. When he was a subject of discussion at all, the conversations focused on his Senate impeachment trial, set to begin in less than two weeks. McConnell was privately telling colleagues he might vote to convict Trump, and momentum seemed to be building to bar him from office for life. Trump was defeated, diminished, and politically toxic.

Until McCarthy threw him a lifeline. News of the meeting broke before McCarthy even left Mar-a-Lago, and Trump's new political organization, the Save America PAC, blasted out a statement recapping it shortly after it was over. "The meeting between President Donald J. Trump and House Republican Leader Kevin McCarthy at Mar-a-Lago in Palm Beach, Florida, was a very good and cordial one," it read. "They discussed many topics, number one of which was taking back the House in 2022. President Trump's popularity has never been stronger than it is today, and his endorsement means more than perhaps any endorsement at any time." A picture of the two of them was attached—Trump grinning from ear to ear, and McCarthy looking as though he'd been ambushed by a photographer and realized he may have just made an enormous mistake.

Several of McCarthy's fellow Republicans believed he had. Two weeks earlier, McCarthy had been saying Trump bore responsibility for the attack on the Capitol and telling his colleagues he was encouraging Trump to resign. Now he was making a pilgrimage to Palm Beach? "McCarthy going to Mar-a-Lago was sort of that initial 'What the fuck?' type of moment," one Republican lawmaker who was generally supportive of McCarthy later told me.[14]

Perhaps to preempt such criticism, McCarthy issued a statement after the meeting making clear why he felt it was necessary. "Today, President Trump committed to helping elect Republicans in the House and Senate in 2022," he wrote. "A united conservative movement will strengthen the bonds of our citizens and uphold the freedoms our country was founded on." Privately, however, McCarthy was telling people the visit to Mar-a-Lago wasn't even his idea. "He's making it sound like I went down to see him, but I was just fundraising [in Florida], and they heard I was down there and called to see if I would come see him," McCarthy explained to a friend shortly after the meeting. "And the minute I go there, he says, 'Let's take a picture.'"

If that's true, it was certainly a savvy move by Trump. The former president's aides told reporters a different story. They insisted McCarthy had requested the meeting to make amends after publicly blaming Trump for the January 6 riot. Within Republican circles at least, the message of McCarthy's pilgrimage was loud and clear: Donald Trump's status as the party's leader was restored. His time in the political wilderness had lasted eight days.

Like RNC chair Ronna McDaniel, McCarthy privately disparaged Trump and was horrified by the president's behavior after the 2020 election. But also like McDaniel, he feared the damage Trump could wreak on the GOP—in the 2022 midterms and beyond—if he turned on its leaders or left the party entirely. Plus, McCarthy knew he would personally need Trump's backing to achieve his lifelong goal of becoming Speaker of the House.

On one level, the strategy worked. Trump remained a Republican, and he played an active role in promoting GOP candidates across the country. McDaniel was reelected chair of the RNC. McCarthy became Speaker of the House.

But what if McDaniel had not begged Trump to remain a Republican? What if McCarthy had not made his trek to Mar-a-Lago? For these Republican leaders, the principled path was the path not taken. Perhaps they would have been replaced by other people who would have done Trump's bidding, adding their names to the long list of Republicans who have had their political careers ruined by the party's conqueror. Perhaps the GOP would have splintered in two, with Trump following through on his threat to found the "Patriot Party."[15] Or perhaps they—and the party—would have been able to turn the page on the Trump era by letting the former president flounder in Palm Beach. We'll never know for sure.

But we do know this: In the years since those decisions were made, the Republican Party has paid a steep price for placating a wounded, vindictive, and angry former president.

The Grim Reaper

There were a number of unique power centers in Donald Trump's Washington. White House officials were often spotted enjoying the happy-hour specials at Union Trust, a bank turned bar a block north of the Treasury Department. Younger administration staffers lived and socialized in Navy Yard, an upstart neighborhood abutting the Anacostia River. The Trump International Hotel, of course, opened on Pennsylvania Avenue in 2016 and served as a gathering place for MAGA celebrities, foreign operatives, and various influence peddlers unbothered by over-priced cocktails or chance encounters with Rudy Giuliani.

But besides the Oval Office, perhaps no physical space was more central to the Trump era than an old brick town house less than one block from the Supreme Court and just two blocks from the US Capitol. Purchased for $2.35 million in 2009 and dubbed the "Breitbart Embassy," the house, built in 1890 during the presidency of Benjamin Harrison, served as the home base for the right-wing media outlet cofounded by Steve Bannon. As the GOP shifted from the party of George Bush and

Mitt Romney to the party of Donald Trump, Republicans looking to climb the ranks knew they'd need to drop by and pay homage to the residents of the three-story building. "The Embassy is where we first started to build [Breitbart]," Bannon told attendees at a fall 2017 book party. "It's a very historic house for the populist, nationalist movement."[1]

I went to visit Bannon there in early 2019 as I was writing *Front Row at the Trump Show*. The place was buzzing with activity. Entering through the basement, I saw several young people working on computers and bumped into Derek Harvey, a former Trump National Security Council official and retired Army colonel who was now working as the Republican staff director of the House Intelligence Committee. After a few minutes, I was whisked out the back door of the house; escorted up a fire escape to the second floor; and directed through the kitchen, down a hallway, and into the dining room. Bannon was seated at a large table, advising members of an advocacy group representing minority bankers how to get through to Trump and his economic team.

For Bannon, these kinds of meetings were part of a daily routine. When I went to see him again a few months later, he was seated at the same dining room table, talking with a woman looking for a job at the State Department. If you wanted something out of the Trump administration, Steve Bannon was an important person to talk to—even, or maybe especially, after he was unceremoniously fired from the White House in August 2017.

In August 2016, Bannon had joined a Trump campaign in disarray, leaving his perch at Breitbart to help the Republican nominee craft a winning message and navigate the last few months before the election. A creature of populist conservative media who had been attacking the GOP establishment for years, he understood Trump's appeal—and his voters—better than anybody. "He's the man with the idea," read a 2016 *Hollywood Reporter* profile by Michael Wolff in which Bannon declared himself the Thomas Cromwell to Trump's King Henry VIII.* "If Trumpism is to represent something intellectually and historically coherent, it's Bannon's job to make it so."[2]

I witnessed this dynamic for myself covering the White House early in Trump's term. While the president would rant and rave about trivialities like the size of his inauguration crowd or whatever was on cable news that morning, Bannon—officially Trump's chief strategist and senior counselor—was methodically pushing to implement the radical policy changes Trump had talked about as a candidate. A whiteboard hung on the wall of his West Wing office listing nearly every promise Trump had made on the campaign trail—and whether the fledgling administration had yet followed through.

Bannon's downfall—in the White House, at least—came when the press began to catch on to the magnitude of his role. Article after article began referring to the advisor as Trump's "brain,"[3] and an ominous-looking Bannon—branded "THE GREAT MANIPULATOR"—was featured on the cover of *Time* magazine in February 2017. "Is Steve Bannon the Second Most Powerful Man in the World?" asked the story's headline.[4] That same week, *Saturday Night Live* began with a skit showing Bannon, depicted as the Grim Reaper, walking into the Oval Office and booting Trump (played by Alec Baldwin) out of the Resolute Desk. Trump is then shown playing with a toy at a mini desk while Bannon does the real work in the president's chair.[5]

---

* Apparently, it didn't bother Bannon that Cromwell went from being the power behind King Henry's throne to being beheaded for treason.

The Trump-Bannon breakup was ugly, and it was made even uglier by comments Bannon made about his former boss's family in Michael Wolff's January 2018 book, *Fire and Fury*. Ivanka Trump? "Dumb as a brick." Donald Trump Jr.? A dimwit who was largely responsible for a "treasonous" and "unpatriotic" 2016 meeting with a group of Russians at Trump Tower.[6] Trump responded in kind, labeling the often disheveled-looking Bannon as "Sloppy Steve"[7] and claiming he'd both "cried" and "lost his mind" when Trump fired him. "[Bannon] spent his time at the White House leaking false information to the media to make himself seem far more important than he was," Trump said at the time.[8]

But the breakup didn't last long. Bannon apologized for his remarks—saying his support for the president was "unwavering"[9]—and Trump would later refer to his former strategist as "one of [his] best pupils," adding that he "loved working with him."[10] In 2019, Bannon launched a daily video podcast called *War Room: Impeachment* aimed at guiding the White House's response to the first Trump impeachment, and he changed the show's name to *War Room: Pandemic* in early 2020.

If you were listening to Bannon, very little that transpired in the months following the 2020 election should have come as a shock. On October 31—in audio obtained by *Mother Jones* magazine—Bannon told a group of associates that Trump was planning to declare victory on election night even if he lost.[11] On January 5, 2021, Bannon repeatedly told his podcast audience, "All hell is going to break loose tomorrow." According to White House phone records, he'd already spoken to Trump that day—and would again both later that evening and the following morning, on January 6. "All I can say," Bannon told his listeners, "is strap in."[12]

Bannon has done more than just about anyone to boost Trump's political career, but perhaps more than any Trump confidant, he is also willing to call out the former president's deficiencies. As Trump launched his third presidential campaign, Bannon told me the former president was "phoning shit in" and lacking his typical "swagger" and "mojo." The two have a mutually beneficial relationship: Bannon's political instincts keep Trump aligned with his voters, while Trump has provided Bannon a vessel through which he can impose his nationalist worldview on both the Republican Party and the country.

"He gets it; he gets it intuitively," Bannon said of Trump in late 2016. "You have probably the greatest orator since William Jennings Bryan, coupled with an economic populist message and two political parties that are so owned by the donors that they don't speak to their audience. But he speaks in a non-political vernacular, he communicates with these people in a very visceral way."[13]

In October 2022, Bannon told me he had been asked by some un-named Republicans to try to convince Trump to play the role of party kingmaker in the upcoming presidential race—effectively choosing the next Republican nominee instead of running again himself. He said he responded this way: "Have you lost your fucking mind? He's not going be a kingmaker. The moment he's the kingmaker, it's on to the other guy and he's in the back. It's never going to work. They don't understand his psychology. Whether you like it or not, it's a reality you have to deal with."

"So," I said, "it has to be Trump as long as—"

"As long as he can fog a mirror," Bannon said before I could finish the sentence.

And sure enough, the two were back together again in 2023, with Bannon interviewing now presidential candidate Trump for a special episode of *War Room* recorded at Mar-a-Lago in late April.[14] The former chief strategist was back in Trump's good graces, just like old times. "I've never seen him better," Bannon told me. "You do understand, we're going back to the White House. I feel it."

"What happens if Trump loses?" I asked him. "Aren't you at all worried that violence could break out again?"

"I'm not worried about that at all," he responded. "Because we are going to win."

CHAPTER THREE

THE CHOKER

O n January 6, Donald Trump was confronted with a crisis that demanded presidential leadership—and he failed to show leadership of any kind, for good or for bad. As his most fervent supporters stormed the Capitol on his behalf, he did nothing to help them—and for hours, nothing to stop them. He failed as a president. *And* he failed as a would-be coup plotter. But extensive new information has come to light, through the sworn testimony of his closest aides and newly released White House documents, revealing the extent of Trump's failure on January 6 is even greater than it appeared at the time.

In his speech at the White House Ellipse that day, Donald Trump infamously told his supporters to march to the Capitol and promised, "I'll be there with you." Then the commander in chief couldn't even get his own Secret Service agents to take him where he wanted to go. FDR rallied the Allied forces to defeat Nazi Germany and Imperial Japan. Ronald Reagan helped bring down the Soviet Union. Donald

Trump couldn't get his Secret Service driver to take him down Pennsylvania Avenue.

To say Trump choked on January 6 is not to say he wasn't responsible for what happened. Of course he was responsible. None of it would have happened without him. The people who stormed the Capitol made it perfectly clear who sent them and why. The world heard Donald Trump tell them to "fight like hell." And to erase any doubt about the purpose of the whole thing, the rioters draped those two massive TRUMP 2020 banners outside the building before breaking in.

The House Select Committee to Investigate the January 6th Attack (January 6 Committee)—with its ten televised hearings and thousands of hours of sworn testimony from the key players—added substantially to our understanding of what happened in meticulous and often riveting detail. So did Special Counsel Jack Smith's criminal investigation of Trump's desperate effort to stop the certification of Joe Biden's election victory. And the court filings of the hundreds of people prosecuted by the Department of Justice for the assault go even further in laying out the actions and motivations of the attackers. But months before the first conviction of a rioter and long before the creation of the January 6 Committee, it was Republican leaders in Congress who said exactly what happened and who was responsible.

"There's no question—none—that President Trump is practically and morally responsible for provoking the events of that day," declared Republican Senate leader Mitch McConnell less than a month after Trump left the White House. "The people who stormed this building believed they were acting on the wishes and instructions of their president." McConnell called the attack "a foreseeable consequence of the growing crescendo of false statements, conspiracy theories, and reckless hyperbole which the defeated president kept shouting into the largest megaphone on planet Earth."

That statement by Senator McConnell—clear, concise, and without equivocation—could easily have come from the opening lines of the January 6 Committee's final report or its criminal referral. But McConnell said it minutes after he'd voted not guilty in Trump's second impeachment trial. He didn't want anybody to think he actually believed Trump wasn't responsible for what had happened; his not-guilty vote on impeachment was based on a technicality—he said he didn't believe an ex-president could be impeached. Perhaps McConnell will one day acknowledge that he regrets that not-guilty vote of a defeated president who he believed was guilty in every other sense of the word.

In the immediate aftermath of the attack, Republican House leader Kevin McCarthy also declared that Trump "bears responsibility" for what happened. And despite the efforts by so many, including McCarthy himself, to later downplay the horror of that day, at the time he spoke with uncharacteristic clarity about how bad it was.

"The violence, destruction, and chaos we saw earlier was unacceptable, undemocratic, and un-American," McCarthy said shortly after the rioters were ejected from the Capitol building on January 6. "It was the saddest day I've ever had serving as a member of this institution."

And it didn't take an investigation for Republicans to see that January 6 was something far more damaging than a riot or an attack on a government building.

"Today the People's House was attacked, which is an attack on the republic itself," said Republican representative Chip Roy of Texas after Congress reconvened that night. "There is no excuse for it. A woman died, and people need to go to jail. And the president should never have spun up certain Americans to believe something that simply cannot be."[1]

Investigations by Congress and the Justice Department, as well as by journalists, added to our understanding and confirmed the immediate judgment of Republicans like McConnell, McCarthy, and Roy—and so many other friends and foes of Donald Trump—about who was responsible for setting in motion the events that led to the assault on the Capitol.

Donald Trump's actions before the attack clearly show he was responsible for what happened, but his actions during the attack are the most revealing moments of the Trump presidency, demonstrating his utter failure as a leader. The full story of Trump choking once the assault on the Capitol was underway is told in the words of his own senior advisors, in another example of a fundamental truth about his presidency—the most damning condemnations of his actions often come from the people closest to him. Under the threat of subpoena, virtually everybody who encountered the president on January 6 testified to what they witnessed, several of them revealing their real-time revulsion at his behavior.

For me, the most surprising revelation to come out of the investigation was that Trump actually did want to go to the Capitol with his supporters. Like everybody else watching that day, I heard him say "I'll be there with you," and when I interviewed him at Mar-a-Lago two months later, he told me that he wanted to go to the Capitol. But I didn't believe him. I figured there was no way Trump would do anything that could potentially put himself in danger. But we now know that as soon as he got in the presidential vehicle following his speech—at precisely 1:17 P.M., according to the official White House log of the president's movements—Trump directed the driver to take him to the Capitol. In sworn testimony, both the driver and the lead Secret Service agent charged with protecting the president, Robert Engel, testified that Trump made this request within thirty seconds of getting into the vehicle and was told by Engel that they couldn't take him to the Capitol.*[2]

The driver testified that Trump was "pushing pretty hard to go." When Engel told Trump he couldn't make the trip because the Secret Service didn't have enough people to take him there safely, Trump said to him, "I'm the president and I'll decide where I get to go." Engel again told Trump they could not make the trip safely. Trump, according to the driver, dismissed the security concerns, saying that "it would be fine and that the people there [marching to the Capitol] were [Trump] supporters."

Trump lost that argument. He wanted to go to the Capitol but was instead taken back to the White House. There is some dispute about just how angry he became when Engel refused to take him where he wanted to go. In riveting live testimony before the January 6 Committee, White House aide Cassidy Hutchinson described Trump becoming so irate that he tried to grab the steering wheel and lunged at Engel, even trying to grab him by the neck. Hutchinson said that this is what she was told that afternoon by Secret Service agent Tony Ornato and that Engel was present when Ornato described the scene and didn't dispute the account. Ornato and Engel both told the committee they didn't recall that conversation. Both Engel and the driver denied Trump tried to grab the steering wheel.

---

*The Select Committee agreed not to name the Secret Service agent who was driving to protect his privacy.

But regardless of the extent of the presidential eruption of anger, this much is without dispute: Trump demanded to go to the Capitol after his speech, and his own Secret Service detail refused to take him. When he returned to the White House, Trump asked the White House valet, a Navy veteran named Walt Nauta,* what he thought of the speech. Nauta explained he didn't see the whole speech because the television networks were instead showing live video of the assault on the Capitol.

"Sir, they cut it off because they're rioting down at the Capitol," Nauta told him.

Trump asked him what he meant.

"They are rioting down there at the Capitol," Nauta said again.

"Oh really?" Trump responded. "All right, let's go see."

And with that, Trump walked over to his personal dining room adjacent to the other side of the Oval Office. A single photograph, taken by White House photographer Shealah Craighead, captures the moment. Trump is still wearing his overcoat, his shoulders somewhat hunched, and he has an expression that looks both angry and defeated. The photo was taken at 1:21 P.M.—and from that moment until 4:03 P.M., the White House log, which tracks all the official movements of the president, is blank. There's no evidence the records were erased; it's blank because the president, for nearly three hours, sat in his dining room and watched television while the US Capitol was under attack.

---

*US House of Representatives, *Final Report of the Select Committee to Investigate the January 6th Attack on the United States Capitol*, 117th Congress (December 22, 2022), p. 592. The report does not name Walt Nauta, referring to him only as "a member of the White House staff." Multiple sources tell me the employee was Nauta, a White House valet who went to work for Trump at Mar-a-Lago after leaving the White House. Nauta would go on to be indicted in Special Counsel Jack Smith's classified document investigation, accused of obstructing justice by helping Trump conceal boxes containing classified documents and lying to investigators.

As he sat in the dining room, Trump wasn't totally passive. He did act on one element of what he had just learned from the valet, who told him he could not watch his speech because "they cut it off" due to the "rioting down at the Capitol." He tweeted a video of his speech to his millions of Twitter followers, who, like Nauta, might have missed the speech because the cable television networks, including Fox News, had switched over to coverage of the unfolding riot on Capitol Hill.

Some of Trump's allies argue that he didn't intend for the march on the Capitol to turn violent—that he wanted a big, loud protest, but he didn't want his supporters to actually fight the police and storm their way into the building. That's not entirely implausible. In his speech, he did direct his supporters to "fight like hell" but also said, "I know that everyone here will soon be marching over to the Capitol building to peacefully and patriotically make your voices heard."

Trump himself told me he tried to go the Capitol twice that day—once immediately after his speech and a second time after he returned to the White House and saw the attack on the Capitol unfolding on television.

"I wanted to go back. I was thinking about going back during the problem to stop the problem, doing it myself. Secret Service didn't like that idea too much," Trump told me in March 2021. "I could have done that. And you know what, I would have been very well received."[3]

That's an astounding admission from Trump. *And you know what, I would have been very well received.* The rioters, he was telling me, would have welcomed him with open arms.

That's almost certainly true. The rioters were there for Trump, and they would have given him a hero's welcome if he joined them as they assaulted the Capitol.

There is, however, no evidence Trump wanted to stop anything other than the counting of electoral votes and the official certification of his election loss. Just look at what White House counsel Pat Cipollone told Liz Cheney in his sworn deposition:

> LIZ CHENEY: And who on the staff did not want people to leave the Capitol?
>
> PAT CIPOLLONE: On the staff?
>
> LIZ CHENEY: In the White House, how about?
>
> PAT CIPOLLONE: I don't—I—I can't think of anybody, you know, on that day who didn't want people to get out of the Capitol once the, you know, particularly once the violence started, no.
>
> ADAM SCHIFF: What about the president?
>
> LIZ CHENEY: Yeah.
>
> PAT CIPOLLONE: She said the staff, so I answered.
>
> LIZ CHENEY: No, I said in the White House.
>
> PAT CIPOLLONE: Oh, I'm sorry. I—I apologize. I thought you said who—who else on the staff. I—I—I can't reveal communications, but obviously I think, you know.[4]

Trump's unwillingness to take any action whatsoever to call off his supporters or to send reinforcements to protect the US Capitol is now well established. His acting defense secretary, Christopher Miller, testified he received calls while the attack was underway from Vice President Pence and from congressional leaders. They pleaded for him to send the National Guard to the Capitol. He received no call from the commander in chief.

The top military official at the Pentagon at the time, General Mark Milley, chairman of the Joint Chiefs of Staff, said the same thing. "I am not aware of anyone in the Pentagon having a conversation with President Trump on the day of the 6th," Milley recalled. "We talked to members of the House and the Senate leadership a lot, all afternoon. We talked to Vice President Pence. We talked to Meadows in the White House. But never once did we talk to, at least to my knowledge, to President Trump."

Milley says Pence was particularly emphatic.

"There were two or three calls with Vice President Pence. He was very animated, and he issued very explicit, very direct, unambiguous orders. There was no question about that," Milley later said. "He was very animated, very direct, very firm to Secretary [of Defense] Miller: Get the military down here, get the Guard down here, put down this situation, et cetera."[5]

It was precisely the time to show leadership. Violence had broken out at the US Capitol—right down the road from the White House—and Trump was missing in action.

It's not that he wasn't making any calls at all. Press Secretary Kayleigh McEnany testified that as rioters battled the police on the steps of the Capitol, Donald Trump asked for a call list of senators. He was still trying to whip votes for the lost cause of getting a majority in Congress to reject Joe Biden's electoral votes. Those calls didn't go well. Trump managed to get through to Senator Tommy Tuberville but only after calling Senator Mike Lee by accident. The White House phone list had the two senators' numbers mixed up.

Tuberville took the call from Trump about fifteen minutes after rioters broke into the Capitol and at a point of maximum danger for Pence. Secret Service agents had just whisked the vice president out of the Senate chamber. A few minutes later, at 2:24 P.M.,[6] Trump posted his infamous tweet saying, "Mike Pence didn't have the courage to do what should have been done to protect our Country and our Constitution." Just two minutes after Trump posted that tweet, rioters came within a mere forty feet of Pence as the Secret Service rushed him down the stairwell behind the Senate chamber on his way to a loading dock below the Capitol.

The crowd's reaction to Trump's tweet proved the rioters were taking their cues from him. In video presented by the January 6 Committee, a man with a bullhorn can be seen on the steps of the Capitol reading the tweet to the crowd. After the man reads the tweet, the crowd starts chanting, "Bring out Pence! Bring out Pence!" Those chants soon changed to the more direct and unforgettable chants of "Hang Mike Pence! Hang Mike Pence!"

With all that going on and the senators themselves about to be evacuated, Tuberville took Trump's phone call. Here's how he described his first call from a president as a United States senator:

"I basically told him, I said, 'Mr. President, we're not doing much work here right now because they just took our vice president out, and, matter of fact, I'm going to have to hang up on you,'" Tuberville said, recounting the conversation weeks later. "I've got to leave because the Secret Service and Capitol Police want us out."[7]

And with that, the newly minted freshman senator from Alabama hung up on the president of the United States.

Once again, Mitch McConnell's description of the state of the play was spot-on.

"A mob was assaulting the Capitol in his name," McConnell said after casting his vote in the Senate impeachment trial. "These criminals were carrying his banners, hanging his flags, and screaming their loyalty to him. It was obvious that only President Trump could end this. He was the only one."[8]

That fact was blatantly obvious to most of the people at the White House that day—especially the most junior among them. Sarah Matthews, a twenty-five-year-old deputy press secretary, testified that she watched the events unfold on a television in the West Wing with twenty-eight-year-old Ben Williamson, an aide to White House chief of staff Mark Meadows. "We both recognized that the situation was escalating and it was escalating quickly, and that the president needed to be out there immediately to tell these people to go home and condemn the violence that we were seeing," Matthews said.[9]

Cassidy Hutchinson, Meadows's twenty-four-year-old personal assistant, described her reaction to the situation unfolding. "I remember feeling frustrated, disappointed," she testified. "I was really sad. As an American, I was disgusted."[10]

Judd Deere, another deputy press secretary, testified that he believed the president's tweet saying Pence lacked courage was "extremely unhelpful" and that he told his boss, Press Secretary Kayleigh McEnany, that the White House needed to put out a message telling the rioters to go home.[11]

Most of the senior players in the White House were saying the exact same thing. As White House counsel Pat Cipollone testified, "There needed to be an immediate and forceful response, statement, public statement, that people need to leave the Capitol now."[12]

Trump, as we now know, wasn't listening to any of it. Kevin Mc-Carthy said that as he was being evacuated from the Capitol, he called Trump and told him, essentially, the same thing those junior aides in the White House were saying—that he needed to tell his own supporters to go home. Trump shrugged it off, telling McCarthy the rioters just cared more about the stolen election than McCarthy did.

When Hope Hicks, who had worked for Trump even before he announced his 2016 presidential campaign and had been as close to him as anybody in the White House, watched the assault on the Capitol unfold on television, she reacted with a mix of anger and horror. She hadn't gone to the White House that day, but she told me several people, including longtime Trump advisor Kellyanne Conway, had called her to say they had tried to reach Trump to tell him to call off the rioters. Hicks herself decided not to call because she didn't think it would do any good.

"I didn't call him because I felt like if the people who reached out to me to say they tried to talk to him and get him to tell people to go home weren't successful, I wasn't going to be either," Hicks told me. "I was really sad. I was really angry."[13]

As the rioters broke into the Senate chamber, Trump lamely tweeted again:

Donald J. Trump
@realDonaldTrump

Please support our Capitol Police and Law Enforcement. They are truly on the side of our Country. Stay peaceful!

2:38 PM · Jan 6, 2021

Still no condemnation of the violence. Still no call for his supporters to leave the Capitol. And we now know, Trump had to be browbeaten by his own daughter to include the words "Stay peaceful!" in a message to a group of people who were anything but peaceful. Press Secretary Kayleigh McEnany told her deputy, Sarah Matthews, "The president did not want to include any mention of peace in that tweet."[14]

The most radical of Trump's supporters heard his message loud and clear. Intercepted communications of those leading the assault on the Capitol captured their real-time reaction to Trump's tweet, with one member of the Oath Keepers militia saying, "That's saying a lot by what he didn't say. He didn't say not to do anything to the congressmen."

And he didn't say "go home."

Chief of Staff Mark Meadows received a blizzard of text messages while the riot was underway. The messages, which Meadows turned over to the January 6 Committee, provide a window into the real-time thinking of many of those closest to Trump outside the White House. Even Trump's own son Donald Trump Jr. begged Meadows to get his father to do something, texting, "He's got to condemn this shit ASAP. The Capitol Police tweet is not enough." Meadows replied, "I am pushing it hard. I agree."

In reality, it didn't seem Meadows was pushing hard at all. Not because he didn't want the violence to stop, but because he was resigned to the fact that no matter what he did or said, Trump was not going to act.

Hutchinson, Meadows's assistant, had her desk right next to his office and described the chief of staff as sitting on a couch and scrolling through his phone as others pleaded for Trump to call off the rioters.

She testified that Cipollone rushed to Meadows's office at one point saying, "The rioters have gotten to the Capitol, Mark. We need to go down and see the President now."

"He doesn't want to do anything, Pat," Meadows said.[15]

Among the text messages to Meadows uncovered by the January 6 Committee was one I personally sent him as the riot was underway.

"What are you going to do to stop this?" I texted Meadows at 2:53 P.M. "What is the president going to do?"

About fifteen minutes later, Reince Priebus, Trump's first chief of staff, texted Meadows in all caps: "TELL THEM TO GO HOME NOW!!!"

There was at least one dissenting voice in the White House to the idea of Donald Trump making a live address to the country to call off the mob. Retired Army general Keith Kellogg Jr., who spent all four years of the Trump presidency as a senior National Security Council official, said that a live press conference by Trump could actually make things worse.

"I remember saying very distinctly, 'Boy, I don't recommend a press conference,'" Kellogg recalled telling Press Secretary McEnany, "because in my experience in four years, there wasn't a single clean press conference we had."[16]

Think about that. At precisely the moment that demanded presidential leadership the most, Trump couldn't be trusted to make a live appearance in the White House briefing room.

It's unclear how hard Meadows was pushing Trump to act, but whatever he was saying in private, it wasn't having any impact. And with Congress under attack and his own vice president's life at risk, the president of the United States sat in his office and watched the chaos unfold on television.

"'They're literally calling for the vice president to be effing hung,'" Hutchinson recalled Cipollone saying. "And Mark [Meadows] had responded something to the effect of, 'You heard him, Pat. He thinks Mike deserves it. He doesn't think they're doing anything wrong.' To which Pat said something like, 'This is effing crazy, we need to be doing something more.'"[17]

McEnany mirrored the president's passivity. As I reported on the events of January 6 for ABC News, I repeatedly attempted to reach her—calling, texting, and emailing. The utter lack of response on such a critical day was so dumbfounding that at 7:42 A.M. the next morning I sent McEnany a message intended to note for history that a White House press secretary had been missing in action on a day that looms large in the history of the United States. For the subject line of my message I wrote, "Message to the National Archives":

> **From:** Karl, Jonathan D.
> **Sent:** Thursday, January 7, 2021 7:42 AM
> **To:** Gilmartin, Kayleigh M. EOP/WHO
> <Kayleigh.McEnany@who.eop.gov>
> **Subject:** Message to the National Archives
>
> Thanks to the Presidential Records Act, White House emails will be preserved for history; the process of releasing them to the public will begin in 15 years.
>
> Let the record show that throughout the extraordinary events of January 6, multiple emails, text messages and phone calls to the White House press secretary have gone

> unanswered. Attempts to get answers to basic questions
> this morning have also been fruitless.

I didn't receive a response to that email either, but at least I know it's there for posterity somewhere in the National Archives along with all the other unanswered queries I sent McEnany on January 6.

I would later learn that McEnany's own deputies were pleading with her to condemn the violence and call off the rioters. She had the honor and responsibility of being the lead spokesperson for the White House and did absolutely nothing. Sarah Matthews described the deliberations in the press office when she said they needed to condemn the violence.

"A colleague suggested that the president shouldn't condemn the violence because they thought it would be 'handing a win' to the media if he were to condemn his supporters," Matthews testified. "And I couldn't believe that we were arguing over this in the middle of the West Wing, talking about the politics of a tweet, being concerned with 'handing the media a win' when we had just watched all of that violence unfold at the Capitol. And so, I motioned up at the TV and I said, 'Do you think it looks like we're effing winning?'"[18]

And with that, Matthews, the twenty-five-year-old junior press aide, displayed more common sense—and acted more decisively—than either the president of the United States or his chief of staff or his press secretary. Matthews submitted her resignation letter at the end of the day.

More than two hours after rioters stormed into the Capitol, Trump finally agreed to make a prerecorded video message telling his supporters to go home. Even at the moment he finally chose to act,

Trump did so with weakness and indecision. The message both told the rioters to go home and justified their actions.

"I know your pain, I know you're hurt," he said, addressing his words directly to the people who were storming the Capitol. "We had an election that was stolen from us. It was a landslide election and everyone knows it, especially the other side. But you have to go home now. We have to have peace."

These people had attacked police officers with flagpoles and riot shields. They had shattered windows and doors as they broke into the building. They rummaged through the desks of US senators and the office of the Speaker of the House. They called for the hanging of his vice president. But even as Trump finally asked them to go home, he added these words:

"We love you, you're very special," he said. "You've seen what happens, you see the way others are treated that are so bad and so evil. I know how you feel. But go home, and go home in peace."

Once again, even the most junior people working at the White House had more sense than the president they served. Nick Luna, a twentysomething assistant whose primary responsibility was carrying the president's bags, testified that he told Trump he thought the statement made it sound like Trump was responsible for what happened at the Capitol.

"It was my interpretation of the words," Luna testified. "I don't write speeches or anything, but the phrase 'these are the things that happen' to me sounded as if—as if culpability was associated with it."[19]

As weak as the message was, the rioters did respond. They went home. And two hours after he taped his video message, Trump made it perfectly clear, again, why he didn't condemn the violence.

> **Donald J. Trump**
> @realDonaldTrump
>
> These are the things and events that happen when a sacred landslide election victory is so unceremoniously & viciously stripped away from great patriots who have been badly & unfairly treated for so long. Go home with love & in peace. Remember this day forever!
>
> (!) This claim of election fraud is disputed, and this Tweet can't be replied to, Retweeted, or liked due to a risk of violence
>
> 6:01 PM · Jan 6, 2021

Perhaps the most disturbing thing about Trump's inaction that day was his utter lack of understanding about the damage done and lack of empathy for those who were hurt. White House phone records show that the very last person Trump talked to that day was Johnny McEntee, the ultra-loyal director of the Presidential Personnel Office.

The January 6 Committee asked McEntee whether Trump, on that call, expressed any regret for what happened that day.

"No," McEntee answered. "I mean, I think he was shocked by, you know, it getting a little out of control, but I don't remember sadness, specifically."[20]

A little out of control?!

The committee asked Ivanka Trump a similar series of questions.

COMMITTEE STAFF: Has he ever expressed to you any sentiment that he did or did not do the right thing in how he responded on the day of the 6th?

IVANKA TRUMP: No.

COMMITTEE STAFF: Has he ever expressed any sentiment about
something that he wished he had done on the day of
the 6th?

IVANKA TRUMP: No.

COMMITTEE STAFF: Has he ever said anything to you about the
people who were injured or who died that day?

IVANKA TRUMP: No.

COMMITTEE STAFF: Has he ever said anything to you about
whether he should or should not continue to talk about
the 2020 Presidential election after the events on the 6th?

IVANKA TRUMP: No.[21]

Trump let down America—but he also let down his most die-hard
supporters. According to the FBI, four days after the attack on the
Capitol, Stewart Rhodes, the head of the pro-Trump Oath Keepers
militia group, attempted to send Trump a secret letter. "Take command like Washington would. Be a Churchill, not a Chamberlain,"
Rhodes wrote to Trump. "I am here for you and so are all my men.
We will come help you if you need us. Military and police. And so
will your millions of supporters."*

Members of the Oath Keepers played a key role in the assault on
the Capitol, marching up the steps of the building in military forma-
tion and helping the mob break into the building. They came with
body armor, but without guns. They left their weapons across the
Potomac River in Virginia, stockpiling them in a room at the

---

*At the trial of Stewart Rhodes and other leaders of the Oath Keepers, witness Jason
Alpers testified that he secretly recorded Rhodes dictating this message to him. But
instead of attempting to pass the letter on to Trump, Alpers turned it over to the FBI.

Comfort Inn in Arlington. The group's insane idea was that Trump would invoke the Insurrection Act, which allows the military to be used for domestic law enforcement, and that their militia would be called into action. It was madness, but it's what they believed Trump wanted them to do.

Days after Trump did nothing of the sort, Rhodes was caught on tape by the FBI complaining to fellow Oath Keepers that Trump wasn't acting on his own words.

"If he's not going to do the right thing, and he's just gonna let himself be removed illegally, then we should have brought rifles," Rhodes can be heard saying on the recording. "We could have fixed it right then and there. I'd hang fucking Pelosi from the lamppost."

The extent of Trump's inability to meet the moment—either to stop the violence or to consummate his plan to overthrow the election—was on vivid display the day after the attack on the Capitol. With growing outrage over his failure to condemn the violence even after the fact, he faced the very real possibility that his own cabinet would convene to declare him mentally unfit for office. Fox News host Sean Hannity, as staunch and unquestioning an ally as Trump has ever had, said it himself in a text message to McEnany after the riot, writing: "No more crazy people. No more stolen election talk. Yes, impeachment and 25th Amendment are real, many people will quit."

With his ability to stay in the White House for the less than two weeks left in his presidency in doubt, Trump was once again cajoled by his senior staff and, most importantly, his daughter Ivanka to make a video statement condemning the violence. He didn't want to do it, but did have enough sense to know that he had to. The video outtakes of the videotaped messages are as damning as any other single piece of evidence uncovered by the January 6 Committee.

As he starts to read the words that have been written for him, Trump becomes disoriented and angry.

"I would like to begin by addressing the heinous attack yesterday," he says, looking uncomfortably at the camera. "And to those who broke the law, you will pay. You do not represent our movement. You do not represent our country. And if you broke the law—I can't say that. I'm not gonna. I already said 'you will pay.'"

He didn't want to say that the people who attacked police officers and broke into the Capitol broke the law.

"The demonstrators who infiltrated the Capitol have defied the seat of—it's 'defiled,' right?" he continued, growing irritated and banging the podium. "I can't see it very well. I'll do this. I'm going to do this. Let's go. But this election is now over. Congress has certified the results."

And then he stops reading the teleprompter.

"I don't want to say 'the election's over,'" he tells the staff in the room. "I just want to say 'Congress has certified the results' without saying 'the election's over,' okay?"

Off camera, Ivanka is heard agreeing to the edit, and Trump starts over.

"I would like to begin by addressing the heinous attack yesterday," he says, slurring the word "yesterday." "'Yesterday' is a hard word for me."

"Just take it out," Ivanka says. "Say 'heinous attack.'"

The whole thing is uncomfortable to watch—a president still unable to speak with clarity a full day after failing to act in time of crisis.

Watching the edited video posted by the White House on January 7, I could see the president uncomfortably condemning the violence. It was overdue, of course, but referring to the actions of his supporters as a "heinous attack" directly contradicted his praise for the rioters the day before—"we love you, you're very special"—and even now neither Trump nor his White House had condemned the threats against Vice President Pence. Trump hadn't checked on his vice president's safety during the riot and over the course of the next few days still hadn't spoken to the man.

Once again, I tried to get a response from the White House press office. My question seemed like an easy one to answer: Does the White House condemn the calls for hanging Mike Pence? I emailed my question to McEnany, and to be absolutely certain she would not miss it, I also sent it to two of her deputies:

> **From:** Karl, Jonathan D.
> **Sent:** Saturday, January 9, 2021 3:49 PM
> **To:** Kayleigh McEnany <Kayleigh.McEnany@who.eop.gov>;
> Brian Morgenstern <Brian.r.morgenstern@who.eop.gov>
> **Cc:** Judd Deere <Judson.P.Deere@who.eop.gov>
> **Subject:** "Hang Pence"
>
> Kayleigh,
>
> Do you or the President have any reaction to the calls for violence against the Vice President by supporters of the president, calls that have become so widespread that "Hang Pence" is trending today on social media?
>
> I appreciate a quick response to this.
>
> Thank you.

Two hours later, there was still no response. So I tried again:

From: Karl, Jonathan D.
Sent: Saturday, January 9, 2021 5:44 PM
To: Kayleigh McEnany <Kayleigh.McEnany@who.eop.gov>;
Brian Morgenstern <brian.r.morgenstern@who.eop.gov>
Cc: Judd Deere <Judson.P.Deere@who.eop.gov>;
Karl, Jonathan D. <Jonathan.D.Karl@abc.com>
Subject: Re: "Hang Pence"

Anything on this? Does the president condemn these
threats against Mike Pence? Does he endorse them? What
about this video of the crowd storming the capitol chanting
"hang Mike Pence!"?

With that, I finally got a response. Not from McEnany herself, but from her deputy Judd Deere: "We strongly condemn all calls to violence, including those against any member of this administration."

Three days after January 6, Trump's press office was still unwilling to specifically criticize those calling for the death of his vice president. I had not seen the one-sentence email from Judd Deere because it got caught by my spam filter and went directly to my junk email folder—perhaps a sign of just how far artificial intelligence had come. Not seeing the response, I sent out a tweet noting that despite repeated inquires, neither McEnany nor her deputies had made any comment on the threats against the vice president's life.[22]

Suddenly, McEnany sprang to life. Three days after Trump had incited an insurrection, his White House press secretary accused me of acting irresponsibly. McEnany issued a tweet saying, "The White

House sent @jonkarl a response condemning all violence at 5:55pm, yet he irresponsibly tweeted at 6:38pm that we did not respond."[23]

The horror!

"The generic statement from your deputy went to my junk mail," I responded on Twitter. "Sorry about that. It also doesn't mention Mike Pence. So, let me ask you again: Does the president condemn the chants of 'Hang Pence' from his supporters."[24]

I never got an answer to that. But when I interviewed Trump for my book *Betrayal* two months later, I got my answer directly from the man himself. He didn't condemn the violence; he offered a justification for it. "The people were very angry," he said. "It's common sense, Jon."

The damage done by Trump's inaction on January 6 was summarized well by a top aide who resigned that day, Deputy National Security Advisor Matthew Pottinger, who said the president's behavior damaged US national security and that, in acting like such a sore loser and failing so thoroughly, Donald Trump allowed our enemies to portray America as a nation in decline and democracy itself as a loser.

"I think it emboldened our enemies by helping give them ammunition to feed a narrative that our system of government doesn't work, that the United States is in decline," Pottinger testified more than one year after the attack on the Capitol. "We've been hearing, for the entirety of US history, from kings and despots, that the United States is in decline, and those kings and despots have been proven wrong every single time. But nonetheless, January 6 helped feed a perception that I think emboldens our adversaries."[25]

CHAPTER FOUR

THE CRAZY FACTOR

Launching her longshot presidential bid in February 2023, former South Carolina governor Nikki Haley announced she wanted to impose a "mandatory mental competency test" for any politician over the age of seventy-five. The proposal had no chance of going anywhere and was probably unconstitutional, but it allowed the fifty-one-year-old candidate to knock the age of President Joe Biden—and, more obliquely, Donald Trump.

Trump, however, was all for the idea—and wanted to expand it. "ANYBODY running for the Office of President of the United States should agree to take a full & complete Mental Competency Test," he posted on Truth Social days later. "Being an outstanding President requires great mental acuity & physical stamina. If you don't have these qualities or traits, it is likely you won't succeed."[1]

Trump was right, of course. The presidency is a grueling job for even the most energetic and sharp individuals. But as you'll see in this chapter, in private, some of Trump's most loyal advisors had serious concerns about his cognitive state as his presidency drew to a close. And for many, those concerns have only intensified since he left office.

Donald Trump faced questions about his mental stability long before he stepped into the White House. His critics pointed to his compulsively self-centered, erratic, and often self-destructive behavior. They tossed around terms like "narcissistic personality disorder" or, more simply, called him "mentally deranged" or "fucking crazy." Most of these allegations came from armchair psychiatrists who'd never met the man, let alone evaluated him—they just didn't like what they saw on TV. But as Trump grew closer to power, some legitimate doctors with impressive credentials got in on the action, too.

On November 29, 2016—just weeks after Trump was elected—a psychiatry professor at Harvard Medical School named Judith Herman wrote an urgent letter to outgoing president Barack Obama with two of her colleagues. At issue: Trump's mental state.

"We are writing to express our grave concern regarding the mental stability of our President-Elect," the letter began. "Professional standards do not permit us to venture a diagnosis for a public figure whom we have not evaluated personally. Nevertheless, his widely reported symptoms of mental instability—including grandiosity, impulsivity, hypersensitivity to slights or criticism, and an apparent inability to distinguish between fantasy and reality—lead us to question his fitness for the immense responsibilities of the office."

These well-credentialed academics "strongly recommend[ed]" Trump undergo "a full medical and neuropsychiatric evaluation by an impartial team of investigators."[2]

Why this letter was addressed to Obama is anyone's guess. What was he going to do? Order his successor and political opponent to spend time in a psychiatric hospital? Declare the election results null and void by reasons of insanity? At least Herman and her coauthors didn't formally declare Trump mentally ill without a proper analysis. As they noted in their letter, professional standards dictated that they couldn't diagnose anyone they hadn't personally evaluated.

Within months, however, some doctors decided it was time to throw those professional standards out the window. In April 2017, Dr. Bandy Lee, a forensic psychiatrist at the Yale School of Medicine, convened a conference in New Haven, Connecticut, entitled "Does Professional Responsibility Include a Duty to Warn?" The assembled psychiatric professionals discussed whether they had an obligation to alert the world if the president of the United States was dangerously unstable. That none of these professional psychiatrists had ever actually met Trump—let alone examined him—didn't seem to matter.

"You don't have to interview him privately in order to, in effect, have an interview with him because he speaks publicly to all of us. The whole public has interviews with him, you know, every single day, three or four tweets at a time," said Dr. James Gilligan, a psychiatrist at New York University. Paraphrasing Bob Dylan, he added, "You don't have to be a weatherman to know which way the wind is blowing."[3]

He described the danger in almost apocalyptic terms. "We have more than enough evidence here that it's important to mention that everybody in America, and in fact everybody in the world, is in danger from the currently most powerful man in the world," Gilligan said. "If we remain silent, I would say we give passive support to people who would make the extremely dangerous and naive mistake of assuming that Trump is a normal politician."

Many psychiatric professionals found this speculation problematic.

The American Psychiatric Association (APA) code of conduct stipulates that it is "unethical for a psychiatrist to offer a professional opinion unless he or she has conducted an examination and has been granted proper authorization for such a statement." Known as "the Goldwater Rule," the guideline dates back to the 1964 presidential candidacy of Barry Goldwater, whom hundreds of psychiatrists labeled mentally ill in a survey published by *Fact* magazine.[4] In truth, the Arizona Republican was nothing of the sort—the psychiatrists just didn't like his politics. He successfully sued the magazine for defamation after the election, winning $75,000 in damages and prompting the APA to institute the Goldwater Rule.*

Impartial observers could look at Herman's letter and Lee's conference and see history repeating itself a half century later: left-leaning academics dressing up concern about a right-wing politician in clinical diagnoses. But questions about Trump's mental state weren't just coming from progressives.

"The presidency is not just another office," conservative *New York Times* columnist Ross Douthat wrote in the May 2017 article "The 25th Amendment Solution for Removing Trump." "One needs some basic attributes: a reasonable level of intellectual curiosity, a certain seriousness of purpose, a basic level of managerial competence, a decent attention span, a functional moral compass, a measure of restraint and self-control. And if a president is deficient in one or more of them, you can be sure it will be exposed. Trump is seemingly deficient in them all."[5]

Trump was certainly aware of all the discussion his brain was generating, and his efforts to prove the haters wrong were often as

---

* The equivalent of about $500,000 today .

funny as they were unconvincing. "I'm a very stable genius!" he famously blurted out at a 2018 NATO summit in response to a question from a Croatian reporter. More than a year later, he sent out a bizarre six-word tweet seeming to refer back to his own comment: "'A Very Stable Genius!' Thank you."[6]

In July 2020—smack-dab in the middle of the pandemic—Trump spent weeks bragging about his performance on a routine cognitive test and his ability to remember a list of five items: person, woman, man, camera, TV. "Yes, the first few questions are easy," the president told Chris Wallace on Fox News when Wallace pointed out that one of the questions on the test was to identify a picture of an elephant. "But I'll bet you couldn't even answer the last five questions. I'll bet you couldn't. They get very hard, the last five questions."[7]

Although Dr. Bandy Lee was eventually let go from Yale, she was able to parlay her Duty to Warn conference into a bestselling book, *The Dangerous Case of Donald Trump: 27 Psychiatrists and Mental Health Experts Assess a President*. The book not only ventured a diagnosis of Trump himself, but it also argued that most of his followers suffered from a "shared psychosis"—or "folie à millions."[8] To her critics, the shtick was more political than scientific. "Psychiatric diagnosis is easily and frequently distorted whenever there is an external incentive to do so," wrote Allen Frances, one of the authors of the *Diagnostic and Statistical Manual of Mental Disorders*, which is used by psychiatrists to identify mental illness. "Diagnosis of public figures at a distance is far too likely to be biased, flat out wrong, and to constitute no more than an unfair form of psychological name calling."[9]

Frances was right—the speculation "at a distance" was dubious. But the diagnoses of Trump's mental state weren't just taking place in ivory towers; they were also coming from within Trump's own White House.

Shortly after he was selected to serve as the president's acting chief of staff in December 2018, Mick Mulvaney suggested some light reading for his fellow senior administration officials: a 2011 book entitled *A First-Rate Madness: Uncovering the Links Between Leadership and Mental Illness*. As I first reported in *Front Row at the Trump Show*, Mulvaney read passages from the book aloud at a retreat he convened at Camp David for top White House staff. He thought it'd help them understand the unique leadership style of the man they served—and provide some reassurance.

"This book argues that in at least one vitally important circumstance, *insanity* produces good results and *sanity* is a problem," Dr. Nassir Ghaemi, director of the Mood Disorders Program at Tufts Medical Center, writes in the book's introduction. "In times of crisis, we are better off being led by mentally ill leaders than by mentally normal ones."[10]

The thesis is not—forgive me—as crazy as it sounds. Ghaemi ticks through a series of case studies and argues that some of history's most effective leaders—including Abraham Lincoln, Franklin Delano Roosevelt, and Winston Churchill—suffered from varying degrees of mental illness. Some eminently sane individuals like Neville Chamberlain and George McClellan, meanwhile, were abysmal failures.

A First-Rate Madness was published more than five years before Trump took office, but Mulvaney presumably found Ghaemi's description of "mania" eerily familiar. "Decisions seem easy; no guilt, no doubt, just do it. The trouble is not in starting things, but in finishing them; with so much to do and little time, it's easy to get distracted," Ghaemi writes. "Mania is like a galloping horse: you win the race if you hang on, or you fall off and never even finish. In Freudian terms, one might say that mania enhances the id, for better or worse."

By recommending the book, Mulvaney seemed to be agreeing with Trump's critics that the president was mentally ill—or, as he often described it to White House colleagues, that Trump's "mind just worked differently." But from Mulvaney's perspective, Trump's supposed condition was an asset, not a liability; what some saw as instability might just be the key to his genius.

It's easy to see why Mulvaney was drawn to Ghaemi's book. "Much of what passes for normal is not found in the highly successful political and military leader, especially in times of crisis," it argues. "If normal, mentally healthy people run for president, they tend not to become great ones."

I reached out to Ghaemi while Trump was still in the White House, and although he wasn't aware his book had become a hit in the West Wing, he certainly understood why it caught on. "I believe [Trump] has mild manic symptoms all the time," he told me, noting the president displayed several attributes of a "hyperthymic temperament," like distractibility, sexual indiscretions, high self-esteem, impulsive behavior, and a decreased need for sleep. But Ghaemi cautioned against overreading his thesis: Not everyone with mental illness is a natural leader, and some can be downright dangerous. As Mulvaney may have noticed, *A First-Rate Madness* included a chapter on Adolf Hitler.

When I first spoke to Ghaemi, in 2019, he pointed out his argument pertained primarily to leaders in times of crisis: Lincoln and the Civil War, Roosevelt and the Great Depression, Churchill and

World War II. In "normal times"—which 2019 arguably was—a leader's mental illness was far more of a drawback. "Such persons are at their weakest in non-crisis situations, when norms need to be followed. They are not effective administrators, and not well organized," Ghaemi wrote to me. "If manic traits occur alone, without any evidence of depressive episodes or symptoms (as apparently with Donald Trump), manic leaders can be very unempathetic toward those they oppose, and unrealistic."[11]

I reached out to Ghaemi again in early 2023 as I was writing this book. Trump had now experienced two crises encapsulating both aspects of the psychiatrist's theory—one (January 6) that was entirely of his own making and one (the pandemic) that was not. Ghaemi pointed to Operation Warp Speed and the rapid development of COVID-19 vaccines as an example of Trump's unconventional thinking paying dividends, but he noted that the downside of Trump's supposed mania was on full display after the 2020 election, when the president exhibited signs of "manic denial" by refusing to accept the reality he had lost.

"The nuance I brought out in my book is that the best leaders are both manic and depressive, not just one or the other, because the mood states have different strengths which complement each other (creativity and productivity and resilience with mania; empathy and realism with depression)," Ghaemi said in an email. "Trump only had half this picture, and it played out to his detriment in the pandemic and the 2020 election due to his extreme lack of realism, i.e., his denial of the truth, since he was manic all the time and never experienced the realism effect of having had depression."

Trump's unconventional mind hadn't rendered him a modern-day Churchill or FDR—he was simply unfit for the office he held.

Following January 6, even Mulvaney seemed to acknowledge as much. He was no longer Trump's chief of staff at that point but had accepted a far more low-key job as the president's special envoy to Northern Ireland. Even that was too much. "It's a small job. It's a part-time gig," he told CNBC the morning after hundreds of Trump supporters stormed the Capitol. "I just—I can't do it. I can't stay."[12]

"I wouldn't be surprised to see more of my friends resign over the course of the next 24 to 48 hours," he added.

Mulvaney's prediction quickly rang true. Deputy National Security Advisor Matt Pottinger had resigned on January 6, as had Stephanie Grisham, Melania Trump's chief of staff. The next day, Education Secretary Betsy DeVos and Transportation Secretary Elaine Chao announced their resignations. "Yesterday, our country experienced a traumatic and entirely avoidable event as supporters of the President stormed the Capitol building following a rally he addressed," Chao wrote. "As I'm sure is the case with many of you, it has deeply troubled me in a way that I simply cannot set aside."[13]

Other members in the administration felt similarly but decided to remain in their posts for the final two weeks of Trump's presidency. They were worried about who would take their place, and at least one cabinet member was willing to stay if her vote would be needed to invoke the Twenty-Fifth Amendment, which would remove Trump from office if the vice president and a majority of the cabinet found him to be "unable to discharge the powers and duties of his office."

Education Secretary DeVos, in fact, stepped down only after she had explored that option and realized it wasn't going to happen. "I spoke with the vice president and just let him know I was there to do whatever he wanted and needed me to do or help with, and he made it very clear that he was not going to go in that direction or that path," she later said in a remarkably candid interview with Ingrid Jacques of *USA Today* about those high-level deliberations. "I spoke with colleagues. I wanted to get a better understanding of the law itself and see if it was applicable in this case. There were more than a few people who had those conversations internally."[14]

One person having those conversations *externally* was Trump's former chief of staff John Kelly. "If I was still there, I would call the cabinet and start talking about the Twenty-Fifth Amendment," he told me as the January 6 riot was still underway. Many of his onetime colleagues who were still in the administration—some of the highest-ranking officials—were thinking the exact same thing, although some of them would later deny it.

Secretary of State Mike Pompeo and Treasury Secretary Steven Mnuchin were two such individuals. Shortly after the Capitol was attacked, I heard from a trusted Republican source close to senior White House officials and congressional leaders that members of the cabinet—including Pompeo and Mnuchin—were discussing the feasibility of using the Twenty-Fifth Amendment to remove Trump from office and limit the damage he could do to the country. These weren't just casual comments, either: A second source close to Pompeo later told me the secretary of state had requested a legal analysis on the procedure. The analysis concluded it wasn't worth pursuing, in part because the process could be subject to legal challenge and would simply take too long considering that Trump had only fourteen days left in office.

Pompeo and Mnuchin were two of the last senior administration officials who had been there since the beginning. They didn't just hold two of the most important jobs in the federal government; they were two of the president's most trusted confidants. That either one of them would even entertain, even briefly, declaring Trump unfit and removing him from office is a testament to just how concerning the president's behavior was to those closest to him. This wasn't just an academic exercise. These were two people in Trump's inner circle questioning whether he needed to be the first president ever expelled from the White House by his own cabinet.

Months passed, and neither Pompeo nor Mnuchin publicly acknowledged the reports—from me and several other journalists—that they had discussed the possibility of invoking the Twenty-Fifth Amendment. I reached out to Pompeo repeatedly in an effort to confirm the story. If those conversations never took place, surely a Trump loyalist like him would want to clear the air. But I got no response.

Until August 2021. In an interview with Trump over the phone, I told the former president what I had learned about Mnuchin's conversations with Pompeo. He told me it was "total bullshit" and that everybody in his cabinet had told him so.

"Is it possible that Pompeo would be pretending to be totally and completely loyal to you?" I asked.

"I think Mike is totally loyal," Trump said, adding that if any other cabinet member had talked to Pompeo about the Twenty-Fifth Amendment, "he would have filled me in immediately."

Shortly after the call ended, I talked to one of Trump's advisors and pointed out that Pompeo had never publicly denied talking about the Twenty-Fifth Amendment and had ignored my repeated questions about it. "If it's not true, why wouldn't he just come out and say it's not true?" I asked.

That did the trick. A few hours later, a spokesman for Pompeo— who had been ignoring my calls and emails for months—finally got back to me and read me a carefully worded denial: "Pompeo through a spokesman denied there have ever been conversations around invoking the 25th Amendment." The spokesman refused to put his own name on the statement—I suspect because he knew it was a lie.

Pompeo would later confirm as much in sworn testimony before the January 6 Committee. "I'm sure the words '25th Amendment' came up in some conversation," he acknowledged. "I have no specific recollection of that. But it was never anything that I had a conversation with anyone that I can recall that was remotely serious."[15]

The typically self-assured Pompeo retreated to different variations of the same phrase as the investigators asked further questions about the Twenty-Fifth Amendment—regarding any discussions he may have had or any legal analyses he may have requested:

"I don't recall it."

"I have no recollection."

"Not that I recall."

"I don't recall."

It's preposterous, of course, that the former secretary of state wouldn't remember talking to someone about declaring the president mentally unfit for office. But being forgetful under oath isn't a crime—lying is.

At least one prominent witness to the conversations suffered no such memory lapse. When the committee asked General Mark Milley, the Joint Chiefs of Staff chairman, if he remembered any conversations about removing Trump from office under the Twenty-Fifth Amendment, he answered in the affirmative. "There was at least one or two occasions when other members of the cabinet mentioned it very brief, like, 10 seconds, 15 seconds," he testified in November 2021. "And then they looked, and they saw that I was standing there, and knowing I'm not a member of the cabinet, they shut up."

"Who were they?" investigators asked.

"Steve Mnuchin, Pompeo," he replied. "I think that's it—those two."[16]

When Mnuchin was deposed nearly a year later, investigators read him Milley's comments verbatim. That jogged his memory. "I mean, I do recall speaking to Secretary Pompeo about the 25th Amendment," the former Treasury secretary admitted. "It came up very briefly in our conversation. We both believed that the best outcome was a normal transition of power."[17]

That didn't stop him from looking further into the possibility. "The only research I did out of curiosity was I googled it," Mnuchin told the committee. "I remember my general counsel asking me if we wanted him to do extensive research on it. I said, no, not at this point."

Not at this point.

If I were asking the questions, Mnuchin would've had to explain exactly what he meant by that. Why was he doing online research about the Twenty-Fifth Amendment? Why was the Treasury Department's general counsel offering to dive deeper on the subject? At what point *would* Mnuchin have wanted additional analysis of the process? We'll likely never know, because the committee's questioner apparently had more pressing subjects to get to:

Q: Let me read you a passage from Jonathan Karl's book.

MNUCHIN: I'm familiar with it, but go ahead.

Q: He said, "Mnuchin did have conversations with other members, plural, of the Cabinet that night, January 6th, and the next morning on a step much more dramatic than issuing a statement. According to a source familiar with the conversations, Mnuchin talked to other members of the Cabinet about attempting to remove Trump from office by invoking the 25th Amendment. Among the Cabinet officials Mnuchin spoke to that night was Secretary of State Pompeo." Again, is that accurate? Does that refresh any recollection?

MNUCHIN: It is completely inaccurate. I can tell you I did speak to Jonathan Karl on background. What I told him—he asked me about the 25th Amendment. I said that I was not going to make any comments on the 25th Amendment, that I didn't think it was appropriate in that format, and that he shouldn't take that as meaning that there were conversations or there weren't conversations.[18]

At least one portion of Mnuchin's response is true: He *did* speak to me in 2021 for my previous book *Betrayal*. But the rest of his answer is either misleading or downright wrong—and I have the audiotapes to prove it. The conversation was on background, meaning that I agreed not to quote him by name. But now that he has talked about the interview and mischaracterized what he told me, I will correct the record with his actual quotes.

"I was aware of all these discussions," Mnuchin said when I asked him about the Twenty-Fifth Amendment. "It would not be an unreasonable assumption to think that people were calling me, okay, and talking about it, whether they were pushing it or not pushing it."

As you can see, he clearly acknowledged that he was aware of discussions about the Twenty-Fifth Amendment, adding it "would not be an unreasonable assumption" to think people were calling him about it. I reached out to Mnuchin again in early 2023 and offered to send him my recording. He did not respond.

Mnuchin and Pompeo both had their own reasons to downplay the significance of their conversations on and shortly after January 6. Mnuchin was deposed as he was building a post-government career centered on his time as Trump's Treasury secretary, and, although he ended up deciding against it, Pompeo testified while he was still considering running for president himself. There may be no quicker way to lose a 2024 Republican presidential primary than to admit you'd considered trying to oust Donald Trump from office.

But Pompeo did exactly that. Mnuchin and DeVos had considered it, too—and that's just who's confirmed their deliberations publicly. And so, by January 2021, the controversial position that a group of left-leaning academics had taken at a 2017 Yale conference—that Trump was mentally unstable and a danger to the country—was a commonly held opinion *within Trump's own cabinet.* And by April 2022, it was a punch line.

"The press often will ask me if I think Donald Trump is crazy," Republican governor Chris Sununu of New Hampshire joked in remarks at the Gridiron Club's annual spring dinner. "And I'll say it this way: I don't think he's so crazy that you could put him in a mental institution. But I think if he were in one, he ain't getting out!"[19]

CHAPTER FIVE

TEAM OF SYCOPHANTS

D onald Trump foreshadowed his presidency—and its downfall—in a little-noticed speech he delivered in late March 2016, just weeks before he clinched the Republican nomination. Speaking to a crowd of students at St. Norbert College in northeastern Wisconsin, he announced he was going to deviate from his usual campaign message.

"When I saw all this youth, these great-looking young people, I said, 'I'm going to talk for a few minutes about success,'" he told the hundreds assembled. "Should I do that?"

After the applause died down, he gave the kind of advice the students could have heard only from Donald Trump.

"You'll find, when you become very successful, the people that you will like best are the people that are less successful than you, because when you go to a table you can tell them all of these wonderful stories, and they'll sit back and listen," Trump explained. "Always be around unsuccessful people, because everybody will respect you. Do you understand that?"

That's right. The future president told those college kids in Wisconsin that the key to success is surrounding yourself with people who are not as successful as you because they will think you are brilliant.

That approach might work for a professional celebrity looking for a fawning entourage, but it didn't lend itself well to running the federal government. During his one term as president and first two runs for the White House, Trump burned through six campaign managers,* four chiefs of staff, six national security advisors, five homeland security advisors, and more lawyers than I can count.† He had vicious fallings-out with both of his confirmed attorneys general and fired both of his confirmed defense secretaries. Some of the people he dismissed along the way may have deserved to be fired or should never have been hired in the first place, but many who got the boot had only committed the sin of not indulging the president's whims.

---

* Technically, there were four campaign managers (Corey Lewandowski, Kellyanne Conway, Brad Parscale, and Bill Stepien), a campaign "chairman" (Paul Manafort), and a CEO (Steve Bannon).

† Here are a few lawyers who worked for Trump outside of government after he became president: Michael Cohen, Rudy Giuliani, Jenna Ellis, Eric Herschmann, Todd Blanche, John Lauro, Susan Necheles, Evan Corcoran, Lindsey Halligan, Christopher Kise, James Trusty, Bruce Castor Jr., David Schoen, Alan Dershowitz, Robert Ray, Jay Sekulow, Christina Bobb, John Rowley, Alex Cannon, Justin Clark, Matt Morgan, Ron Fischetti, Quincy Bird, Jeremy Bailie, Honey Rechtin, Carol Sweeney, Alina Habba, Drew Findling, John Dowd, Dwight Thomas, Michael van der Veen, Jennifer Little, Sidney Powell, John Rowley, John Eastman, William Consovoy, Pam Bondi, Patrick Strawbridge, Joe Tacopina, Cameron Norris, Marc Kasowitz, Michael Madaio, Robert Garson, Yanina Zilberman, Peter Ticktin, Cleta Mitchell, Jamie Alan Sasson, Jesse Binnall, Jane Raskin, Marty Raskin, Tim Parlatore, Kenneth Chesebro, and Boris Epshteyn. There are others. And I'm not including people like Pat Cipollone, Ty Cobb, Don McGahn, and the many other lawyers who worked in the Trump White House—they were government lawyers, not Trump lawyers, even if Trump didn't seem to understand the difference.

The result, by the very end of his presidency, was an administration full of two types of people: true believers whose Trump fanaticism was their only qualification for their roles, and those who had learned that the key to survival was to keep their head down.

From the very beginning, the upper levels of the Trump administration seemed chock-full of Trump devotees, and he claimed to be enormously proud of the team he had assembled. "We have a phenomenal team of people," he told the White House reporters he'd summoned to witness his first full cabinet meeting in June 2017. "A great group of talent."

For Trump, it was a moment of triumph; the man few people believed would ever come anywhere near the presidency now had his entire cabinet confirmed by the Senate and assembled for the world to see. Over the course of his campaign, Trump had promised to hire "only the best and finest" for his administration. Now that those top officials were in place, he wanted each and every one of them to say a few words before the television cameras.

"I'm going to start with our vice president," he said once the reporters were in place. "Where is our vice president?"

Mike Pence was sitting about four feet away, directly across from him. Apparently, the man who Trump had said looked like he came right out of "central casting" for the role of vice president didn't stand out in a crowd like this. But Pence took his cue and kicked things off with remarks that set the tone for the meeting, and the rest of the Trump presidency.

"It's the greatest privilege of my life to serve as vice president to a president who is keeping his word to the American people," Pence said as Trump nodded in approval.

What followed was the strangest televised cabinet meeting in the history of the presidency. One by one, the men and women Trump had brought in to lead his administration extolled the brilliance of the man they served.

There was Nikki Haley, the new US ambassador to the United Nations, who declared that, thanks to Trump, "we now have a very strong voice" on the international stage. Attorney General Jeff Sessions spoke of all the praise he was hearing from local and federal law enforcement because Trump had "set the exact right message" on fighting crime. Tom Price, secretary of the Department of Health and Human Services, looked at Trump and said, "I can't thank you enough for the privilege that you have given me and the leadership that you've shown." As the cameras made their way around the table, each cabinet member seemed determined to outdo the obsequiousness of the last. The ego-stroking reached its divine apex with chief of staff Reince Priebus: "We thank you for the opportunity and the blessing that you've given us to serve your agenda."

Abraham Lincoln had a team of rivals. Donald Trump had a team of sycophants.

One of the few who didn't join in the adulation for Trump was the man sitting immediately to his left, Secretary of Defense James Mattis. When his time to speak arrived, he said nothing about Trump, instead expressing gratitude for the sacrifices made by the men and women in the military.

One of those who attended the meeting later told me he found the whole thing embarrassing, comparing it to the kind of gathering North Korean dictator Kim Jong-un might convene, with subordinates speaking glowingly about their Dear Leader out of fear that insufficient praise might lead to death by firing squad. What alarmed this senior official even more than the newly minted cabinet secretaries' puffery was just how much Trump seemed to be enjoying it all. The circle of adoration was bizarre, but it was exactly what Trump wanted.

"I was looking at him, and I was thinking, 'You made billions of dollars, and you think you have to do this?'" the official recalled.

Attorney General Jeff Sessions had been pushing a version of the MAGA agenda decades before Trump made it his own. The Alabama Republican was the first US senator to endorse Trump in the 2016 presidential primary, and one of Sessions's top aides, Stephen Miller, played a key role in Trump's campaign, writing many of his speeches and crafting some of his most polarizing policies. "This isn't a campaign," Sessions had said when he announced his support for Trump in 2016. "This is a movement."

Trump rewarded Sessions by tapping him to be attorney general, one of his very first cabinet picks. Sessions may have been the perfect nominee to translate Trump's rantings and ravings into law—the president-elect characterized him as a "world-class legal mind"—but once in office, he turned out to have too much integrity for Trump's taste. Sessions's refusal to put an end to fraud and insider-trading charges against two Trump-supporting congressmen infuriated Trump—why was he prosecuting Republicans? But it was Sessions's decision to recuse himself from the Justice Department's investigation into Russian election meddling—because he himself was a potential subject of the investigation—that really made Trump irate.

"The Russian Witch Hunt Hoax continues, all because Jeff Sessions didn't tell me he was going to recuse himself," Trump tweeted a few months before he would fire his attorney general. "I would have quickly picked someone else. So much time and money wasted, so many lives ruined."[1]

That very well might have been the *nicest* thing Trump said about Sessions while he served as attorney general. Behind closed doors, the president mocked him as "an idiot,"[2] "mixed up and confused,"[3] and a "dumb Southerner."[4] He repeatedly compared him to Mr. Magoo, the clumsy and dim-witted cartoon character from the mid-twentieth century, and at one point he even called Sessions "the first mentally retarded attorney general."[5]

I asked Sessions about that last insult years later, wondering how he felt about the man he'd helped become president having such a low opinion of him. He chuckled and told me, "There was nobody in his cabinet that understood his agenda and was more supportive of it than I was."[6] Yes, the person who arguably understood and supported Trump's agenda more than anyone else in the cabinet was the one Trump labeled "mentally retarded."

But Trump wasn't content to just humiliate Sessions and denigrate his honor—he destroyed his career, too. After the president finally fired him in November 2018, Sessions began to plot his next steps and announced a campaign for his old Senate seat the following November. Before he'd joined the Trump administration, you'd be hard-pressed to find a politician more popular in his or her state than Sessions was in Alabama. First elected to the US Senate in 1996, his margin of victory ballooned from 7 percentage points that year to 19 in 2002 and to 27 in 2008. Democrats didn't even bother nominating a candidate to oppose him in 2014, when he won an astounding 97 percent of the vote. "Professionals said I was the most popular politician in Alabama," Sessions told me in late 2022.[7]

"Was" is the operative word in that sentence. Sessions's comeback bid fell flat. The man who won his Senate seat in 2014 with 97 percent of the vote was trounced in the 2020 Republican primary, losing to former Auburn University football coach Tommy Tuberville by more than 21 percentage points. Trump was the decisive factor—endorsing Tuberville and attacking his former attorney general. "You know, you make choices," Sessions said when I asked him why he never hit back at the man who ruined his career. "I just made up my mind I was not going to undermine [or] get in an argument with the president who appointed me, and [was] advancing an agenda I basically believed in. So I just took it."[8]

Others in the Trump cabinet were far less willing to just take it. Mattis was quoted saying that Trump had the understanding "of a fifth- or sixth-grader."[9] Trump responded by calling the man he'd made secretary of defense "the world's most overrated general." Just weeks after that first cabinet meeting, Rex Tillerson, the ExxonMobil executive turned secretary of state, described Trump as a "moron."[10] Tillerson so openly disparaged Trump that Vice President Pence felt the need to intervene, counseling Tillerson on ways to suppress his true feelings about the man who'd appointed him. Trump fired Tillerson in March 2018, claiming that he was "dumb as a rock" and that he "couldn't get rid of him fast enough."[11] Apparently not. Tillerson served as secretary of state for thirteen months before Trump got around to firing him.

Quick decision-making seemed to be an issue for Trump. He would later say he couldn't fire John Kelly fast enough, either.[12] Kelly served in the Trump administration for nearly two full years, first as secretary of homeland security and then as White House chief of staff—a job he kept for seventeen months, by far the longest tenure of the four people who held that role for Trump. After he fired him, Trump retroactively accused the retired four-star Marine general of being "unable to handle the pressure" and "in way over his head" the entire time.

Kelly—who, as commander of Task Force Tripoli, led thousands of Marines into Saddam Hussein's hometown of Tikrit—had a different recollection of events. He compared dealing with Trump to "French-kissing a chainsaw"[13] in addition to calling him "the most flawed person I have ever met in my life."[14]

Most of the people sitting around the table at that first cabinet meeting had either quit or been fired long before January 6, 2021. Two of them announced their resignations the next day—Education Secretary Betsy DeVos and Transportation Secretary Elaine Chao. The attack on the Capitol didn't seem to trouble Trump much, but Chao's denunciation of it sure did. He spent the next two years branding the only Asian American member of his cabinet—and one of the few senior officials he kept around for the entirety of his term—"Coco Chow" and a "sellout to China."

Trump described his top advisors that day in June 2017 as a "phenomenal team of people," but he was singing a far different tune by the end of his term. In his own assessment, he had assembled a cabinet full of "retarded," "overrated," and "dumb-as-a-rock" bureaucrats who were "in way over their heads" and "unable to handle the pressure." Maybe he was just following the advice he had given those St. Norbert students years earlier: "Always be around unsuccessful people, because everybody will respect you."

But even as president, that "respect" eluded Donald Trump. He never garnered the reverence and admiration that had historically accompanied the office he held—especially among those who served him. An astonishingly high number of people who held senior positions in his administration came to believe that he was woefully unfit for the presidency. And his cabinet—which featured more talent and honor than he gave it credit for—had a front-row seat to his failings as a president.

Though Trump boasted throughout his term he was accomplishing more than any president since George Washington, White House officials could see he had only a rudimentary understanding of how the federal government worked, and little interest in learning more. There were a few things he cared about—building the wall on the Mexican border, insisting our allies pay more for our mutual self-defense, slapping higher tariffs on our trading partners, picking the color scheme for the new version of Air Force One—but everything else was the "boring politics" he often decried on the campaign trail. Most days, Trump opted not to receive the President's Daily Brief, the regular intelligence update designed to give the president an overview of the greatest threats facing the United States. For Trump, it was more like the President's Weekly Brief—and even then he'd agree to sit down for it only later in the morning, after he'd watched a couple of hours of *Fox & Friends*.

His national security team frequently found briefing him on just about any subject to be a chore. One such briefing came in early December 2018, when Mattis, General Joseph Dunford, who was then the chairman of the Joint Chiefs of Staff, and other national security officials were in the Oval Office to discuss the Pentagon's upcoming budget. Trump, however, wasn't interested in what they had to say. "I know more about nuclear weapons than anybody," he interjected. "I know more about nukes than all you people." Kelly, Trump's chief of staff, was standing with others in the back of the room when another attendee heard him muttering under his breath: "Jesus, this fucking bastard."

Kelly was far from the only administration official to exhibit such disdain for the commander in chief. Just about everyone who worked in the Trump White House has stories of being frustrated—or even worse, embarrassed—by the president's behavior. One such senior official who sometimes attended Trump's meetings with foreign leaders told me about a time he was so mortified by Trump during a meeting with Chinese president Xi Jinping that he deliberately tuned out his boss. Members of each delegation were provided headphones that played out real-time translations—from Mandarin to English or English to Mandarin, depending on which channel the headphones were tuned to. As Trump droned on, extolling his own brilliance to the president of China and failing to bring up the issues on the agenda for the meeting, this White House official switched over to the Chinese feed and cranked up the volume. He may have appeared to be paying attention to the president, but he couldn't understand a word. 纯粹的幸福。

That was the Trump administration in a nutshell. Hundreds of officials—from four-star generals to deputy press secretaries—doing everything they could to drown out the president's absurdities and live to fight another day. Staffers throughout the executive branch were instructed to ignore Trump's tweets, as the 280-character missives were not considered orders no matter what they said. Trump's spoken words were often treated just as flippantly. "The President thinks out loud," a senior national security official told *The New Yorker*'s Dexter Filkins in early 2019. "Do you treat it like an order? Or do you treat it as part of a longer conversation? We treated it as part of a longer conversation." By refusing to consider the president's various musings as directives, he continued, "we prevented a lot of bad things from happening."[15]

Mortified White House staffers and lawmakers would provide glimpses into the alternate universe where Trump's impulses went unchecked, quietly telling stories about how they prevented the president they served from doing even more damage to the country than he had already done. On multiple occasions administration officials tried to explain to me just how much worse things could have been if Trump's own advisors had done everything he wanted them to do. Early on in his tenure as chief of staff, Kelly joked with me about what he'd title a book about his first few weeks in the White House: *Tweets Not Sent, Decisions Not Made.*

The noncompliance infuriated many of Trump's ideological allies in Congress and in the media, who argued the "deep state"—their contemptuous term for the career civil servants who make up the bulk of the federal government and national security apparatus—was thwarting the agenda the American people elected him to enact. "Intentionally misrepresenting a matter of national security to the commander in chief is a dereliction of duty and should be punished," GOP representative Jim Banks of Indiana, a fervent Trump supporter in Congress, told *National Review* after a Trump administration official bragged publicly about disobeying the president's orders. "I can't think of anything more dishonorable."[16]

At issue was an interview James Jeffrey, Trump's Syria envoy, gave days after the broadcast networks projected Joe Biden as the winner of the 2020 presidential election. "We were always playing shell games to not make clear to our leadership how many troops we had [in

Syria]," he said, noting there were "a lot more" soldiers still deployed there than the two hundred Trump had agreed to leave in place a year earlier, after initially trying to bring them all home. "What Syria withdrawal?" Jeffrey added wryly. "There was never a Syria withdrawal."[17]

On one hand, Trump's backers have a point: Unelected bureaucrats should not be undermining the wishes of the duly elected commander in chief, to whom the Constitution grants sweeping authority over the military. Officials who are unwilling to carry out an order can resign, but they have no authority to thwart the orders of a duly elected president. Mattis spent much of his tenure as defense secretary working to divert Trump's more destructive whims before they became orders. But when Trump made the order to withdraw from Syria, which Mattis opposed, he resigned.

"You have the right to have a Secretary of Defense whose views are better aligned with yours," Mattis wrote in his resignation letter. "My views on treating allies with respect and also being clear-eyed about both malign actors and strategic competitors are strongly held and informed by over four decades of immersion in these issues."

But the ease with which Trump administration officials undermined the president they served is a reflection of Trump's leadership abilities. A competent commander in chief who understands how the government operates would certainly notice his or her orders weren't being carried out—and do something about it.

Because the president had so little interest in the day-to-day responsibilities of governing, it was often months or years before he realized his own people weren't doing what he wanted. Jeffrey, for example, was a staunch Trump opponent in the 2016 Republican primary and was never supportive of his plans to pull US troops out of the Middle East, but was appointed to his post in 2018 on the recommendation of Secretary of State Mike Pompeo. Jeffrey held the role for more than two years, and Trump very well may have had no idea what he was up to—or even who he was.

Jeffrey himself survived until the end of the term, but many like him had been weeded out over four years—either they did something to attract Trump's attention and wrath or they resigned of their own volition. The result was an administration that looked markedly different in January 2021 than it did in January 2017. At the end, there were more Trump loyalists and fewer guardrails, making something like January 6 possible, if not inevitable.

After the horrors of that day, however, even the loyalists began to turn on the president. "In one day he ended every future opportunity that doesn't include speaking engagements at the local proud boys chapter," longtime Trump aide Hope Hicks texted another White House staffer as the attack on the Capitol was unfolding. "We all look like domestic terrorists now."[18]

Hicks had been with Trump for nearly a decade at that point. She stuck by him through thick and thin. Hicks was the first person on the 2016 campaign to learn of the *Access Hollywood* "grab 'em by the pussy" tape—and helped craft the "locker room" talk response.[19] She admitted before the House Intelligence Committee in early 2018 she had told "white lies" on Trump's behalf.[20]

But Trump's falsehoods about the 2020 election were a bridge too far. Hicks told the January 6 Committee—candidly and under oath— that she never bought into Trump's voter-fraud conspiracy theories and that she barely interacted with him after Thanksgiving 2020. "I just felt like it was extremely damaging to his legacy and was taking away from everything that he accomplished," she said. "It wasn't a good message. It wasn't good optics. It was nonsense, actually."[21]

Later, Hicks would tell friends she hoped Trump would read the transcript of her testimony once it was published. If he did, she said, he'd hopefully never want to talk to her again.

"Only One"

Donald Trump's relationships with other world leaders throughout his presidency were . . . awkward, to say the least. In keeping with his "America First" mantra, he tended to view interactions with foreign governments—even US allies—as competitions to be won rather than opportunities for collaboration. This outlook manifested in some strange ways.

When Japanese prime minister Shinzo Abe came to visit the White House in February 2017, for example, Trump made a point to grip his hand tightly for some twenty seconds, yanking the Japanese prime minister back and forth while the cameras clicked away. When Trump finally let go, Abe pulled his hand away, leaned back in his chair, and made an animated expression of relief as he mouthed the word "wow." Trump, meanwhile, turned toward the press in the room and grinned. "Strong hands," he said, prompting Abe to laugh nervously.

To Trump, the handshake wasn't a gesture of friendship. It was a chance to assert dominance.

Other leaders were paying attention. When Trump traveled to Paris to meet with French president Emmanuel Macron a few months later, Macron squeezed Trump's hand tightly and wouldn't let go. Both men's knuckles turned white, and Trump made two unsuccessful efforts to pull himself away. Only once his point had been made did Macron relax his grip. "My handshake with him—it wasn't innocent," the French president later acknowledged. "That's how you ensure you are respected. You have to show you won't make small concessions—not even symbolic ones."[1]

Trump returned from that Paris trip with some grand plans. Macron had invited him to the country's massive Bastille Day military parade, and Trump knew immediately he had to have a military parade of his own back in Washington—only bigger. Once home, the president tasked the Pentagon with coming up with plans for such a parade the following Fourth of July, where tanks and oversized missiles would roll down Pennsylvania Avenue while fighter jets flew by in the skies overhead.

James Mattis, then Trump's defense secretary, privately told his top aides he'd "rather swallow acid."[2] Such parades, the retired four-star general thought, were better suited for tyrants in places like Moscow and Pyongyang. Pentagon leaders slow-walked Trump's request, hoping he would eventually move on to another shiny object and forget about it. He did, never getting a chance to show the world he could put on a bigger military parade than his French counterpart.

Running for president, Trump repeatedly argued global leaders didn't take the United States seriously, claiming the country had become the laughingstock of the entire world. But addressing the United Nations General Assembly after taking office, Trump became the first president to literally be laughed at on the world stage. "In less than two years, my administration has accomplished more than almost any administration in the history of our country," he boasted. The audible chuckling from the assembled leaders caught him so off guard that Trump stopped speaking for a moment. "Didn't expect that reaction," he said, "but that's okay."

That wouldn't be the only time Trump found himself the object of a world leader's mockery. At a reception during a NATO meeting in London the following year, Canadian prime minister Justin Trudeau was caught on a hot mic laughing with Macron, British prime minister Boris Johnson, and others about the meeting Macron had just had with Trump, which the US president had turned into an impromptu press conference. "You just watch his team's jaws drop to the floor," Trudeau recounted in disbelief as the others looked on in amusement. Asked about the comments the next day, a clearly irritated Trump labeled the Canadian prime minister "two-faced."[3]

Among Trump's relationships with US allies, Trump and German chancellor Angela Merkel's was the most strained of all. The German leader—who had been in power since 2005—couldn't hide her contempt for the American president. During a tense 2018 G7 summit in Canada, the German government released a photo that perfectly captured Trump's status with the heads of the world's leading democracies. With the leaders of Japan, France, and the United Kingdom standing next to her on the other side of a table, Merkel glares down at Trump as he sits in a chair, grinning with his arms folded across his chest.

By July 2020, Merkel's exasperation with Trump was evident to even the most casual of observers. "You cannot fight the [COVID-19] pandemic with lies and disinformation any more than you can fight it with hate or incitement to hatred," she said in comments clearly referencing the US president. "The limits of populism and denial of basic truths are being laid bare." In August of that year, Ric Grenell, the former US ambassador to Germany, preposterously claimed during a speech at the 2020 Republican convention that Trump had "charmed" Merkel. A reporter asked Merkel about those comments a few days later. The German chancellor smiled and asked back, "He did what?" The reporter repeated that Grenell said Trump had "charmed" her. "Oh, I see," she replied with a laugh before moving on to the next question.[4]

As Merkel's contempt for Trump became more obvious, Trump made an effort to let people know the German chancellor actually really liked him—or at least, as he saw it, had tremendous respect for him.

One prominent member of Congress—a Trump ally—told me that the president, on two separate occasions, claimed Merkel had complimented him on the large crowds he attracted when he spoke.

"She told me that she was amazed at the size of the crowds that came to see me speak," Trump told the Republican congressman. "She said she could never get crowds like that. In fact, she told me that there was only one other political leader who ever got crowds as big as mine."

Only one! In history!

The Republican congressman couldn't believe the insinuation was lost on Trump. "And I'm thinking," he told me while recounting his interaction with Trump, "'you know who she's talking about, right?'"

Which would be more unsettling: that he didn't or that he did?

CHAPTER SIX

TRUMP'S ESSENTIAL MAN

To understand what a second Trump administration would look like, consider Johnny McEntee, the cheerful and upbeat young aide who became Trump's essential man in the waning days of his presidency. In McEntee, Trump had the ultimate loyalist: He never hesitated to carry out the president's orders, and he made it his mission to find and remove anyone in the executive branch who was not as devoted to the president as he was. If Trump makes it back to the White House, it would likely be McEntee—or someone like him—doing the hiring and enforcing loyalty.

I reported extensively on McEntee's role in my last book. But in the years since *Betrayal* was published, I have come to learn McEntee's role was even greater than I had realized—especially during Trump's postelection tantrum. At just thirty years old, McEntee had become such a powerful figure in the West Wing by late 2020 that one senior staffer described him to me as effectively the deputy president.[1] Having finally realized many of his own advisors were thwarting his wishes—often because they considered them danger-ous or illegal—Trump enlisted McEntee to do the things his more senior aides would not.

McEntee was just twenty-five years old when he volunteered to work on the Trump campaign in 2015. He didn't have much experience—he was a production assistant on the news desk at Fox News at the time—but he was eager, confident, and willing to work hard. Most importantly, he loved Donald Trump. A former quarter-back at the University of Connecticut, he achieved short-lived inter-net fame in 2011 when a video of him throwing trick passes went viral. Trump liked having him around and soon made him his per-sonal assistant, taking him along whenever he traveled. As the cam-paign ramped up, he became Trump's "body guy," carrying the candidate's bags and relaying messages.

McEntee reprised the role in the White House after the 2016 elec-tion, but was fired in early 2018 by then-chief of staff John Kelly when a background check turned up a serious gambling habit that was con-sidered to pose a national security risk. He didn't leave for long, though. After Kelly himself was fired, McEntee returned to the White House in February 2020.

His second stint in the administration proved to be more conse-quential. McEntee resumed his role as Trump's body guy with a seat just outside the Oval Office, but he was also named director of the Presidential Personnel Office, which is responsible for the vetting, hiring, and firing of the four thousand political appointees who serve in the executive branch. McEntee may have never hired or fired any-body before in his life, but he was fiercely loyal—and for Trump, that made him the perfect choice for the job.

McEntee's efforts to root out Trump infidels in the administration were often comically petty, but they came with the force of a presidential mandate. Just weeks before the 2020 presidential election, for example, somebody on McEntee's staff discovered that a young woman in the office of Housing and Urban Development Secretary Ben Carson had liked an Instagram post by pop star Taylor Swift that included a photo of Swift holding a tray of cookies decorated with the Biden-Harris campaign logo. The transgression was brought all the way to White House chief of staff Mark Meadows, who placed a call to Carson's top aide. The message: We can't have our people liking the social media posts of a high-profile Biden supporter like Taylor Swift.

When it wasn't monitoring Trump administration staffers' social media activity, McEntee's office conducted interviews with employees throughout the federal government to gauge loyalty to the president. Months after Trump left office, Andrew Kloster, a member of McEntee's staff who had helped conduct these loyalty interviews, described them as a way of identifying people who claimed to support Trump but weren't *really* on the team. "I think the first thing you need to hire for is loyalty," Kloster explained on a podcast. "The funny thing is, you can learn policy. You can't learn loyalty."[2]

McEntee's Presidential Personnel Office had about thirty employees, many of them in their twenties and at least a couple without college degrees. In both attitude and mission, they were a Trumpian version of the Red Guard youth of Mao's Cultural Revolution in the late 1960s who rooted out intellectuals and "class enemies" in the upper ranks of Chinese society. There also seemed to be another requirement: One senior White House official told me McEntee had hired "the most beautiful twenty-year-old girls you could find, and guys who would be absolutely no threat to Johnny in going after those girls." Some inside the White House called McEntee's staff "the Rockettes and the Dungeons and Dragons Group." And in fact, one of McEntee's assistants had performed with the Radio City Rockettes.[3]

McEntee's team reached the apex of its power after Trump lost the election in 2020. Within days, they orchestrated sweeping changes to the civilian leadership at the Pentagon that resulted in Defense Secretary Mark Esper and other top officials being fired. In preparing for Esper's ouster, McEntee and his team created a memo listing the Pentagon chief's sins against Trump, arguing he "consistently breaks from POTUS' direction, and has failed to see through his policies." Among Esper's supposed transgressions:

- Vowing to be apolitical;
- Opposing the president's direction to utilize American forces to put down riots;
- Barring the Confederate flag on military bases;
- Focusing the department on Russia;
- Actively pushing for diversity and inclusion; and
- Contradicting the reasoning for and disagreeing with the president's decision to withdraw troops from Germany.

Trump fired Esper and replaced him with McEntee's preferred successor, National Counterterrorism Center director and Army Special Forces veteran Christopher Miller. To serve as Miller's senior advisor, McEntee recruited a retired Army colonel named Douglas Macgregor, whose regular appearances on Fox News had caught the White House's attention. Chief among his qualifications was his penchant for praising Trump's approach to US military involvement and calling for martial law along the US-Mexico border.

Before leaving for the Pentagon, Macgregor sat down in McEntee's office to go over the acting defense secretary's sweeping agenda for the final seventy-three days of the lame-duck period before Joe Biden would be sworn into office. As first reported by *Axios*, on a piece of paper, McEntee jotted down four quick bullet points that, if carried out, would represent a dramatic shift in the global order:

- Get us out of Afghanistan.
- Get us out of Iraq and Syria.
- Complete the withdrawal from Germany.
- Get us out of Africa.[4]

The January 6 Committee's investigation unearthed the extraordinary story of what happened next—but the information didn't make it into any of the committee's hearings or its final report. What follows is based on the sworn testimony of the key players, including McEntee and Macgregor, as well as National Security Advisor Robert O'Brien and General Mark Milley, the chairman of the Joint Chiefs of Staff.

Three days after Macgregor arrived at the Pentagon, he called McEntee and told him he couldn't accomplish any of the items on their handwritten to-do list without a signed order from the president.

"Hey, they're not going to do anything we want, or the president wants, without a directive," Macgregor told him, emphasizing the need for an official White House order signed by Trump.[5] The Pentagon's stonewalling made sense, of course: You don't make major changes to America's global defense posture based on a glorified Post-it note from the president's body guy.

The order, Macgregor added, should focus on the top priority from McEntee's list—Afghanistan—and it had to include a specific date for the complete withdrawal of all uniformed military personnel from the country. He suggested January 31, 2021.

McEntee and an assistant quickly typed up the directive, but they moved the Afghanistan withdrawal timeline up to January 15—just five days before Trump was set to leave office—and added a second mandate: a complete withdrawal of US troops from Somalia by December 31, 2020.

McEntee, of course, didn't know the first thing about drafting a presidential directive—let alone one instructing the movement of thousands of servicemen and -women. He had two jobs in the White House—only one of which he was qualified for—and neither one had anything to do with national security or the military. An order even 10 percent as consequential as the one McEntee was drafting would typically go through the National Security Council with input from the civilian leadership at the Pentagon, the Joint Chiefs of Staff, and the military commanders in the region. Instead, the guy who usually carried Trump's bags was hammering it out on his computer, consulting with nobody but the retired colonel the president had just hired because he had seen him on cable TV.

The absurdity of the situation was captured in McEntee's interview with the January 6 Committee:

Q: Is it typical for the Presidential Personnel Office to draft orders concerning troop withdrawal?

MCENTEE: Probably not typical, no.[6]

Because they were so out of their depth, McEntee and his assistant ended up reaching out to Macgregor again—they didn't know how to arrange the document they were working on. "I was called on the phone by one of McEntee's staffers who was having trouble formatting the order and getting the language straight," Macgregor recalled.[7] The retired colonel told the thirty-year-old staffer to open a cabinet, find an old presidential decision memorandum, and copy it.

Easy enough. The duo wrote up the order, had the president sign it, and sent it over to Kash Patel, the new acting defense secretary's chief of staff.

Chaos ensued.

Upon receiving the order from his chief of staff, Christopher Miller called Joint Chiefs chairman Mark Milley to his office to discuss next steps. After reading the order, Milley told the January 6 Committee, he looked at Patel, who had just started working at the Pentagon three days earlier.[8]

"Who gave the president the military advice for this?" Milley asked him. "Did you do this?"

"No," Patel answered. "I had nothing to do with it."

Milley turned to the acting defense secretary. "Did you give the President military advice on this?" he asked.

"No. Not me," Miller answered.

"Okay, well, we've got to go over and see the president," Milley said, noting his job required him to provide military advice to the commander in chief. "I've got duties to do here, constitutional duties. I've got to make sure he's properly advised."

And with that, Miller and Milley went to the White House to see Robert O'Brien, Trump's national security advisor.

"Robert, where's this coming from?" Milley asked O'Brien. "Is this true?"

"I've never seen it before," O'Brien told him.

They were joined in the meeting by retired lieutenant general Keith Kellogg, the national security advisor to Vice President Pence.

"Something is really wrong here," Kellogg said, reading through the order. "This doesn't look right."

"You're telling me that thing is forged?" Milley responded in disbelief. "That's a forged piece of paper directing a military operation by the president of the United States? That's forged, Keith?"

Despite McEntee's best efforts—which included not only the advice from Macgregor but several minutes of searching the internet—the only part of the document that looked anything like an official presidential order was Trump's signature at the bottom. But even that, Kellogg thought, could have been the work of an autopen used to mimic the president's autograph on thousands of unofficial letters sent out by the White House.[9]

"Let me see if I can get to the bottom of this," O'Brien told the group, before heading to White House counsel Pat Cipollone's office on the second floor of the West Wing.

Cipollone, whose office was responsible for reviewing all presidential orders, said he hadn't seen the document and knew nothing about it. When Derek Lyons, the White House staff secretary responsible for filing and transmitting official presidential orders, told them he hadn't seen the directive either, the group knew they needed to go see the president himself.

They found him where he spent most of his time after the November election—in his private dining room next to the Oval Office, where the television on the wall was almost always on. Once the president confirmed he had indeed signed the document, O'Brien and Cipollone explained to him that such an order should go through some sort of process, and that an abrupt movement of so many US troops would be dangerous and unwise without proper planning. At the very least, they told him, such an order should be reviewed by White House lawyers.

"I said this would be very bad," O'Brien recalled telling Trump. "Our position is that because it didn't go through any proper process—the lawyers hadn't cleared it, the staff [secretary] hadn't cleared it, NSC [National Security Council] hadn't cleared it—that it's our position that the order is null and void."[10]

According to O'Brien, the president didn't object. Trump's bold plan for ending the war in Afghanistan before the end of his term was dashed as quickly and apathetically as it was slapped together. "It's rescinded. It's over," O'Brien said when he returned to his office, where the acting defense secretary and Joint Chiefs chairman had been waiting for about fifteen minutes. Milley breathed a sigh of relief. "Okay, fine," he said. "So it doesn't exist."

Trump's backers will likely read this story and see yet another example of the "deep state" thwarting the president on an issue important to him and the people who elected him. But in reality, the episode demonstrated once again that the president of the United

States couldn't get the people *he* appointed to carry out his policies because he couldn't be bothered to learn how to implement them. As soon as he realized an Afghanistan withdrawal would require more work than having McEntee scribble up a note, he dropped it entirely.

When McEntee wasn't busy attempting to remake the United States' defensive posture around the globe, he was helping the president with his increasingly desperate efforts to overturn the results of the 2020 election. McEntee, Trump realized, was willing to take on legal work he couldn't convince his own White House lawyers to do—perhaps because McEntee was not a lawyer.

Trump's body guy, for example, was there at the genesis of Trump's most brazen idea for overturning Biden's election victory—the notion that Vice President Pence could single-handedly toss out Biden's electoral votes when he presided over the ceremonial counting of those votes on January 6.

Shortly after Trump first stumbled across the the plan for his vice president, he ran the plan by his chief of staff, Mark Meadows, and White House counsel, Pat Cipollone. When he didn't get the response he wanted, the president turned to his body man, conveniently sitting at his post right outside the door to the Oval Office. Trump asked McEntee to look into whether a vice president had ever swayed the results of a presidential election while presiding over the counting of electoral votes. The peculiarity of the request was not lost on the January 6 Committee.

Q: Do you have any idea why the President would ask you to do that, given that he's got a White House Counsel's Office, a

Justice Department, a whole lot of lawyers representing the campaign?

MCENTEE: Probably because, like, he would see something maybe in three weeks, and I could get it to him in, like, 20 minutes.

Such corner-cutting was par for the course in the Trump White House—as was the dark humor in what came next. Joined by a young lawyer on his Presidential Personnel Office staff named Dan Huff, McEntee began searching online for anything resembling a precedent for such a move. They couldn't find anything comparable, so they settled on what they considered the closest match: the election of 1800, when Vice President Thomas Jefferson presided over the counting of electoral votes that would certify his own White House victory. Jefferson didn't reject any slates of electors, but he did accept electors from Georgia despite some technical issues with the document conveying the state's votes.

McEntee knew the situations were apples and oranges. "I just remember thinking it's slightly different, but it's the only time we've seen anything even remotely close to this," he later admitted to the January 6 Committee. "Pretty vague, you know, but that's all I could find."

The memo he wrote for Trump on the issue, however, was far less circumspect. "JEFFERSON USED HIS POSITION AS VP TO WIN," the all-caps title read at the top of the page.

Having operated in Trump's orbit for half a decade at that point, McEntee knew the key to climbing the ranks: Tell the boss what he wants to hear. Even if he didn't personally believe the Jefferson and Pence situations were analogous, McEntee left the president with the implication that they were. At one point during his deposition, an investigator for the January 6 Committee asked McEntee if he ever raised his inner reservations about the Jefferson-Pence connections. "Nope," he replied. "I just passed it along."[11]

The mere mention of Jefferson was more than enough to capture Trump's imagination, and the president never let go of the false comparison. In fact, he was still talking about it when I interviewed him at Mar-a-Lago six weeks after he'd left the White House. "Unfortunately, Mike [Pence] was not Thomas Jefferson," Trump told me, insisting he would still be president if his vice president had acted like John Adams's second in command.

Before Pence ultimately did the correct and honorable thing on January 6, McEntee was tasked with at least one more book report intended to convince the vice president to take another path. Rather than the vice president outright rejecting some of Biden's electoral votes, this scenario—later expounded on in more detail by far-right lawyers John Eastman and Jenna Ellis—would have Pence send some of them back to the states for reconsideration. Once again, McEntee accepted the assignment and got to work.

Together with Huff, the young Presidential Personnel Office lawyer, McEntee began preparing a new memo entitled "PENCE CAN LET THE STATES DECIDE."[12] It took the duo just a few hours to come up with what they considered to be a far more reasonable plan, whereby half the contested electoral votes would be sent back to the states to be reconsidered and Biden would be left without the majority needed to be certified as the president-elect. "The VP doesn't need to declare Trump the winner, or to reject ALL the ballots of a disputed state," the memo began. "There is a middle path that is a way out for everybody."[13]

That "middle path" made its way to Meadows and Trump with a handwritten note from its author: "THIS IS PROBABLY OUR ONLY REALISTIC OPTION BECAUSE IT WOULD GIVE PENCE AN OUT. —JOHNNY." The memo and accompanying note—like so many documents Trump came into contact with—were each torn into two pieces, and later retrieved by a White House staffer who turned them over to the National Archives, which pieced them back together again. Testifying before the January 6 Committee months later, McEntee confirmed the handwriting was his.

Unlike some of the others in Trump's inner circle—including Meadows and former chief strategist Steve Bannon—McEntee voluntarily told his story to the January 6 Committee. Although his memory was conveniently foggy on several key points, he didn't act as if he had anything to hide, directly answering questions about his role in Trump's White House. If anything, he seemed proud of his role as the president's enforcer.

Trump never seemed to fear McEntee would say anything to hurt him, either. In fact, the former body guy was at Mar-a-Lago shortly after he received a subpoena to testify before the committee. Sitting alongside Trump's personal secretary, Molly Michael, and his social media advisor Dan Scavino, McEntee told Trump about the summons.

The former president reacted with a short diatribe about the committee's supposed illegitimacy and persecution of him, but he also told McEntee not to worry about it and gave him the green light to testify. As a bonus, McEntee was told his legal bills would be paid by Trump's political organization. McEntee wouldn't have to worry about lawyer fees, and Trump wouldn't have to worry about anything incriminating spilling out into the open.

McEntee may or may not return to the White House if Trump wins another term, but he's positioned himself to play a major role in a future Trump administration if he wants one. He's kept in touch with the former president; in May 2023, the pro-Trump Heritage Foundation launched an initiative called Project 2025, designed to set the agenda for the next Republican administration. Announcing the initiative, the Heritage Foundation made it clear Johnny McEntee would be involved:

"McEntee will play a vital role supporting the personnel pillar of Project 2025," the Heritage Foundation said in the press release announcing the initiative. "Embracing the motto that 'personnel is policy,' Project 2025 is launching the database to collect résumés and vet thousands of potential applicants in advance of Jan. 20, 2025, when the next president takes office."

While he waits for Trump to win back the White House, McEntee is also working with some of his old Trump administration colleagues—including Dan Huff, the guy who helped him write those legal memos about the viability of the vice president overturning a presidential election—on a business venture called The Right Stuff. It's billed as a dating service for conservatives that "hasn't gone woke."

"Personally, I have never and would never date anyone who doesn't share the same political views as me," McEntee explained in an essay for *Newsweek* when he launched the project. "Perhaps if this were a different period in American history, that would be fine—but right now it seems there are two separate world views and we're living in two very different places. I just don't think it would work."[14]

Trump approved. "He thought it was a great idea," McEntee remembered. "He was super excited about it and loved the name."

The status McEntee earned in service to Trump will provide a road map for future strivers in a hypothetical second term: If you want to advance your career and accumulate power, nothing matters more than loyalty to Donald Trump.

Toward the end of his interview with the January 6 Committee, McEntee was asked about Trump's darkest day as president, a day when even his own children were disturbed by his actions.

Q: Were you in any way dissatisfied with the President's conduct as it related to January 6?

MCENTEE: No.

That's the kind of loyalty a would-be tyrant can appreciate.

Martial Law

With the clock running out on his presidency in mid-December 2020, Donald Trump dispatched his most loyal and trusted White House aide on an urgent mission. Two US military leaders had just issued a statement President Trump believed was insubordinate, and he wanted the aide, Johnny McEntee, to let the Pentagon know the remark was entirely unacceptable. If it happened again, heads would roll.

"There is no role for the U.S. military in determining the outcome of an American election."

This joint statement—issued by Army Chief of Staff James McConville and Army Secretary Ryan McCarthy—seemed so obvious and uncontroversial that it barely attracted any attention beyond a narrow band of military reporters. Who were they refuting? Was anyone thinking the US military *did* have a role in determining the outcome of an American election?

Yes, actually.

Michael Flynn, a retired three-star Army general and former director of the Defense Intelligence Agency, had just given an interview to a right-wing television network, flatly stating the military could enforce a "rerun" of the 2020 election in states Trump had lost. "He could order, within the swing states if he wanted to, he could take military capabilities, and he could place them in those states and basically rerun an election in each of those states," Flynn told Newsmax host Greg Kelly.[1]

In the interview, Flynn made clear he wasn't "calling for" martial law—but he wasn't *not* calling for it, either. "It's not unprecedented," he said. "I mean, these people out there talking about martial law like it's something that we've never done. We've done—martial law has been instituted sixty-four, *sixty-four*, times."*

These may have sounded like the rantings of a madman, but they weren't coming from just *any* madman. Flynn had briefly served as Trump's national security advisor before resigning over undisclosed conversations with Russian officials and, more recently, had regularly appeared at rallies with Sidney Powell, the lawyer who was helping lead Trump's efforts to challenge the election. Plus, Flynn still had serious military connections: His former associates were in key positions throughout the Pentagon, and his brother was a senior Army official who had just been promoted to four-star general. A few weeks earlier, Flynn had reached out to one of his former subordinates, undersecretary of

---

* Flynn actually undersold his point here. According to a 2020 report from the Brennan Center for Justice, martial law—the temporary supplanting of civilian governance with military authority—has been declared at least sixty-eight times in US history, most recently in 1963. But nearly all those declarations came from governors seeking to respond to natural disasters or put down civil unrest—think the Great Chicago Fire in 1871 or Seattle anti-Chinese riots in 1886. Only two presidents have issued such a declaration: Abraham Lincoln during the Civil War and Franklin Delano Roosevelt following the attack on Pearl Harbor. Declaring martial law to "rerun" an election in states the president lost would represent a . . . departure from the norm. (Joseph Nunn, "Guide to Declarations of Martial Law in the United States," Brennan Center for Justice, August 20, 2020.)

defense for intelligence Ezra Cohen, asking for unspecified help with Trump's push against the election results. Cohen was so alarmed by the request, he reported it to the acting secretary of defense.

Under these extraordinary circumstances, McConville and McCarthy decided a statement reassuring the American people was warranted. They wanted to make perfectly clear the military would not take part in a coup. "If we don't say anything," McCarthy figured, "it's going to scare people."[2]

"It seemed like a pretty, you know, straightforward statement," McConville later recalled.[3]

Trump, however, was outraged. And he wanted McEntee—the thirty-year-old aide whose primary role was to seek out and punish disloyalty in the ranks of the Trump administration—to do something about it.

Thanks to the National Archives, we know what that "something" was. After relaying Trump's disapproval of McConville and McCarthy's joint statement to acting defense secretary Chris Miller, McEntee jotted down some updates for the president and White House chief of staff Mark Meadows. "Chris Miller spoke to both of them and anticipates no more statements coming out," the note read. And in parentheses: "If another happens, he will fire them."[4]

After reading McEntee's note, Trump did what he often did with sensitive White House documents: He ripped it up. But fortunately, somebody on the White House staff retrieved the pieces of torn paper from the trash and sent them off to the National Archives, where they will be forever part of the recorded history of Trump's presidency.*

---

* This was a fairly common practice. Staff at the White House often gathered the remnants of official White House documents ripped up by Trump; preserved them, as required by law; and sent the pieces off to the National Archives, which would then attempt to tape the documents back together.

McCarthy remembered receiving a call from Miller—who was en route to Afghanistan—the day after the statement was issued. "You could get the sense that, from the Secretary of Defense to call you from an airplane at 8:30 on a Saturday morning, that it was pretty serious," McCarthy said. Asked by investigators if he was told a repeat offense would cost him his job, he told them that "it was implied."[5]

Looking back, it's clear why McConville and McCarthy's statement had angered Trump so much: It had ruled out a course of action—imposing martial law and ordering the military to "rerun" the election—the president was legitimately considering. As the Army leaders' comments made clear, members of the military wouldn't violate the Constitution they had sworn to uphold—even if the commander in chief ordered them to.

Hours after Miller got off the phone with McCarthy, Flynn—the man who'd set these wheels in motion—was at the White House, joining Trump and his lawyers Sidney Powell and Rudy Giuliani for more than four hours of discussions. The meeting of the minds wouldn't disband until well after midnight, and at 1:42 A.M. on December 19, 2020, Trump sent a tweet that changed the course of history. "Big protest in D.C. on January 6th," it read. "Be there, will be wild!"[6]

He'd have to rely on a ragtag group of supporters armed with flagpoles and rage, fueled by the lie that the presidential election had been stolen. The US Army would have nothing to do with it.

CHAPTER SEVEN

"FIX IT NOW!"

In March 2022, Republican representative Mo Brooks received a call on his cell phone from Donald Trump. This wasn't an unusual occurrence; the congressman from Alabama was as die-hard a supporter of the former president as anybody on the planet. He was the first lawmaker to announce plans to challenge the Electoral College vote certification of Biden's election victory, and on the morning of January 6, he was speaking at the president's rally outside the White House, wearing body armor and telling the crowd it was time to "start taking down names and kicking ass."[1]

Brooks was now a candidate for the US Senate in Alabama. He had Trump's endorsement and was hoping to ride it to victory. But there was a problem. Trump had become increasingly upset about something Brooks had said at a Trump rally the previous August in Cullman, Alabama. His speech that day started off perfectly on-message for a Trump rally. He denounced "massive voter fraud" in the 2020 presidential election. He attacked "weak-kneed Republican

RINOs" and argued that real Republicans must beat "godless, evil, amoral, socialist Democrats" in the upcoming 2022 midterm elections and "put Donald Trump back in the White House in 2024." But then he crossed a line.

"There are some people who are despondent about the voter fraud and election theft in 2020," Brooks said. "Folks, put that behind you. Put that behind you."

The crowd immediately erupted in boos and jeers, with attendees shouting, "NO! NO!" and angrily gesturing toward the stage. Brooks, clearly taken aback by the response, replied: "Look forward! Look forward! Look forward! Beat them in 2022!" When that only inflamed Trump's supporters further, he threw his arms up in the air and tried to win them back over.

"All right, well, look back at it, but go forward and take advantage of it," he said. "We have got to win in 2022. We've got to win in 2024."

As Brooks attempted to forge ahead, the boos turned into chants. "Fix it now! Fix it now!" the crowd roared. Before long, the Alabama congressman had joined in: "Fix it now!"

Trump heard it all from backstage and grew increasingly irate. What the hell was Brooks doing telling the crowd to move beyond the 2020 election? In Trump's mind, the battle over the 2020 election was far from over: There was a huge, privately funded "recount" going on in Arizona, and Trump allies in Wisconsin, Georgia, and Michigan were still fighting to somehow overturn the results of an election that had been certified months earlier. Brooks knew he had upset his most important political ally, so he tried to make amends. "Let me be clear, the 2020 election was fraught with voter fraud & election theft on a massive scale," he tweeted shortly after the rally was over. "I support audits of state 2020 election results, & I eagerly await their findings."[2]

For a while, that mea culpa placated Trump. But months later, in an interview with an Alabama radio station, Brooks was asked about a wacky online conspiracy theory—that Trump could soon be reinstated as president—and his answer further irritated Trump. "I am baffled by the view that we can do something right now to put Donald Trump into office today," Brooks told the interviewer. He said he'd love to have Trump back in the White House, but it just wasn't feasible until the 2024 election.

Not long after that interview, his phone began to ring. Brooks recognized the number.

"Hello, Mr. President," he answered.

Trump had no time for pleasantries. He was unhappy with what Brooks had said about the 2020 election and made a series of demands. If Brooks didn't do as he was told, Trump said, he could kiss the former president's endorsement goodbye. But Trump's requests weren't just baffling—they were insane. He wanted Brooks to issue a statement calling for Joe Biden—who had already been president for fourteen months at this point—to be evicted from the White House and for Trump to be reinstated immediately as president of the United States.

"President Trump asked me to lie to the public in four different ways," Brooks later told me. "First, he asked me to publicly call out for rescission of the election, which violates the United States Constitution and federal law. So that's not a remedy. Second, he asked me to call for the immediate removal of Joe Biden from the White House. And there's no right that Donald Trump or anybody else has to do that. Third, he asked me to publicly state that Donald Trump should be allowed to move back into the White House, reinstated as president. And fourth, Donald Trump asked me to publicly call for a special election for the presidency of the United States."

Brooks had heard Trump say plenty of deluded things about the 2020 election. Heck, Brooks himself had repeated many of them. But this was a new level of absurdity. "All four of those things are not supported by law," Brooks told me. "And all four of those things would have been untrue statements had I uttered them."

"No, I'm not going to do it," he remembered telling Trump. "It's not the truth."

According to Brooks, Trump grew enraged, yelling profanities into the phone before hanging up on him. "It's pretty clear he's used to people doing what he says," Brooks told me. "Even if it violates the law."

Brooks immediately knew the magnitude of what had just happened. "This does not look good for my Senate race," he told his wife after the call ended. "He's a vengeful, spiteful person. And if you don't do exactly what he says, he's demanding you do, then he's the kind of person who likes to get even."

And sure enough, Trump did get his vengeance, issuing a statement on March 23 retracting his endorsement of Brooks and accusing the congressman—one of the most conservative in the House—of going "woke." Because Brooks wouldn't go along with the deranged idea the 2020 election could be overturned more than a year into Biden's presidency, Trump made it his mission to take Brooks down. He succeeded, too—Brooks went on to get trounced in Alabama's Republican Senate primary a few months later.

After Brooks recounted the whole bizarre episode to me, I had one final question.

"Do you think that he really believed this?" I asked him. "Do you think he really believed that he could be reinstated as president?"

"I sure hope not," Brooks responded. "Because if he truly believed that, then he was way outside the bounds of reality."

Well, guess what? Diving into the reinstatement theories circulating at the time and what Trump actually thought of them, I found the preponderance of evidence supported the idea Trump *was* outside the bounds of reality. Trump knew he lost the election and was willing to promote any allegation, no matter how absurd or thoroughly disproven, to convince people that his "victory" was stolen from him. But unlike many of his other lies about the election, his reinstatement fantasy was something, for the most part, that he spoke about privately and to the people closest to him. And he did so persistently. Even two years after leaving the White House, Trump seemed to really believe Biden could be ejected from office and he himself could be restored to the presidency before the 2024 election.

I had personally asked Trump about this idea on July 23, 2021—months before Brooks first set him off—when I spoke to the former president for a final interview over the phone before finishing my book *Betrayal.* He sounded cranky and tired. "Jonathan, let's waste a little time," Trump said to kick off the conversation. "You're not going to write it like it is. Let's waste a little time, Jonathan." Before I could finish my first question, he jumped in to interrupt me.

"Are you seeing the polls, how strong the polls are right now? With people having tremendous buyer's remorse? Not that I didn't win it, because we did," he said. "And the information coming out of the election, that the fake news doesn't like talking about, is very strong, so strong, to put it mildly. But you'll be seeing that. You won't write it, but you'll be seeing it."

Boasting about polls was not unusual for Trump, of course. He did it even when his polls were awful, as they often were. But there was a weariness to his voice. The days when he could drive national news coverage and move markets with a single tweet were over. He seemed increasingly irrelevant. In May he had launched, with much fanfare, a website called "From the Desk of Donald Trump" where he would spread the Trump gospel one statement at a time. But the venture failed and he had taken the website down, eliciting the kind of mockery he truly hates.

"Twenty-nine days after it was launched, Donald Trump's blog, once hailed by fans as his triumphant return to the internet, was taken down on Wednesday," *Politico* reported. "It was just less than three Scaramuccis old. Noah's Ark had a longer run."[3]

Now Trump was reduced to emailing statements to the list of reporters who had once covered his presidency but no longer paid him much attention. He tended to blast out several such statements a day, many of them just a line or two long—like a tweet. But these statements received a fraction of the viewership Trump's tweets used to get. He was essentially shouting into an empty canyon, and there wasn't even much of an echo. Not only did mainstream news organizations mostly ignore these emails; so did many of the conservative outlets that had hung on his every word while he was president.

About a month before I called him for that interview, Trump had issued a particularly rambling statement complaining about *Saturday Night Live* and other "100% one-sided shows [that] should be considered an illegal campaign contribution from the Democrat Party." His train of thought was all over the place, bouncing between criticism of the performance of actor Alec Baldwin, campaign finance laws, and the "Fraudulent Election" of 2020. The final line in the statement was just three words long: "2024 or before!"[4]

I began the conversation with no intention of asking Trump about the reinstatement fantasies I had seen circulating among some of his most extreme supporters, but as he droned on about the "very strong" information I'd soon be seeing coming out about the election, he sounded like someone who genuinely believed his 2020 defeat could still be overturned. So I asked what he meant when he wrote in his statement "2024 or before!"

"You don't really think there's a way you would get reinstated before the next election, do you?" I asked.

"I'm not going to explain it to you, Jonathan," he replied, "because you wouldn't either understand it or write it."

I didn't think much about Trump's response at the time. I was focused on documenting his multipronged efforts to overturn the election while he was still *in* the White House—the legal challenges, the pressure he put on Republican governors and local officials, the demands he made of Vice President Pence, and all the rest. But listening back to my audio recording of that interview almost two years later, I realized he wasn't just complaining about the election and spouting false claims about fraud—he was still intent on overturning the results. Far from denying that he believed the preposterous idea he could be reinstated as president, Trump was signaling to me that he actually thought it could happen.

I'm not going to explain it to you, Jonathan, because you wouldn't either understand it or write it.

I moved on and asked him to respond to some of the revelations I would be reporting in my upcoming book. After about ten minutes, the interview became quite contentious when I asked him about Pence, who had recently given a speech at the Ronald Reagan Presidential Library saying he was "proud" of what he'd done on January 6, when he'd defied Trump's demand to overturn the election. Trump told me Pence had made a "terrible mistake" when he didn't reject Biden's electoral votes from the states Trump falsely claimed he had won—including Arizona, Pennsylvania, Georgia, Michigan, and Wisconsin.

"Not a single one of those states that you were challenging sent an alternative batch of electors," I reminded him. "Not a single one. I mean, you asked Michigan to do it. You asked Georgia to do it. And they didn't do it."

Trump then claimed, as he has many times since, that the legislatures in those states wanted and expected Pence to send the electoral votes back when he presided over the joint session of Congress on January 6. Now I was frustrated: Trump was either lying to me or living in an alternate reality. Each of those states had reviewed all the election challenges Trump and his allies had brought and went on to certify Biden's election victory anyway. Some of his allies had put together fake slates of electors, but contrary to Trump's assertions, no state legislative leader had indicated they expected Pence to reject the electoral votes they had sent to Washington.

I told him as much: "None of the leaders of those legislatures have said that. Not one of them."

The further I pressed, the more deranged Trump became. He pointed to an electoral audit his allies had commissioned in Arizona—a bizarre spectacle led by an obscure company called Cyber Ninjas that involved searching ballots for traces of bamboo to determine whether China had shipped in thousands of ballots for Biden. More states were going to be doing the same.

"You take a look at what's going on in Georgia, you take a look at what's going on in Wisconsin, look at what's going on in Pennsylvania," Trump told me. "Look at what's going on even in Texas now. Texas wants to do an audit, and other states."

"But you won Texas," I interjected.

"Now even states that I won want to do audits," Trump said.

When I told him I didn't get that logic, he seemed exasperated. "Why don't you understand it, Jon?" he asked. "Is it that complicated to you?"

None of it made any sense at all. It's one thing to obsess over an election loss. It's quite another to insist on recounting votes that had already been recounted—over and over again—nearly a year after the election took place. And now he was excited about the possibility of a recount in a state he had won?

The conversation was going nowhere, so I pressed ahead. I had one more thing to ask him about—one more way to test whether Trump had truly lost his mind.

"Italygate."

The competition was fierce, but Italygate was the nuttiest theory to have emerged since the 2020 election. Adherents of this hypothesis allege that Italian spy satellites had somehow been used to take control of voting machines in the United States and to flip thousands—perhaps millions—of votes from Trump to Biden. I had tracked the idea to a con artist and part-time real estate agent in Virginia who went by several different names and was known by some in the Pentagon simply as "the heiress." She even had ties to pirates in Somalia who knew her as "Amira," or "Princess."[5] As I documented in *Be-trayal*, this woman managed to bring the Italygate theory to the attention of both the White House and Trump himself.[6] And in early January 2021, I had learned, White House chief of staff Mark Meadows had asked both the Justice Department and the Pentagon to investigate the claims. Now I wanted to know why.

"You'd have to ask Mark [Meadows] about that," Trump told me. "Mark Meadows is a good man, did a very good job. He was a really great chief."

"You don't really believe there was somehow foreign control of the voting machines, do you?" I asked incredulously. "You don't really believe—"

"I think, frankly, there was so much voter fraud and irregularities, where it came from, I can't tell you," he replied. "But I can tell you there was a lot of voter fraud and irregularities."

In the final days at the White House, Trump was prepared to believe anything—no matter how absurd—that would prove the election had been stolen from him. It was almost sad. This was a former president so unable to accept his own defeat that he had constructed his own alternate reality. Whether he had come to believe his own lies about the election or was just confident he could fool enough people into believing them, Trump was living in a fantasy where at any moment the nefarious forces who conspired against him would be exposed and he would once again be made president of the United States.

The idea that Donald Trump would be reinstated as president began to circulate online almost immediately after Joe Biden was sworn into office. Many versions of this concept were put forward in the weeks and months after the inauguration, and while each iteration was obviously ludicrous and unworkable, some theories were more absurd than others.

Take, for instance, the QAnon-style narrative involving an arcane nineteenth-century statute and the Twentieth Amendment. Popularized by a far-right blog on the day Biden was set to take office, the theory outlined a scenario in which Trump would leave Washington, DC, on January 20 as part of a mission to wrest back control of the *true* United States, which had been seditiously converted into a corporation and sold off to a foreign entity 150 years earlier. Trump had to leave the capital, because he could not preside over a sovereign nation while on foreign soil.[7]

"We are literally watching the reclaiming of the United States of America," the blog post read. "Watch and see how this plays out. It is a genius move. God is in charge of this nation and is now leading his elect [*sic*] to restore this great nation called by his name."[8]

When that reckoning failed to materialize and Biden was sworn in as president, some QAnon adherents despaired—but others pivoted. Because the United States had ceased to be a real country in 1871, they reasoned, any law enacted after that date—including the Twentieth Amendment, which moved Inauguration Day from March 4 to January 20—was invalid. Trump, therefore, wasn't gone for good; he was just biding his time until March 4, when he'd be sworn in, the theory went, as the first truly legitimate US president since Ulysses S. Grant.

There's no evidence Trump himself put much stock in this particular theory—and some QAnon followers eventually began to worry they were being set up—but it gained enough traction that top officials cited it in their decision to keep National Guard troops in

DC through mid-March. "Some of these people have figured out that apparently 75 years ago the President used to be inaugurated on March 4," Democratic representative Adam Smith, then chair of the House Armed Services Committee, said in a February 2021 hearing. "Why that is relevant, God knows. At any rate, now they are thinking, maybe we should gather again and storm the Capitol on March 4."[9]

The day came and went without much fanfare, but before too long the push to reinstate Trump began anew. And this time, the former president was paying close attention.

"Donald Trump will be back in office in August," Mike Lindell, the conspiratorial pillow salesman, declared on Steve Bannon's *War Room* podcast in late March. "All the evidence I have, everything is going to go before the Supreme Court, and the election of 2020 is going bye-bye."[10]

Wearing a salmon-colored golf polo and speaking in the thick Minnesota accent familiar to anybody who has seen his ubiquitous pillow commercials on Fox News, Lindell started to pick up steam, blowing through Bannon's attempts to interject. "It was an attack by another country—communism coming in," he asserted, referring to the 2020 election. "I don't know what they're going to do with it after they pull it down, but it's going down."[11]

It wasn't "going down," of course. Judges—including Trump-appointed judges—had already rejected dozens of challenges to the election *before* it was certified, and the Supreme Court certainly wasn't going to reverse the 2020 results months *after* they had been made official. Even if Lindell had the goods—which he didn't—there's no constitutional or legal mechanism for undoing an election. The remedy he was seeking simply did not exist.

Even some of Trump's staunchest supporters understood this.

"The election was lawless, six states allowed their delegates to vote by false certifications, but the [Electoral College] process happened," Jenna Ellis—who, alongside Rudy Giuliani, led Trump's failed legal efforts after the 2020 election—tweeted in late May. "The Constitution has only one process for removal of a sitting president: impeachment and conviction. No, President Trump is not going to be 'reinstated.'"[12]

Trump's own daughter-in-law, Lara Trump, also quickly dismissed the theory. "I have not heard any plans for Donald Trump to be installed in the White House in August," she said in an interview on *Fox & Friends* a few days later.[13] The push was too out there even for Representative Marjorie Taylor Greene. "I want people to be careful in what they believe," she told Bannon in early July. "It's going to be very difficult to overturn the 2020 election, and so I'd hate for anyone to get their hopes up thinking that President Trump is going to be back in the White House in August. Because that's not true."[14]

But one person "getting their hopes up" was Trump himself. Not only did the former president confirm as much to me in our late-July call—"You wouldn't understand," he told me—but Bannon would later tell me Trump was "100 percent all in" on the theory. "Remember, at that time there was not a lot of Mar-a-Lago activity," he said, noting Trump was more or less left to his own devices. "He was a lion in winter at that time."

One of Trump's relatively junior aides at Mar-a-Lago told me that he was so concerned about how much Trump was talking about it, he urged the former president to give it a break. "If you really think it's true, then stop talking about it. Just let it happen," the aide said he told Trump. "If you keep talking about it so much, people will think you are crazy."

"You say that because you aren't a true believer!" Trump told him. "No," he told his boss. "I just believe in the Constitution."

By July 2021, there were scattered reports that Trump was talking to those around him about the idea of returning to the White House. "Trump has been telling a number of people he's in contact with that he expects he will get reinstated by August," Maggie Haberman of *The New York Times* tweeted in early June.[15] Shortly after, Will Sommer and Asawin Suebsaeng reported in *The Daily Beast* that the former president was "quizzing confidants about a potential August return to power" and telling them a lot of "highly respected" people were letting him know it was possible. Lindell took credit: "If Trump is saying August, that is probably because he heard me say it publicly."[16]

Charles C. W. Cooke, a conservative writer for *National Review*, corroborated the stories a few days later. "I can attest, from speaking to an array of different sources, that Donald Trump does indeed believe quite genuinely that he—along with former senators David Perdue and Martha McSally—will be 'reinstated' to office this summer after 'audits' of the 2020 elections in Arizona, Georgia, and a handful of other states have been completed," Cooke wrote. "I can attest, too, that Trump is trying hard to recruit journalists, politicians, and other influential figures to promulgate this belief—not as a fundraising tool or an infantile bit of trolling or a trial balloon, but as a fact.[17]

"The scale of Trump's delusion is quite startling," he continued. "This is not merely an eccentric interpretation of the facts or an interesting foible, nor is it an irrelevant example of anguished post-presidency chatter. It is a rejection of reality, a rejection of law, and, ultimately, a rejection of the entire system of American government. There is no Reinstatement Clause within the United States

Constitution. Hell, there is nothing even approximating a Reinstatement Clause within the United States Constitution. The election has been certified, Joe Biden is the president, and, until 2024, that is all there is to it."[18]

Yet Lindell kept chugging along, growing more confident over the summer with each appearance he made on Bannon's podcast. "We have a clear path to pull this election down," he said in June, now claiming his evidence was so strong, the Supreme Court ruling would be unanimous.[19] And at some point, his vague promises of "August" began to get more specific. "The morning of August 13, it'll be the talk of the world," Lindell said on another far-right show in early July. "Hurry up! Let's get this election pulled down, let's right the right, let's get these communists out that have taken over. You'll see."[20]

At the center of Lindell's plan was what he was labeling his "cyber symposium," a three-day event scheduled for August 10 to 12 in Sioux Falls, South Dakota, where he promised to finally reveal to the world the thirty-seven terabytes worth of "evidence" he and his team had collected. The files were supposed to include packet captures (pcaps)—or intercepted network data—that made clear Chinese hackers had accessed voting machines and flipped votes to Biden. As the symposium began, however, Lindell produced none of the evidence he'd promised. "This is incredibly frustrating," tweeted Robert Graham, a prominent cybersecurity analyst who attended the conference. "Lindell invited 'cyber experts' and 'fact checkers' to come and confirm the 'packet captures'—and has yet to provide us any packet captures.... To be clear: he gave us experts NOTHING today, except random garbage that wastes our time."[21]

The same drama played out over the next two days of the symposium. Lindell would make sweeping promises to provide attendees the irrefutable proof he'd been hyping up for months, only to waffle when it came time to deliver. Either he'd come up with an excuse to delay the reveal a few more hours or flash a series of fast-moving numbers on the screen that were essentially meaningless. Even Josh Merritt, one of the cyber experts Lindell hired to comb through the data, came away unimpressed. "We're not going to say that this is legitimate if we don't have confidence in the information," Merritt told the conservative *Washington Times* on the second day of the conference. Lindell, he added, had provided nothing to prove Chinese hackers had interfered in the election.[22]

Lindell was not deterred—he just pushed his timeline back yet again. "Originally, I had hoped for August and September," he admitted in a late-September appearance on Bannon's podcast. "We will have this before the Supreme Court before Thanksgiving. That's my promise to the people of this country. We're all in this together. We worked very hard on this!"[23]

Bannon had long known Lindell was full of crap, subtly pushing back on his assertions on the podcast and mocking him behind the scenes. "I knew we had a problem when Kristi Noem [the Republican governor of South Dakota] had a 'previously scheduled appointment' before that cyber symposium in Sioux Falls," Bannon later told me with a laugh. "She couldn't come down and give us ten minutes? I knew the reinstatement thing was going to be a problem at that time."

Noem may not have made it to the cyber symposium held in her home state, but there was another high-profile Republican woman in attendance—we just didn't know it yet. Among the hundred or so attendees at Lindell's event was a former Phoenix television news anchor named Kari Lake, who had launched a long-shot bid to be Arizona's governor two months earlier. The Arizona contingent in Sioux

White House press conference, March 24, 2020. No presidential press conferences in American history featured more disinformation or fewer reporters than those Donald Trump held during the COVID-19 pandemic. *(Photo by Doug Mills)*

In *Betrayal*, I published unreleased White House photographs showing how the Trump campaign took over the Map Room of the White House on election night 2020. Here in th book, I am publishing more images from election night 2020 taken by an official White House photographer that have never before been made public. *(White House photo)*

Trump Campaign manager Bill Stepien briefs three Trumps—Ivanka, Lara, and Eric. *(White House photo)*

There was no way to spin the results— it didn't look good for Trump. From left to right: Trump campaign lawyer Justin Clark, Bill Stepien, Lara Trump, Ivanka Trump, Eric Trump, and Donald Trump Jr. *(White House photo)*

...ery grim group of Trump
...isors takes the White House
...vator upstairs to see a very
...ry President Trump after Fox
...ws projected Joe Biden the
...nner in Arizona. From left to
...nt: Bill Stepien, Eric
...schman, Head White House
...her Timothy Harleth, Justin
...rk, and Jason Miller.
...ite House photo)

THE WHITE HOUSE

CHRIS MILLER SPOKE
TO BOTH O.C. THEM
AND ANTICIPATES NO
MORE STATEMENTS
COMING OUT. (IF
ANOTHER HAPPENS, HE
WILL FIRE THEM)

In December 2020, the Secretary and Chief of Staff of the Army infuriated Trump by putting out a statement saying, "There is no role for the US military in determining the outcome of an American election." This is a note Johnny McEntee, Trump's most unwaveringly loyal aide, wrote to the president informing him that the Army leaders would be fired if they ever put out a statement like that again. The note was torn into pieces and later reconstructed for the National Archives. *(National Archives via January 6 Committee)*

This photo is out of focus—but it documents a key moment on January 6 as Trump meets the Oval Office with family and staff shortly before he heads out to give his speech at the White House Ellipse. *(National Archives via January 6 Committee)*

Trump backstage before his January 6 speech with his son Eric and daughter Ivanka. *(National Archives via January 6 Committee)*

e Trump family returns to the West Wing after Donald Trump's speech on January 6.
ational Archives via January 6 Committee)

January 6, 2021

Minute 11

This photo captured Trump as he walked alone into the Oval Office after his speech on January 6. He had just been told by White House valet Walt Nauta about the violence at the Capitol. *(National Archives via January 6 Committee)*

Trump speaks to Mike Pence on the morning of January 6.
(White House photo via January 6 Committee)

This remarkable photograph was taken just moments after Pence was evacuated from the Senate chamber to a nearby ceremonial office. His wife, Karen, is seen pulling the curtains shut to prevent the mob outside from seeing where they were. Minutes later, Pence was evacuated to a loading dock below the Capitol. *(White House photo by Myles Cullen)*

Pence sat in his Secret Service vehicle, but he refused to let them close the door because he did not want to be removed from the Capitol complex. *(Photo by Myles Cullen via January 6 Committee)*

Trump reviews his January 6 videotaped statement. "We have to have peace. So go home. We love you. You're very special." *(National Archives via January 6 Committee)*

Another remarkable photo. Pence, at the loading dock below the Capitol, can be seen watching Trump's video message released at 4:17pm on January 6, where he finally tells his supporters to go home, but also adds, "We love you. You are special." *(Photo by Myles Cullen via January 6 Committee)*

Republican House leader Kevin McCarthy meets with Donald Trump eight days after Trump left the White House in disgrace.
(Trump press release)

The January 6 hearing presents one of the searing images from the attack on the Capitol—the gallows set up by the rioters, some of whom were chanting, "Hang Mike Pence." *(House Creative Services)*

Some of the most forceful voices heard by the January 6 Committee were young women who worked for Donald Trump and were horrified by what they saw. One of them was Deputy White House Press secretary Sarah Matthews. *(House Creative Services)*

Three Justice Department officials appointed by Donald Trump who stood up to Trump's efforts to overturn the 2020 election. From left to right: Steven Engel, Jeffrey Rosen, and Richard Donaghue. *(House Creative Services)*

true profile in
ourage, Arizona's
epublican Speaker of
e House Rusty Bowers
fused to use his
osition of authority to
ullify Joe Biden's
ctory in Arizona.
Photo by Jonathan Karl)

No major candidate in 2022 echoed Donald Trump's lies about the election more aggressively than Kari Lake. I interviewed her shortly before the election. She ran for governor of Arizona. She lost. And like Trump, she refused to concede. *(Photo by Meghan Mistry)*

The scene outside Mar-a-Lago on November 15, 2022, as Donald Trump announced he would be running for president again in 2024. *(Photo by Jonathan Karl)*

Most of the people who worked in the Trump White House and Cabinet were no-shows at Trump's presidential announcement. But convicted felon Roger Stone was there. *(Photo by Jonathan Karl)*

Mike Lindell, who peddles lumpy pillows and conspiracy theories, was also at Mar-a-Lago for Trump's announcement. *(Photo by Jonathan Karl)*

little more than halfway through Donald Trump's big announcement speech, attendees at Mar-a-Lago started heading for the exits. Eventually the security staff blocked the doors, telling people they had to wait until the speech was over. *(Photo by Jonathan Karl)*

This painting is displayed prominently on the wall at Mar-a-Lago. *(Photo by Jonathan Karl)*

Steve Bannon with Trump at Mar-a-Lago in April 2023. "I've never seen him better," Bannon told me. "You do understand—we're going back to the White House." *(Photo by William M. Blair)*

...ys after her defeat in Wyoming, I interviewed Liz Cheney in the room where the January [6] Committee held its hearings. "People continue to believe the lie. People continue to believe [wh]at he is saying, which is very dangerous," Cheney told me. "Larger portions of our party, [inc]luding the leadership of our party, is very sick." *(Photo by Quinn Scanlan)*

[M]y view from the House chamber
[as] Kevin McCarthy struggled to
[get] elected Speaker of the House.
[Ph]oto by Jonathan Karl)

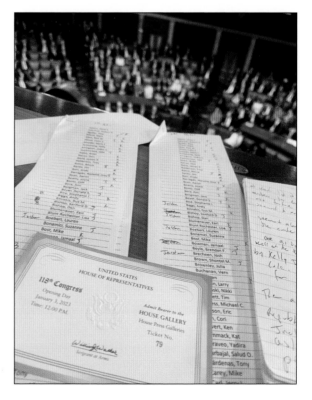

Jack Smith's first indictment of Trump included photos of the various places Donald Trump kept his boxes filled with White House documents, some of them highly classified. These boxes were stored in an ornate bathroom at Mar-a-Lago. *(Office of the Special Counsel)*

Another inglorious first: a mugshot of a former president, also known as inmate No. P01135809, after he was indicted for allegedly leading a criminal conspiracy to overturn the results of the 2020 presidential election in Georgia. *(Fulton County Sheriff's Office)*

Falls also included state senator Wendy Rogers, a self-described member of the Oath Keepers militia known for her extreme views and her allegiance to Trump; and Mark Finchem, a far-right member of the Arizona House of Representatives who had marched to the Capitol on January 6 and was a candidate for Arizona secretary of state.[24] Lake and Finchem were on the fringe of Arizona politics, but their support for Lindell's fantasies caught Trump's attention, and eventually his endorsement, helping them win the GOP nominations for two of the state's most important offices and transforming them into two of the state's most prominent Republicans going into the 2022 midterm elections.

Lake didn't publicly endorse Lindell's idea that Trump would be reinstated at the end of the symposium on August 13, but the idea seemed to intrigue her. As she tweeted from Sioux Falls at the start of Lindell's gathering on August 10, three days before the predicted Trump reinstatement: "When it's not God's time, you can't force it. When it is God's time, you can't stop it."

The "evidence" never made it before the Supreme Court, of course, and Donald Trump, as of this writing, was never reinstalled as president. The whole push was so absurd that, by early March 2023, even Lindell was starting to distance himself from the claims. "I never said [August 13]," he shot back when reporter Declan Garvey asked him at the Conservative Political Action Conference about his previous comments and whether he thought Trump's reinstatement was still possible. "On August 13, I said everybody's going to be *talking* about it. That's what I said. . . . It had nothing to do with overturning an election."

That wasn't true, of course. As I have documented in this chapter, Lindell had repeatedly declared Trump would be reinstated on August 13. He said it with certainty. And to this day, you can still find a video clip online of Lindell telling Steve Bannon, "Donald Trump will be back in office in August" and "the election of 2020 is going bye-bye."[25]

The idea had obvious appeal for Donald Trump. The pillow salesman had been promising him something his lawyers and all his political advisors had failed to get him: a path back to the White House. And while that path wouldn't work for Trump, Lindell and his cyber symposium were just the beginning.

Lying to the Vatican

As Donald Trump traveled aboard Air Force One en route to Rome on his first foreign presidential trip, he had a decision to make: Who would he bring with him for his meeting with Pope Francis at the Vatican? State visits with the pope follow a strict protocol: Even the president of the United States can bring only a small entourage to meet the pope.

Deputy chief of staff Joe Hagin, who was handling the logistics for the May 2017 trip, explained to Trump that the Vatican would allow only ten people to accompany him and the First Lady. He needed to submit the names before Air Force One landed in Rome.

"There are a lot of people on this plane who would love to go with you to the Vatican," Hagin, who had handled logistics for two previous Republican presidents, told Trump. "I suggest you invite the people who helped you get here."

Trump jotted down the names on a piece of paper and handed it to Hagin. The list included his daughter Ivanka and son-in-law Jared Kushner, as well as several high-level White House staffers, including H. R.

McMaster, Gary Cohn, Hope Hicks, Dina Powell, and Dan Scavino. Noticeably absent was the person who seemed more eager to meet the pope than anyone else on the trip: Press Secretary Sean Spicer, a devout Catholic, had been telling people for days that he was excited to get a chance to see the pope in person and that he had brought his rosary beads to be blessed.

"Don't you want to include Sean on this list?" Hagin asked. "It would mean the world to him."

"No," Trump answered curtly. Trump would never explain why he decided to cavalierly crush Spicer's plan to meet the pope. For previous presidents, it was standard practice to bring the press secretary along for a meeting with the pope. But Spicer, the proud Catholic, would be iced out. And there would be more drama to come.

Upon arriving in Rome, Hagin notified the people on Trump's list that they would be part of the presidential delegation going to the Vatican— and two of them were surprised to be included. Gary Cohn and Dina Powell—neither of whom are Catholic—suggested to Hagin that others for whom the opportunity would be more spiritually meaningful should go in their place.

Hagin explained it was too late to change the names, but based on his experience on previous presidential trips to meet the pope, he said he didn't think the Vatican would check the IDs of the president's entourage. If they wanted to give away their spots on the visit, whoever took their places would simply have to identify themselves to the guard at the door as Gary Cohn and Dina Powell.

With that, Powell gave her spot on the Vatican visit to Julie Radford, Ivanka Trump's chief of staff, and Cohn let Brian Hook, a senior State Department official, take his place. Both of the substitutes were devout

Catholics who were thrilled about the chance to meet the pope, even if it meant telling a little white lie to get into the room.

Here is where the story takes a decidedly Trumpian turn.

When Trump's entourage arrived at the pope's offices, there was a person checking names but, as Hagin had said, not checking IDs. Brian Hook was let in as "Gary Cohn." But when Julie Radford walked up to take Dina Powell's spot, she was stopped in her tracks.

"No!" said the Vatican gatekeeper. "Dina Powell has already gone in!"

What happened? Dina Powell wasn't there. Who was?

Another member of Trump's team had learned of Cohn and Powell's plan, and according to three people present at the Vatican, this official managed to snag Powell's slot before Radford could get into the meeting with the pope.

When confronted by her colleagues, the official denied lying her way into the meeting. Nobody believed her, but who would call her out? Is it really a sin to deceive your colleagues at work when they are already lying to the Vatican?

CHAPTER EIGHT

RAZING ARIZONA

Getting married at Mar-a-Lago isn't cheap, but where else can you expect Donald Trump might crash the party and share some words of wisdom with the bride and groom? Even while he was president, Trump would occasionally make an appearance as newlyweds tied the knot at his club.

One such appearance came in February 2018, when then Speaker of the House Paul Ryan had made the trek down to Palm Beach for a meeting with the president. As Trump gave his guest a tour of the property, the two men stumbled upon a wedding ceremony in progress. Noticing that the attendees' attention had begun to shift from the bride walking down the aisle to the two politicians on the veranda behind her, the genteel Ryan suggested they turn back. He didn't want to upstage the wedding party's big day.

"No," Trump responded, giving a thumbs-up to the wedding guests. "They love it. This is why they come here." He was probably right. If you're someone who wants to get married at Mar-a-Lago, you're likely not going to mind the club's owner stopping by and briefly stealing the spotlight.

But after Trump left the White House as a defeated president and had more time on his hands, his cameos became a little less brief—and a lot weirder. "I just say, 'Do you miss me yet?'" he asked reception guests in a video that surfaced from a wedding on March 27, 2021.[1] Trump, wearing a black tuxedo, had just regaled his audience with a rant about Joe Biden's handling of the southern border, China, and Iran. A drummer and bass player can be seen in the background, waiting to get the dance floor bumping again. They'd have to hold tight a little bit longer.

"We did get seventy-five million votes—nobody's ever gotten that," Trump continued. "They said, 'Get sixty-six million votes, sir, and the election is over.' Well I got seventy-five million." He added, somewhat cryptically: "A lot of things happening right now."

With Trump banned from just about every major social media platform and almost never on television, snippets like these—often posted to TikTok or Instagram by wedding attendees themselves—were just about all the American public saw of the man who had dominated the national psyche for half a decade. And they provided unique insight into what was on his mind as he transitioned back to life as a private citizen.

More often than not, Trump was thinking about the 2020 election—and how it might still be undone. Although the former president didn't explain what he meant by "a lot of things happening right now" at the wedding reception, he had recently been informed of a development in Arizona that wouldn't be announced publicly for four more days: Republicans in the state senate had contracted the company Cyber Ninjas to conduct a massive audit of every single ballot cast in the state's biggest county, Maricopa, during the 2020 election.

Trump believed it was the start of something big—as he explained in a similar Mar-a-Lago video that emerged a few weeks later. "I wouldn't be surprised if they found thousands and thousands and thousands of votes," he told attendees of a charity gala at his club in late April, with yet another band sitting idle behind him. "So we're going to watch that very closely. And after that, you'll watch Pennsylvania, and you'll watch Georgia, and you're going to watch Michigan, and Wisconsin, and you're watching New Hampshire—they found a lot of votes up in New Hampshire just now, you saw that? Because this was a rigged election, everybody knows it, and we're going to be watching it very closely."[2]

Trump was describing what had become known among many of his most ardent followers as the "domino theory." Once Cyber Ninjas discovered Trump was the true victor in Arizona, the theory went, lawmakers in all the other swing states Trump lost in 2020 would have no choice but to conduct similar probes, and the Democrats' mass voter fraud campaign would be laid bare. Before the year was out, some of these people believed, Trump would be back where he belonged: behind the Resolute Desk at 1600 Pennsylvania Avenue.

Trump wasn't hoping just to prove a point or set the record straight with these audits. As I explained in the previous chapter, there is overwhelming evidence he actually believed he could still be reinstated as president. And he wasn't exactly hiding this bizarre belief. In a little-noticed statement he issued in May 2021, Trump touted a "bombshell" report out of Michigan that he claimed showed a "MASSIVE" number of votes were switched from Trump to Biden.

"If a thief robs a jewelry store of all of its diamonds (the 2020

Presidential Election), the diamonds must be returned," he wrote. "The Fake News media refuses to cover the greatest Election Fraud in the history of our Country. They have lost all credibility, but ultimately, they will have no choice!"

At least one media organization agreed, breathlessly covering every twist and turn of Cyber Ninjas' audit in Arizona. In the name of "transparency," Republicans in the Arizona State Senate had allowed the installation of a camera to broadcast a 24/7 livestream of the audit, and the relentlessly pro-Trump One America News (OAN) network was chosen as the broadcast partner.

But the relationship between OAN and Arizona Republicans went deeper than that. In addition to OAN airing the recount, we'd later learn, one of the audit's largest funders was an organization called Voices and Votes, set up by two prominent OAN personalities, Chanel Rion and Christina Bobb, the latter of whom worked as a lawyer for Trump.[3]

"Arizona is just the beginning, and they need our help as much as we need their audit results," Bobb told viewers of an OAN broadcast in early May, plastering the Voices and Votes home page on the screen. "The audit is dangerously underfunded. If you can support the audit, I humbly ask you to do so."[4]

Going all-in on Arizona may or may not have been a smart business decision—OAN has since been dropped by Verizon and DirecTV after disputes over carriage fees—but the move earned it a very high-profile viewer. "One America News (OAN), one of the fastest growing networks on television, and the 'hottest,' is doing a magnificent job of exposing the massive fraud that took place," Trump said in a statement emailed out on May 15. Days earlier, he had alerted everyone on his email list that "the Arizona recount and examination will be on live TV (OAN) for all to watch."[5]

Trump, according to multiple people close to him, was obsessed. One of his confidants told me the former president was constantly checking in on the OAN feed. He even referred to it during one of his Mar-a-Lago appearances that spring. "Just take a look, it's on," he encouraged the crowd. "It's on closed-circuit, I guess it's on all over the place because everyone's talking about it."[6]

In pursuing the Cyber Ninjas' audit, Arizona Republicans insisted they were simply hoping to provide voters "additional assurance" and "bring integrity to the election process."[7] This reasoning was suspect even at the time—Maricopa County already had conducted both a forensic audit and a hand recount of select precincts that detected no irregularities.

The previous audits confirmed a fact that was both indisputable and inconvenient to the state's Republican Party—Trump's loss in Arizona was a historic embarrassment. He was the first GOP presidential candidate to lose the state in nearly a quarter century, and he lost massive Maricopa County—which includes Phoenix and its suburbs and accounts for more than 60 percent of the state's population—by more than 45,000 votes. The last Republican to lose the county? Thomas Dewey, who was defeated by Harry Truman in 1948.[8]

And Trump lost even as other Republican candidates won in lower-profile down-ballot races. The GOP retained control of the state legislature and won nearly all of Maricopa's countywide elections. Trump and Republican senator Martha McSally both lost, but most of the party's other candidates were celebrating on election night.

"If indeed there was some great conspiracy, it apparently didn't work, since the county election official who's a Democrat lost, and other Republicans won," Arizona's Republican attorney general Mark Brnovich said a few days after the election. "What really happened, it came down to people split their ticket. People vote for Republicans down-ballot; they didn't vote for President Trump and Martha McSally. That's the reality. Just because that happened doesn't mean it's fraud."[9]

But other Arizona Republicans disagreed, launching their audit a few months later. Curiously, they decided to look at only two races: Trump's loss to Biden and McSally's loss to Democratic US Senate candidate Mark Kelly.[10] Apparently, there was no need to reexamine the votes in all those races Republicans won.

When Arizona Republicans began looking into their audit, they received bids from a number of election technology companies to lead the process, including at least one—Clear Ballot Group—that was certified by the US Election Assistance Commission. But Senate Republicans—led by Karen Fann—didn't choose them. Despite receiving warnings from many of her advisors—including her outside legal counsel—the state senate president assembled a team of four companies that would be led by a small cybersecurity firm based in Sarasota, Florida, that had never conducted an election audit: Cyber Ninjas.

Only Fann knows for sure why she went with Cyber Ninjas—she would later tell the Associated Press she couldn't recall how she found them,[11] and there is no evidence the company submitted a formal bid—but it's hard to believe the politics of the company's founder and

CEO, Doug Logan, didn't play a role. In the months leading up to the audit, Logan had been promoting some of *the* most far-fetched theories about the 2020 election—not just questions about how some states changed their voting laws during the pandemic, but full-on conspiracies featuring the late Venezuelan dictator Hugo Chávez, hacked voting machines, and alleged ties between China and Dominion Voting Systems.[12] As of this writing, a document Logan authored—which suggests rigging the election was part of a Chinese plan set in motion in 1963 to "take over America without firing a shot"—is still featured prominently on former Trump lawyer Sidney Powell's website.

After a lengthy court battle, Logan's Cyber Ninjas was given access to all 2.1 million paper ballots cast in Maricopa County in 2020, as well as the voting machines that counted them. To accommodate the enormous amount of paperwork, the state senate leased Veterans Memorial Coliseum, an enormous arena in downtown Phoenix that, until 1992, was the home of the NBA's Phoenix Suns. The count was originally expected to take just a few weeks but ended up dragging on for more than four months.

If that sounds expensive, that's because it was. As the audit sputtered along, its price tag ballooned—well past the $150,000 the state senate originally agreed to pay Cyber Ninjas out of its own taxpayer-funded budget. Stephen Richer, the Republican recorder of Maricopa County, told me that, altogether, he believed the endeavor ended up costing "close to twenty million."

It's difficult to pin down the exact price of the boondoggle because so many of the auditors' undertakings were shrouded in secrecy, but we know from public records it climbed well into the millions. Security to guard the ballots, portable air-conditioning units, and janitorial services all cost thousands of dollars, and the state senate racked up more than half a million dollars in legal fees alone, as it sparred with Maricopa County officials over access to election equipment and data.[13] Those costs, however, pale in comparison to the more than $5 million in payroll and labor costs associated with the audit.[14] "I don't like wasting taxpayer dollars," Fann told *The Arizona Republic*. "But this is part of our job as the Senate: writing laws."[15]

Apparently also part of the senate's job? Making Maricopa County's vote-counting machines inoperable and forcing taxpayers to spend about $3 million to replace them. Because Cyber Ninjas was not accredited by the Election Assistance Commission, the Department of Homeland Security advised Arizona's Democratic secretary of state, Katie Hobbs, to decertify the equipment for future use over concerns the auditors had tampered with it. "The frustrating thing is, those were perfectly good machines which passed all of our accuracy tests from the time we first got them in 2019," Maricopa County Board of Supervisors chairman Jack Sellers said. "When Senate leadership chose novices to conduct their audit rather than reputable, certified companies, they wasted an expensive investment that had served Maricopa County voters well in 2019 and 2020."[16]

Taxpayers ended up footing the bill for many of these costs, but they were at least somewhat offset by funds raised and donated by some of the most extreme and conspiracy-minded figures in Trumpworld. In addition to about $600,000 from the OAN hosts' organization Voices and Votes, Cyber Ninjas' effort was also supported by more than $3 million from a group led by former Overstock.com CEO Patrick Byrne, nearly $1 million from an organization affiliated with former Trump national security advisor Michael Flynn, and more than $500,000 from Sidney Powell's Defending the Republic.[17]

Pro-Trump groups aggressively raised money off the audit and fun-neled some of those funds back to keep it going.

Sellers, the Board of Supervisors chairman and a Republican, called the whole effort "a grift disguised as an audit."[18]

Ken Bennett, Arizona's Trump-supporting former secretary of state, who served as a "liaison" between the state senate and the audit, later told me it was a big mistake to rely on groups so closely tied with Trump and his claims that the election had been rigged. "They had a vested interest in what they wanted the result of the audit to show," he said. That's an understatement: These groups had been relentlessly pushing election conspiracy theories and hyping the audit as a chance to prove Trump had really won.

Bennett told me he later learned there had been a series of daily meetings during the audit between Cyber Ninjas' Logan and state senator Wendy Rogers, the member of the Oath Keepers militia who touted her total support for all things Trump. These meetings, ac-cording to Bennett, were convened to provide updates on the audit's progress to the people funding the effort and possibly Trump him-self.

In truth, the recount was adhering closely to Maricopa County's official count. But by excluding Bennett from these meetings, Logan and Rogers were able to present "evidence" they "uncovered" that simply didn't exist. "They couldn't keep the money flowing if the re-ports were coming out that they were confirming that the county was accurate," Bennett told me. "They had to be feeding these people the possibility of major variances or deviations to keep the money flow-ing."[19]

The search for those major variances or deviations led the auditors down some kooky rabbit holes. Early on, the arena's livestream showed counters scanning ballots with what appeared to be ultraviolet light. We'd later learn they were searching for secret watermarks supposedly imprinted on the paper, but didn't find any. A few weeks later, an official helping manage the audit explained why volunteers were taking pictures of the ballots with a special 5K camera. They were searching for those telltale traces of bamboo.

"There's accusations forty thousand ballots were flown in to Arizona and it was stuffed into the box, okay?" John Brakey, founder of AUDIT Elections USA, told a reporter with Phoenix television station CBS 5 News. "And it came from the southeast part of the world, Asia, okay? And what they're doing is to find out if there's bamboo in the paper."[20]

Brakey was quick to clarify that he didn't believe the theory himself, but he argued that taking the time to check could help convince those who did. "That is part of the mystery that we want to ungaslight people about," he said. "And this is a way to do it."

Ostensibly, that was the purpose of the entire audit. "Everybody keeps saying, 'Oh, there's no evidence,' and it's like, yeah, well, let's do the audit, and if there's nothing there, then we say, 'Look, there was nothing there,'" Fann told the Associated Press. "If we find something—and it's a big if—but if we find something, then we can say, 'Okay, we do have evidence, and now how do we fix this?'"[21]

But if that was truly the mindset Fann and her state senate colleagues were bringing to the recount, nobody told Trump. "So many people would like to thank the brave and patriotic Republican State Senators from Arizona for the incredible job they are doing in exposing the large scale Voter Fraud which took place in the 2020 Presidential Election," he wrote in a statement issued shortly after the process began.[22] His misplaced excitement in what the audit would turn up was surpassed only, perhaps, by the auditors themselves. As the official Twitter account of the audit tweeted in early May: "THE GREATEST AUDIT IN THE GALAXY CONTINUES!!"

Greatness, in this case, was in the eye of the beholder. "In more than a decade working on elections, audits and recounts across the country, I've never seen one this mismanaged," Jennifer Morrell, a US Air Force veteran who helped run elections in Utah and Colorado from 2009 to 2018, wrote in *The Washington Post* after observing Cyber Ninjas' recount. "I was stunned to see spinning conveyor wheels, whizzing hundreds of ballots past 'counters,' who struggled to mark, on a tally sheet, each voter's selection for the presidential and Senate races. They had only a few seconds to record what they saw. Occasionally, I saw a counter look up, realize they missed a ballot and then grab the wheel to stop it. *This process sets them up to make so many mistakes*, I kept thinking."[23]

At one point the auditors considered going door-to-door in certain precincts to ask people directly about their votes. The plan was scrapped after the Department of Justice sent a letter to the senate president on May 5, 2021, warning that such a move might violate federal law. "The Department enforces a number of federal statutes that prohibit intimidation of persons for voting or attempting to vote," Pamela Karlan, principal deputy assistant attorney general of the Justice Department's Civil Rights Division, wrote. "This description of the proposed work of the audit raises concerns regarding the potential intimidation of voters."[24]

The Arizona secretary of state's office dispatched several people to observe the audit, and those onlookers were astounded by the sloppiness they encountered. Security gates were left open, a confidential technical manual was left unattended, officials carelessly unlocked the cage where ballots were being stored so anyone could see the access code, and black and blue pens capable of altering the ballots were allowed onto the counting floor.

The people counting the ballots were reportedly being paid fifteen dollars an hour, but the audit was perpetually understaffed—and the people who *did* volunteer were . . . not always the best fit. Former state lawmaker Anthony Kern, for example, was eventually barred from participating in the process after officials realized his name appeared on the ballots being recounted, as a candidate—and that he was at the US Capitol on January 6. "He was here for two or three days," Bennett said at the time. "Once it was identified that that wasn't the best optics, I think the contractor removed him from the counting tables."[25]

The clownishness of the audit didn't seem to bother its biggest fan. "I want to send our profound and everlasting gratitude to every Arizona Republican who had the fortitude and the backbone to defy the lying media," Trump said that summer in remarks at Turning Point USA's Student Action Summit in Phoenix. His shout-outs to obscure individual lawmakers made clear just how closely he'd been paying attention the last few months. "State senators J. D. Mesnard, Kelly Townsend. Kelly, you've been so incredible," he gushed, as if he were meeting characters from his favorite reality show. "Sonny Borrelli, he's great. Where's Sonny? There he is. I recognize that man from television!"

After singing the praises of state senator Wendy Rogers—who would later be censured by her Republican and Democratic colleagues alike for speaking at a conference organized by a well-known white supremacist and calling for the public execution of political "traitors"—Trump stumbled upon a new catchphrase. "Wendy, Kelly, Borelli. What a group. I wouldn't want to fight you," he mused. "Wendy, Kelly, and Borelli: That's going to be a very famous statement someday, I suspect."

About halfway through his nearly two-hour speech, Trump finally stopped talking about ballot signature-matching standards and Maricopa County's network routers and moved on to criticizing the Biden administration. But not before he singled Rogers out for backing his evidence-free claims of fraud from the get-go. "You knew the answer early on, Wendy," he said. "We're waiting for results, but you knew the answer."[26]

For Trump, those results couldn't come fast enough. They would not only serve as the domino that would set in motion his plan to decertify the election and be reinstated, but they would finally quiet all the people who had been mocking his claims for months. "When the real numbers are released people will be shocked, but this is a concerted effort of the Fake News Media to discredit and demean," Trump said in a written statement in July 2021. "There has never been anything like it. Numbers will be released shortly, and they are extraordinarily big and highly determinative!"

Trump was right: People *were* shocked when the "real numbers" were released.

Cyber Ninjas' final report was finally made public in late September 2021—and it found 99 *more* votes for Biden and 261 *fewer* for Trump. After all that, the final recount showed Biden won Arizona by a slightly *larger* margin than the original official count.

In testimony before the state senate about their final report, Logan and his fellow auditors brushed past that 360-vote swing, arguing their search was less about the raw vote totals and more about whether those votes were fraudulent. But the questions they raised—about potential duplicate ballots, signature matching, deceased voters, and changed addresses—were summarily rebuffed by county officials, and even Karen Fann, the Republican state senate leader who had started the audit in the first place, had seen enough. "Truth is truth and numbers are numbers," she said as the auditors presented their report.[27]

Ken Bennett put it in even simpler terms during my conversation with him: "The audit confirmed Biden won Arizona."

The implications were devastating to those clinging to the belief Trump would be proved to be the true winner in 2020. "If Trump and his supporters can't prove it here, with a process they designed, they can't prove it anywhere," David Becker, the executive director of the Center for Election Innovation and Research, told *The New York Times*.[28]

Trump frantically tried to spin the results as anything other than a massive disappointment, issuing six increasingly desperate-sounding statements on the day the report was released. "The Fake News is lying about the Arizona audit report!" read one issued late in the morning. By 6 P.M.—when it was clear Cyber Ninjas hadn't upended the national narrative as he'd hoped—Trump was despondent.

"It is not even believable the dishonesty of the Fake News Media on the Arizona Audit results, which shows incomprehensible Fraud at an Election Changing level, many times more votes than is needed," he claimed. "The Fake News Media refuses to write the facts, thereby being complicit in the Crime of the Century. They are so dishonest, but Patriots know the truth!"[29]

If the audit report was truly as damning as Trump claimed, he and his allies should've been content to let it stand on its own. But within hours of Cyber Ninjas releasing their findings, a second version of the report—which branded itself as the "real" one and concluded the election "should not be certified" because the "results are not reliable"—was rocketing around the pro-Trump internet, amplified by QAnon influencers and even former Overstock.com CEO Patrick Byrne, who helped fund the audit. One popular Telegram post insinuated Cyber Ninjas CEO Logan and his family had been threatened to prevent the truth from being revealed.

The problem was that this second report was a complete fabrication—and even the audit's biggest proponents admitted it. "There is a false version of the Executive Summary of the Maricopa County Forensic Election Audit report that is circulating," Logan told *Vice*. "This false version claims to be an earlier version of Cyber Ninjas Executive Summary, but because of supposed threats from the [Arizona State] Senate, it was not used. This is absolutely false."[30] One of the audit's cochairs told the *Arizona Capitol Times* that the second report was a "fake document" and that there was "never a discussion about decertifying."[31]

A week or so later, Logan joined far-right activist Joe Oltmann's podcast and acknowledged that someone on his audit team wrote the false report—but that he didn't agree with it. "I know that sounds shocking to everybody, but one of the things that I think uniquely qualifies me in a lot of this audit work is how objective I go about things and how much I'm looking for proof on things," he said. That frustrated Oltmann, who revealed he leaked the unauthorized report to the public, saying he was trying to take some heat off Cyber Ninjas after they failed to deliver what Trump and his allies had been hyping. "I put out that draft to protect you," he told Logan. "I did it for you. I did it because people came to me and said, 'Doug is under constant attack, they've [gone after] his family.'"

In other words, the story went that Logan—the guy who promoted Hugo Chávez conspiracy theories endorsed by Sidney Powell, and who had been cheered on by Trump as he spent four months on a wild-goose chase looking for voter fraud—was receiving threats from the former president's supporters who believed he had sold out when the audit didn't prove what they wanted it to. Asked on the podcast whether he'd ever lead another election audit, Logan said the answer was no—unless he felt compelled after praying on it. "Quite frankly, it's not because of the left, it's because of the right," he said. "It's because the attacks, the many messages I've gotten [from people] who think that I did not do enough."[32]

Almost exactly three months later, Cyber Ninjas folded, facing a court-imposed $50,000-per-day fine after being found in contempt for failing to turn over audit-related documents in accordance with public records laws. One day earlier, Maricopa County election officials had released a comprehensive report disproving just about every assertion the auditors had raised in their September hearing, concluding that twenty-two of the auditors' claims were "misleading," forty-one were "inaccurate," and thirteen were "demonstrably false."[33]

But the fevered dream wouldn't die.

A few weeks after Cyber Ninjas shut down, GOP state representative Mark Finchem—who was part of the pro-Trump mob outside the US Capitol on January 6—introduced HCR 2033, a concurrent resolution that would "decertify and set aside" the 2020 Arizona electors. And two months after that, Trump took a swing at Mark Brnovich, the state's Republican attorney general who had launched a bid for US Senate. "Attorney General Brnovich of Arizona was given massive information on the fraud and so-called 'irregularities' that took place in the 2020 Presidential Election," he wrote. "He did a report, and he recites some of the many horrible things that happened in that very dark period of American history but, rather than go after the people that committed these election crimes, it looks like he is just going to 'kick the can down the road' and stay in that middle path of non-controversy. He wants to be politically correct.

"The good news is Arizona has some very good people running for election to the U.S. Senate," Trump continued. "I will be making an Endorsement in the not too distant future!"[34]

The Club Champ

March 28, 2022, was a momentous news day. Representatives from Russia and Ukraine were preparing to meet in Turkey to discuss a possible cease-fire in what would become Europe's deadliest conflict since World War II. President Joe Biden released his $5.8 trillion proposed budget for fiscal year 2023. Florida governor Ron DeSantis officially signed into law a controversial bill restricting classroom instruction on issues related to sexual orientation and gender identity. And Donald Trump had an announcement of his own.

"Many people are asking, so I'll give it to you now, it is 100% true," he wrote in a lengthy statement blasted out to reporters that evening. "While playing with the legendary golfer, Ernie Els, winner of four Majors and approximately 72 other tournaments throughout the world, Gene Sauers, winner of the Senior U.S. Open, Ken Duke, and Mike Goodes, both excellent tour players, I made a hole-in-one."

No detail was spared in the former president's recounting of what had transpired. The fortuitous stroke took place on the 181-yard seventh hole at Trump International Golf Club in West Palm Beach. There was "a slight wind." He used a five iron. The ball sailed "magnificently" with approximately five feet of cut. "It bounced twice and then went *clank*, into the hole," he concluded. "Anyway, there's a lot of chatter about it, quite exciting, and people everywhere seem to be asking for the facts."

For all his faults, let's not take this away from Donald Trump: The man says he is a pretty good golfer. And on the face of it, why wouldn't he be? He owns more than a dozen golf courses and he plays all the time. Even during his four years as commander in chief, faced with the crushing demands of the presidency, he managed to get more than 250 rounds in.[1] That's not a record—Woodrow Wilson played more than 1,200 times over his two terms in office *before* he suffered a debilitating stroke—but it does place Trump among the most prolific golfers in presidential history. Although he constantly railed at Barack Obama for how often he was out on the course, Trump ended up playing about twice as often as his predecessor did.

That wasn't his plan going in—or, at least, it's not what he told voters during his first campaign. "Believe me, if I win this I'm not going to be playing much golf," he told a 2016 South Carolina crowd. "There's a lot of work to be done."[2] He repeated the promise in Virginia several months later, assuring his supporters he'd be too busy fighting for them to get out on the links.[3] At one point, he said he probably wouldn't leave the White House much at all. "If you're at the White House and you have so much work to do," he said in March 2016, "why do you leave so much? You'd think you'd want to work, work, work."[4]

On the final day of Trump's term, a tally by Philip Bump of the *Washington Post* found he'd visited one of his properties on 428 out of the 1,461 days in his presidency, and "probably"* played 261 rounds of golf over that span.[5]

The frequency picked up after he left the White House, with the former president often playing five times a week. In January 2023, he even won the Senior Club Championship at Trump International Golf Club in Palm Beach. "A great honor," he wrote on Truth Social announcing the victory. "Competed against many fine golfers, and was hitting the ball long and straight."[6]

He insisted he wasn't bragging—he was proving fitness for office. "The reason that I announce this on fabulous TRUTH is that, in a very real way, it serves as a physical exam, only MUCH tougher," Trump added. "You need strength and stamina to WIN, & I have strength & stamina— most others don't. You also need strength & stamina to GOVERN!"[7]

Securing the Senior Club Championship at "one of the best courses in the country" would have been impressive enough on its own, but Trump's feat was magnified by the fact that he managed to do so while skipping the entire first day of the two-day competition. As senior members of the golf club teed off on Saturday morning, Trump was hundreds of miles away, delivering a eulogy at a memorial service in North Carolina for Ineitha Lynnette Hardaway—better known as Diamond of the Diamond and Silk duo who often performed as an opening act at Trump campaign events.

---

* The analysis, from Philip Bump, included the "probably" because Trump's staff didn't always disclose what the president was doing when he visited one of his clubs. If the 261 estimate is correct, Trump played a round of golf every 5.6 days of his presidency. Obama averaged a round every 8.8 days.

On Sunday, according to the *Daily Mail,* golfers participating in the club championship were surprised to find out they were competing against—and already losing to—the former president. Although Trump had missed the first day of the tournament, he decided he was going to enter anyway—and just use his score from a round he'd played earlier in the week. Miraculously, he was now ahead of the pack with a commanding five-stroke lead.[8]

As it turns out, Trump had been winning amateur golf tournaments at his own golf clubs in this manner for decades. In one particularly brazen example—documented by sportswriter Rick Reilly in his book *Commander in Cheat: How Golf Explains Trump*—the former president "won" a senior championship against one of the best players at Trump National Golf Course in Bedminster, New Jersey, by entering a score from another, easier golf course.

"Having zero chance at beating the guy, he went up to his Trump Philadelphia course on the day of the tournament and played with a friend there," Reilly wrote. "Afterward, according to a source inside the Bedminster club, he called the Bedminster pro shop and announced he'd shot 73 and should be declared the winner." His caddy would later tell Reilly's source Trump had "maybe" shot an 82—and that was being generous.

If you ever visit a Trump golf club, you'll be amazed to see just how many club tournaments Donald J. Trump has won throughout the years. If you didn't know any better, you'd assume he's one of the best golfers on the East Coast. But another anecdote in Reilly's book, recounting a moment when Trump walked into the Bedminster clubhouse as an employee was hanging up a championship plaque, explains what's really going on.

"Hey, I beat that guy all the time," Trump said, according to multiple sources. "Put my name up there instead."

"Really, sir?"

"Yeah, yeah," the future president continued. "I beat that guy constantly. I would've beaten him. Put my name up."[9]

CHAPTER NINE

THE BIGGEST LOSER

A fter two years of desperately working to undo the results of the last election—and pursuing preposterous schemes to eject the current president and get back into the White House—Donald Trump looked at the 2022 midterms as the moment he would complete his political comeback the old-fashioned way: leading his party to victory in a new election. Republican candidates— many of whom were essentially chosen by Trump over the past year—were widely expected to do very well, not only winning back control of both chambers of Congress from Democrats, but also taking back governors' mansions, secretaries of state offices, and state legislatures across the country. And if they did, Trump—who'd made himself a central figure in the election by issuing hundreds of endorsements and holding rallies in eight states during the campaign's final month—could plausibly claim to once again be the clear leader of the GOP.

"I think if [Republicans] win, I should get all of the credit," he told

NewsNation as polls opened on November 8, 2022. Almost as an afterthought, he added, "And if they lose, I should not be blamed at all."[1]

By that point, Trump's hedge seemed unnecessary. The party in power almost always faces a shellacking in the midterm elections, and Democrats—led by an unpopular president in Joe Biden—were considered particularly vulnerable. Voters routinely listed high inflation and rising crime among their biggest concerns, and tended to blame Democrats' policies.[2] When the election analysts over at *FiveThirtyEight* published the final preelection update on November 8, they projected a range of possible outcomes that had Republicans winning an average of 230 House seats to the Democrats' 205—with the potential for the tally to grow even more lopsided.[3]

Republicans themselves were more bullish. At a preelection National Republican Campaign Committee briefing I attended, the operatives spearheading the party's efforts to take back the House gave me a list of seventy-four Democratic seats they believed Republicans had a realistic shot of winning—enough to win not just a majority but the largest Republican majority in more than one hundred years. In the Senate, the GOP needed to flip only one seat to take back the majority, and party leaders thought they could pick up as many as four. "I am incredibly optimistic," Senator Ted Cruz of Texas told Fox News the day before the elections. "I think this is going to be, not just a red wave, but a red *tsunami*."[4]

Things were looking so good for Republicans, in fact, that in the days leading up to the election, Trump's biggest concern was whether he'd receive sufficient credit for all the victories. To ensure he earned the recognition and gratitude he believed he deserved, the former president cooked up a scheme: He'd announce his 2024 presidential bid *before* the midterms. Such a move would not only win back the national spotlight he missed so much but allow him to claim the GOP wins as his own.

Essentially everyone in Trump's orbit thought this was a terrible idea, and GOP leaders hated it even more. Republican operatives had spent hundreds of millions of advertising dollars in recent months hammering Democrats on two things: inflation and crime. Democrats, meanwhile, figured their only hope was to desperately try to brand even the most moderate and traditional Republicans as "ultra MAGA" Trump acolytes. A Trump presidential campaign announcement would play right into their efforts to make the midterm elections a referendum on the deeply unpopular former president instead of the deeply unpopular current president. And as much credit as Trump hoped to snag with his early entry into the race, his advisors worried he'd receive even more blame if he announced and Republicans underperformed.

Trump didn't care. As Election Day approached, he continually brought up the idea in meetings with his political advisors, who repeatedly reminded him why they believed it was wiser to wait until after the midterms to kick off his 2024 presidential campaign. It became a near-daily routine: Trump would say he was moving forward with an announcement, and his advisors would talk him out of pulling the trigger. There were, however, still several close calls.

"I ran twice. I won twice—and did much better the second time than I did the first," Trump falsely told the assembled crowd at an October 22 rally in Robstown, Texas. "And now, in order to make our country successful, safe, and glorious again, I will probably have to do it again." His fans were ecstatic, erupting immediately into a familiar chant: "USA! USA! USA!"

Almost two weeks later, I traveled to Sioux City, Iowa, for my first

Trump event since the 2020 campaign. It was billed as a rally for Iowa Republicans, but as I made my way there, I got an urgent call from a source close to the former president, who told me Trump was now talking about making his 2024 announcement right there in Iowa. Once again, he held back, but only barely. "In order to make our country successful and safe and glorious," he told the crowd, "I will very, very, very probably do it again."

"Get ready," he added. "That's all I'm telling you. Get ready."

That was November 3, the Thursday before the midterms. Two days later, I spoke to one of the political operatives Trump had hired for a major role on his expected presidential campaign. He sounded exasperated—and on the verge of quitting. "If he does this, you have to ask yourself, 'What's the point?'" the advisor told me after venting about his recurring conversations with Trump. "If he's not going to listen to any of our advice, why are we here?"

Trump was at it again the day before the election, telling his advisors he wanted to announce his presidential campaign that night in Ohio at a rally he was holding for Senate candidate J. D. Vance. As he boarded his plane in Palm Beach to fly to Dayton for his final midterm rally, Trump's political team truly didn't know whether he would go through with it. But once again, he held off. "I'm going to be making a very big announcement on Tuesday, November fifteen, at Mar-a-Lago in Palm Beach, Florida," he said. "We want nothing to detract from the importance of tomorrow."

Trump's advisors may not have wanted him to announce his third presidential campaign before the midterms, but they were confident enough in a "red tsunami" materializing on November 8 that they planned an election night party, inviting supporters, club members, and reporters to Mar-a-Lago to watch the results roll in—and to see the former president bask in the glow of a triumphant election night for the first time since 2016. Trump wanted an audience for his recoronation as the leader of the Republican Party.

As attendees filtered into the main ballroom at Mar-a-Lago that Tuesday evening, they were met with magnificent chandeliers and a row of American flags. Enormous television screens had been wheeled into the room so guests could watch Fox News as election updates trickled in, and Trump—joined by high-level staffers on his campaign-in-waiting—sat at a table that was cordoned off by a velvet rope at the front of the room. Next to his table was a stage with a podium, where the former president—and future presidential *candidate*—would deliver celebratory remarks as results started rolling in.

As the clock struck 7 P.M. and polls began to close along the East Coast, everything seemed to be going according to plan. In Florida, Governor Ron DeSantis and Senator Marco Rubio were quickly projected to win their respective bids for reelection, and Democratic representatives from New York began dropping like flies. "To start the night, Republicans are already +4 in the House—just in Florida," conservative activist Matt Schlapp tweeted shortly after 8 P.M. "If these trends continue nationwide Democrats are in for a very long night."[5] Donald Trump Jr. was even more optimistic: "Bloodbath!!!"[6]

But before long, the tide began to turn. Josh Shapiro, the Democratic gubernatorial nominee in Pennsylvania, was projected the winner over Republican Doug Mastriano—the first of several Trump candidates destined to lose in a landslide. As the night wore on, a clear pattern began to develop: Republicans in competitive races who'd shown some independence from Trump were winning, while those who'd tied themselves closely to the former president were losing.

In New Hampshire, for example, Republican governor Chris Sununu, a frequent Trump critic, trounced his Democratic opponent, while the GOP's election-denying Senate candidate, Don Bolduc, was beaten decisively by Maggie Hassan—arguably the Democrats' most vulnerable incumbent senator. The difference was astounding: Republican Sununu won by more than 15 percentage points, while Republican Bolduc lost by more than 9. Georgia was playing out the same way. Governor Brian Kemp—who had often clashed with Trump and refused to go along with his effort to overturn the 2020 election results in his state—easily won reelection against Democrat Stacey Abrams, while Herschel Walker, the former football star Trump had recruited to run for Senate, was trailing Raphael Warnock, another Democratic incumbent Republicans believed would be easy to beat.

For Trump, it would only get worse. Most of the candidates he had endorsed in ruby-red states and districts were winning as expected, sure, but in the contested races, most of Trump's candidates were going down. And on top of that, Florida governor Ron DeSantis—then considered the strongest challenger to Trump for the 2024 Republican presidential nomination—had secured perhaps the most impressive victory of all, despite Trump attacking him as Ron "DeSanctimonious" just days before the election. He defeated Democrat Charlie Crist by 19.4 percentage points after Trump had won Florida by just 3.3 points two years earlier.

Sitting around that table in the Mar-a-Lago ballroom with his advisors, Trump knew exactly what was happening. He seemed to want to leave the party, but he also didn't want to be seen walking out. As one Trump confidant who was with him that night told me, almost no one wanted to be near the former president as he grew more and more agitated: "Boris was the only one who wanted to sit next to him," the confidant said, referring to Boris Epshteyn—widely viewed as one of Trump's most sycophantic advisors.

Earlier in the evening, a more confident Trump had told reporters he'd be making remarks after the results came in. When Trump finally went up to the podium, he gave one of the briefest—and most timid—speeches I've ever seen him deliver. "Well, thank you very much everybody," he started off. "This has been a very exciting night. We have some races that are hot and heavy, and we're all watching them here. And some of you like the music so much that you'd rather hear the music—and I understand that very well."

All told, he spoke for just over four minutes, trying to spin his colossal failure into a win. But even the Trump-endorsed candidates who prevailed had underperformed. Ted Budd, Trump's candidate in North Carolina, won his race by just over 3 percentage points, six years after Richard Burr, the retiring senator he'd be replacing, had won the seat by nearly twice as much. J. D. Vance got a shout-out for his 6-point triumph in Ohio, even though Mike DeWine—Ohio's more traditional Republican governor, whom Trump despised—won by 25 points. Trump highlighted Marco Rubio's landslide reelection— he'd held a rally with the Florida senator days earlier—but neglected to mention DeSantis had won by even more.* "We have a lot of big

---

* After DeSantis launched his own presidential campaign in May 2023, the Florida governor still seemed hurt that Trump didn't acknowledge his big reelection victory. "We

races going on right now, so enjoy that," Trump concluded. "Enjoy the food and enjoy everything."

After thanking the crowd one more time, he gave attendees a half-hearted fist pump and walked off the stage and directly out of the ballroom, not to be seen again that night. "For those many people that are being fed the fake narrative from the corrupt media that I am Angry about the Midterms, don't believe it," he'd later post on Truth Social. "I am not at all angry."[7]

For some Republicans, November 8, 2022, managed to do what January 6, 2021, did not: wake them up to the dangers of sticking with Trump, and give them the courage to speak out against him. "The voters have spoken and they have said that they want a different leader," Virginia's GOP lieutenant governor Winsome Earle-Sears, who in 2020 had served as cochair of a group called Black Americans to Re-Elect the President, told Neil Cavuto on Fox Business. "And a true leader understands when they have become a liability."[8]

In January 2021, former Speaker of the House Paul Ryan had condemned Trump's efforts to overturn the 2020 election on moral and constitutional grounds, arguing it was "difficult to conceive of a more anti-democratic and anti-conservative act." After the awful Republican performance in the 2022 midterms, Ryan appealed to his fellow Republicans' instinct for political survival.

"With Trump, we lose," he told me shortly after the midterms. "It's just evidence. We lost the House in '18. We lost the presidency in '20.

---

won the biggest election landslide that Florida Republicans have ever won. And did he ever say anything like 'Attaboy, good job'? No, he attacked me three days before the midterm election," DeSantis told reporters in Iowa.

We lost the Senate in '20. And now, in 2022, we should have—and could have—won the Senate. We didn't. And we have a much lower majority in the House because of that Trump factor."[9]

It took several days for all the votes to be tallied—particularly in Arizona, Nevada, and California—but Ryan was right: Republicans underperformed not only their own outsize expectations but also decades of historical midterm trends. Those seventy-four Democratic House seats they believed they had a chance to flip? They lost sixty-four of them. And in the Senate, the GOP needed to pick up only *one* Democratic seat to retake the majority and bring Biden's agenda to a screeching halt. They lost every single one of them. In fact, *Democrats* increased their majority by winning retiring Republican Pat Toomey's Senate seat in Pennsylvania.

"I think my party needs to face the fact that if fealty to Donald Trump is the primary criteria for selecting candidates, we're probably not going to do really well," Toomey told Erin Burnett on CNN November 10. "All over the country, there's a very high correlation between MAGA candidates and big losses—or at least dramatically underperforming."[10] Republicans being honest with themselves were immediately able to identify what went wrong.

When I interviewed Donald Trump in March 2021, he had been eager to prove his influence in the upcoming primaries. "If you got a Ronald Reagan endorsement, it meant nothing other than it was a nice thing to have," he told me. "[But] people have gone up twenty, thirty points [with my endorsement]. People will not get elected without the endorsement. And I don't say that in a bragging tone. I'm just looking at the numbers."

"I would not dispute that you are the single most influential voice in the Republican—"

He cut me off before I could finish the sentence: "In history. In history."

As hyperbolic as that sounded, Trump was probably right. Less than three months after he left office with a 29 percent approval rating—the lowest of his presidency—Republicans were banging down the door at Mar-a-Lago, vying for his support.[11] By the time I sat down with him on March 18, 2021, he'd already offered his "Complete & Total Endorsement" to several GOP senators up for reelection in 2022, as well as to former White House staffers Sarah Huckabee Sanders, who was running for governor in Arkansas, and Max Miller, who was mounting a primary challenge to Representative Anthony Gonzalez in Ohio.

"This is like Grand Central Station," Trump said, ticking through all the candidates who'd made the pilgrimage to Mar-a-Lago seeking his backing. "[I've got] many coming. People that you wouldn't even believe, because there's never been an endorsement like it."

One such candidate who would travel to Palm Beach was David McCormick, a Gulf War veteran and highly successful hedge fund executive who'd held multiple senior roles in the George W. Bush administration. He was born and raised in Pennsylvania, and his wife, Dina Powell, had served as Trump's deputy national security advisor. Between McCormick's military record, deep ties to the state of Pennsylvania, government experience, and ability to finance his own campaign, Republican strategists viewed him as the perfect candidate to succeed retiring GOP senator Pat Toomey.

McCormick brought on several Trumpworld alums to advise his campaign—including Trump's former policy advisor and speechwriter Stephen Miller and former spokesperson Hope Hicks. To win the Republican nomination, McCormick figured he would at least need to be on good terms with the former president. And in December 2021, McCormick made the journey to Mar-a-Lago to personally let Trump know he'd be jumping into the race a few weeks later. He didn't expect an endorsement from the former president, but he didn't think he needed it, either. McCormick figured that as long as Trump stayed neutral, he would be in a good position to secure the nomination.

But the aspiring senator's second Mar-a-Lago visit, in early April 2022, didn't go as well as his first. After the two men exchanged pleasantries, Trump invited McCormick—along with Powell and Hicks—up to his office. As Trump sat behind his desk—which was designed to look like the one he'd used in the Oval Office, sort of like a fake Resolute Desk—he called out to his secretary, Molly Michael.

"Molly, show them the video," Trump said, according to two people who attended the meeting.

And with that, Trump's personal secretary played the group a clip of a little-seen and long-forgotten Bloomberg News TV interview McCormick had done in January 2021—shortly after the attack on the Capitol—in his capacity as CEO of the hedge fund Bridgewater Associates.

"I think what we have to not embrace is the divisiveness that's characterized the last four years and the polarization," McCormick told Bloomberg anchor Erik Schatzker when asked whether the Republican Party should move on from Trumpism. "I think the president has some responsibility—a lot of responsibility—for that."[12]

When the video clip ended, Trump turned back to McCormick.

"That's very bad," he told him. "Why would you say bad things about me?"

In reality, McCormick did not say anything in that old interview that Republican leaders in Congress hadn't said in the days after January 6, when even Kevin McCarthy had argued—on the House floor, not in some obscure interview—that Trump bore responsibility for what happened. As long as Republicans like McCarthy came back into the fold, Trump had shown a willingness to forgive them. "I think it's all a big compliment, frankly," he told the *Wall Street Journal* about those who had once criticized him. "They realized they were wrong and supported me."[13]

McCormick had stopped saying anything negative about Trump well before that April meeting and had even reversed himself in an interview on the podcast *PoliticsPA*[14] after that first visit to Mar-a-Lago, saying he didn't think Trump should be held accountable for January 6. But it wasn't enough. Trump needed him to prove his loyalty—and to pay a price for what he'd said on Bloomberg more than a year earlier. But it was a price McCormick wasn't willing to pay.

"I know Pennsylvania," Trump said after they watched the video clip. "You cannot win unless you say the election was stolen."

"Mr. President," McCormick said, "I cannot do that." He said he agreed there had been some issues with the way the election had played out in Pennsylvania but that it didn't amount to enough to change the election results.

A few days later, Trump issued an endorsement of McCormick's opponent, "the brilliant and well-known Dr. Mehmet Oz." Like McCormick, Oz also hadn't echoed Trump's 2020 election claims. But unlike McCormick, Oz had never publicly criticized the former president, and more importantly, he was a fellow TV star. "I have known Dr. Oz for many years, as have many others, even if only through his very successful television show," Trump said in making the endorsement. "He has lived with us through the screen and has always been popular, respected, and smart."

McCormick's campaign team wasn't thrilled with the development, but they didn't see it as the end of the race. Nearly a month later, in fact, their internal polling still showed McCormick with a narrow lead. But that lead evaporated after Trump held a rally for Oz in Pennsylvania less than two weeks before the primary and levied a series of personal attacks against the guy who had come to see him twice at Mar-a-Lago. "He did want my endorsement very badly, but I just couldn't do it," Trump told the crowd, who had come out to the Westmoreland Fairgrounds in western Pennsylvania despite a rainstorm. "He was with a company that managed money for communist China, and he is absolutely the candidate of special interests and globalists and the Washington establishment."

Oz thought the attack was so brutally effective that he used it as a television ad that ran right up until the election.

McCormick held up remarkably well despite the onslaught from Trump, but Oz eked out the win by fewer than one thousand votes—31.21 percent to 31.14 percent.[15] The race was close enough that there's little doubt Trump's endorsement made the difference—but it was barely a win, and the former president's powers did not extend to Oz's general election against John Fetterman, which Oz lost by just over 5 percentage points. With a progressive record as Pennsylvania's lieutenant governor, Fetterman was clearly beatable. And shortly after the primary, he suffered a stroke that kept him off the campaign trail for most of the race. But Oz's mixed record on social issues rankled some conservative voters, and Fetterman's team routinely mocked Oz as an out-of-touch TV doctor with scant ties to the state.*

McCormick might or might not have won the general election, but he was clearly the more electable candidate—and the one Democrats feared more. A few months after his primary loss, McCormick ran into Senator Chuck Schumer at a party on Long Island, and the Democratic leader told him, "Trump's an idiot. You would've won." It was flattery, but Schumer was probably right.

But to those who went through the Mar-a-Lago circuit in 2022, that didn't seem to be the former president's top priority. "I don't think he gave a shit at all whether we won the Senate," one Republican Senate candidate told me. "It was all about, 'Who has the most allegiance to me?' It was all who was going to be beholden to him."†

In Arizona's primary, for example, Trump endorsed a slate of Republican candidates defined almost entirely by their total commitment to his 2020 election lies. For governor, Trump tapped a long-shot candidate, the former local TV news anchor Kari Lake, who echoed Trump so aggressively that she would soon be talked about as a potential Trump running mate in 2024. One of the ways Lake proved her allegiance to Trump was showing contempt for Trump's former nemesis, John McCain, who had died four years earlier but still managed to draw Trump's ire. In the final days before the election, Lake

---

* Oz had lived in New Jersey for decades before moving to Pennsylvania in late 2020.

† Donald Trump nearly withdrew his endorsement of Joe Lombardo, the Republican gubernatorial candidate in Nevada, because Lombardo declined to say the 2020 election was stolen and called Trump a "sound" president rather than a "great" one during a debate with the Democratic nominee, Steve Sisolak. The crisis was averted after Republican National Committee chairwoman Ronna McDaniel got Lombardo to issue a post-debate statement: "By all measures, Donald J. Trump was a great President and his accomplishments are some of the most impactful in American history." (Shane Goldmacher, "How the 2022 Midterms Became a Squeaker," *New York Times*, November 12, 2022.)

told "McCain Republicans" she didn't want their support.[16] It was an odd move for a Republican—or any candidate—trying to win in Arizona, but it undoubtedly made Trump happy.

Senate candidate Blake Masters won the former president's endorsement after saying he would have voted to overturn Biden's election victory had he been in Congress on January 6. And Trump's choice to be Arizona's secretary of state, Mark Finchem, was part of the mob in Washington, DC, that day. As the attack was underway, Finchem posted a photograph of rioters storming the Capitol on Twitter with the caption "What happens when the People feel they have been ignored, and Congress refuses to acknowledge rampant fraud. #stopthesteal."[17]

All highly unconventional candidates, none of the three would likely have won their respective GOP primaries without Trump's support. And like so many of the other candidates Trump backed in 2022, they all went on to lose their general-election matchups. In a year that was supposed to favor Republicans, Democrats in Arizona swept nearly every statewide office that was up for grabs. The only Arizona Republican to win statewide—state treasurer Kimberly Yee—was the only statewide Republican candidate not endorsed by Trump. She defeated her Democratic opponent by 11 percentage points, earning 220,000 more votes than Kari Lake did.

Trump also played kingmaker in the Pennsylvania and Maryland Republican gubernatorial primaries. He endorsed two fringe candidates who didn't just protest outside the Capitol on January 6—they paid to bring in dozens of other protesters to Washington that day. Trump's man in Pennsylvania, Doug Mastriano, helped organize two buses to DC on January 6; his man in Maryland, Dan Cox, chartered three buses. Mastriano was so deeply involved in the effort to overturn the election that he helped put together a fake slate of Trump electors to replace Biden electors duly certified by the state. As for Cox, while the attack on the Capitol was underway, he tweeted that Mike Pence was a "traitor" for refusing to reject Biden's electoral votes. Larry Hogan, Maryland's outgoing Republican governor, called Cox "a QAnon whack job" and refused to endorse him.[18]

As relatively unknown state legislators, neither would have had much chance of winning their primaries without Trump's support. But with Trump's endorsement, they both prevailed in the Republican primaries—and then, in turn, decisively lost to their Democratic opponents in the general election. Mastriano lost by nearly 15 percentage points, and Cox was beaten by more than 32 points. Cox's defeat stood in stark contrast to the previous governor's race in 2018—a tough year for Republicans nationwide—when Hogan had defeated his Democratic challenger in Maryland by nearly 12 percentage points.

Trump's campaign of vengeance against the ten House Republicans who voted to impeach him was especially destructive to his party. In Washington state, for example, he endorsed Joe Kent—an Army veteran who defended January 6 rioters and speculated the attack was orchestrated by the US intelligence community[19]—to take down Republican representative Jaime Herrera Beutler in the primary. Kent did, and then promptly lost the seat—which Herrera Beutler had held for twelve years—to a Democrat whom *FiveThirtyEight* had given a 2 percent chance of winning.* To Trump, this wasn't a total loss: better a Democratic representative than a Republican

---

* Kent also mimicked Trump in defeat, refusing to concede the race for more than a month. ("GOP's Joe Kent Concedes Washington State Congressional Race," Associated Press, December 21, 2022.)

"traitor"—even if that "traitor" had voted with Trump nearly 80 percent of the time.[20]

Trump was so desperate to oust the so-called Impeachment Ten and other Republicans who had crossed him that, if no primary challenger for a given incumbent emerged naturally, he and his team would actively recruit one of their own. "Any interest from good and SMART America First Republican Patriots to run primary campaigns against Representatives Tom Rice, John Katko, Don Bacon, Don Young, Fred Upton (challenge accepted), Andrew Garbarino, Peter Meijer (challenge accepted), David McKinley (challenge accepted), Nancy Mace, Jaime Herrera Beutler (challenge accepted) and Chris Smith?" Trump asked in a November 13, 2021, email blast. "You will have my backing!"

Trump's team tried especially hard to recruit a candidate to run against popular Michigan freshman representative Peter Meijer, who voted to impeach Trump after serving in Congress for just one week. After several prospective candidates rebuffed his advisors' entreaties, the former president eventually settled on John Gibbs, a former software engineer and far-right commentator known for his conspiratorial social media postings.[21] Democrats helped Trump get his revenge, running ads to help Gibbs in the Republican primary because they knew he would be much easier to beat in the general election than Meijer. They were right. Gibbs narrowly defeated Meijer in the primary, and then got trounced in the general election, losing to Democrat Hillary Scholten by a margin of 55 to 42.[22]

While Trump was trying to elevate handpicked Republicans through various primaries, he also couldn't keep his hands off how those eventual GOP nominees ran their campaigns. Shortly after debating Democratic senator Mark Kelly, for example, Blake Masters received a call from his highest-profile backer that was captured in a Fox News documentary by Tucker Carlson about the campaign.[23]

"I heard you did great in the debate, but bad election answer," Trump could be heard saying over speakerphone. "You want to get across the line, you've got to go stronger on that one thing. That was the one thing, a lot of complaints about it."

Trump was upset with how Masters answered a rather simple question during the debate: "Is Joe Biden the legitimately elected president of the United States?"

"Joe Biden absolutely is the president. My gosh, have you seen the gas prices lately?" Masters responded.

"Legitimately elected?" the debate moderator repeated.

"I'm not trying to trick you. He is duly sworn and certified. He is the legitimate president. He's in the White House, unfortunately for us," Masters answered.

Trump didn't like hearing one of his candidates saying the words "legitimate president" about Joe Biden.

"Look at Kari [Lake]," the former president told Masters, referring to Arizona's Republican gubernatorial nominee. "Kari's winning with very little money. And if they say, 'How is your family?' she says the election was rigged and stolen. You'll lose if you go soft. You're going to lose that base."

"I'm not going soft," Masters assured him.

Masters obeyed Trump's demand from then on—never again calling Biden "legitimate" or suggesting the election was anything but rigged. "I think if everyone followed the law, President Trump would be in the Oval Office," Masters told Fox News days after the debate.[24] And a few weeks later, he lost to Kelly by more than 125,000 votes.

Republican Senate candidate Herschel Walker was also a particularly frequent recipient of Trumpian counsel. Preparing for his one—and only—debate with Democrat Raphael Warnock, Walker received a call from the former president and, according to a senior advisor to the Walker campaign who witnessed the conversation, put the former president on speakerphone so his team in the room could hear the strategic wisdom that was about to be offered.

"Just call him a child molester," Trump said, suggesting Walker make an entirely unfounded allegation against his opponent during the debate.

"But I got no evidence of that," Walker replied.

"Just do it. You can say there was sexual abuse on his watch," Trump insisted, according to the senior Walker advisor who witnessed the call. "Just call him a child molester."

Trump was maliciously referring to abuse that allegedly occurred in 2002 at a Maryland summer camp run by Douglas Memorial Community Church, where Warnock was the senior pastor at the time. When Warnock first ran for Senate in 2020, a former camper came forward alleging a counselor had tossed urine on him and locked him outside his cabin overnight as a punishment for wetting his bed.[25] The story was horrible—the camper reportedly received a financial settlement the following year—but labeling Warnock a "child molester" was ridiculously wrong. There was no allegation of sexual abuse and no allegation whatsoever against Warnock himself. He was the pastor at the church, not the director of the camp.

Walker—who was dealing with domestic violence allegations of his own and with reports he paid for a girlfriend's abortion—didn't take Trump's advice during the debate. But all bets were off once the race went to a runoff. "Y'all know what he did at that camp?" Walker falsely told a crowd of supporters in late November. "This young man said there was sexual abuse and there was physical abuse. I'm like, Who did that? It has to be Senator Raphael Warnock, because he was responsible for it."

Walker would go on to lose the runoff on December 6 by nearly 2 percentage points—yet another Trump-candidate loss to a Democrat Republicans had counted on beating.

The election results for Trump's candidates were part of a larger pattern. Several postelection studies quantified just how much the Trump factor had hurt Republican candidates. An April 2023 study by the nonpartisan group States United Action, for example, found candidates for state offices overseeing voting, who backed Trump's 2020 election lies in 2022, performed 2.3 to 3.7 percentage points worse than otherwise expected. "Voters rejected candidates *specifically because* those candidates refused to support free and fair elections," the report read, noting that "voters who otherwise would have voted for the Republican candidate instead voted for the Democrat" when the Republican repeated Trump's claims that the 2020 election was stolen.[26]

A study from Nate Cohn at *The New York Times* further quantified the damage inflicted by the former president in November. Using the Cook Political Report's primary scoreboard—which sorted GOP nominees into "MAGA" Republicans and "traditional" Republicans—he showed that the MAGA group performed, on average, about 5 percentage points worse than the party's traditional candidates.[27]

An even deeper dive into the numbers by Philip Wallach, a senior fellow at the conservative American Enterprise Institute, arrived at a similar conclusion. In the 114 most competitive general election races of 2022, according to his analysis, Republicans backed by Trump underperformed their districts' historic trend lines by 5 percentage points, while Republicans without Trump's endorsement *outperformed* those trend lines by 2.2 percentage points, suggesting Trump *himself* stopped the red tsunami. "Trump remains quite popular among Republican voters, and his endorsement was decisive in plenty of House primaries this summer," Wallach wrote. "But close association with the twice-impeached president was a clear liability in competitive 2022 House races, turning what would have been a modest-but-solid Republican majority into (at best) a razor-thin one."[28]

Not long after the midterms were over, the Republican National Committee decided to conduct its own after-action report to analyze the party's poor performance with an eye toward avoiding similar mistakes in the next election. A draft that began circulating among RNC members in April 2023 accounted for several factors that may have hurt Republican candidates: The Supreme Court's June 2022 decision overturning *Roe v. Wade*, a longtime Republican goal, effectively put abortion rights on the ballot for the first time in decades. Lackluster GOP fundraising had allowed Democrats to dominate the airwaves. Republican voters' aversion to early and mail-in voting made it difficult for campaigns to bank votes and determine where to focus their resources on Election Day.

The RNC draft report also said the results showed voters are not interested in "relitigating" previous elections. "The Republican candidates in 2022 who delivered results and had a vision for the future did much, much better than those stuck in the past and rehashing old grievances," the report noted. There was really only one reason the Republican Party had been saddled with so many losing candidates intent on wallowing in those past grievances and relitigating the last election. But there were two words that didn't appear anywhere in the report: "Donald Trump."

CHAPTER TEN

SPEAKER TRUMP

After a long and tortuous process that stretched over four days—and fifteen rounds of voting—Kevin McCarthy finally secured the job of his dreams after midnight on January 6, 2023. "My father always told me, 'It's not how you start, it's how you finish,'" he said in an acceptance speech that began at 1:15 A.M. "And now we need to finish strong for the American people."[1]

He went on to express gratitude for the support of his family, his colleagues, and his constituents back in Bakersfield, California. McCarthy made no mention of Donald Trump in this official acceptance speech—the speech that would be memorialized for history in the *Congressional Record*—but leaving the House chamber about an hour later, the newly minted Speaker singled out the man he suggested made his victory possible. "I do want to especially thank President Trump. I don't think anybody should doubt his influence. He was with me from the beginning," McCarthy told reporters assembled in the US Capitol's Statuary Hall. "He would call me and he would call others. And he really was—I was just talking to him tonight—helping get those final votes."

Trump had indeed endorsed McCarthy, and that endorsement played a role in his win. But it didn't play as decisive a role as Trump would have you think—and the former president wasn't exactly with the Californian "from the beginning." In fact, he made McCarthy work for nearly two years to earn his support. Even then, as you'll learn in this chapter, there was a critical moment when Trump wavered—briefly entertaining the possibility of pushing McCarthy aside and wielding the Speaker's gavel himself.

McCarthy's quest to earn Trump's support began less than three weeks after the January 6 attack on the Capitol, when he paid his visit to the disgraced former president at his Mar-a-Lago home. He didn't literally kneel and kiss Trump's ring, as some of his critics described it, but the trip—and accompanying photo op—sent a clear message: Trump was still a leader of the Republican Party despite his loss and false claims of a stolen election. His brief time in exile was over.

McCarthy faced significant blowback over the visit with Trump, and not just from Democrats. Many of his fellow Republicans were privately exasperated he was helping bring Trump back from the political dead. As I noted in Chapter Two, one member of Congress who was generally supportive of McCarthy later described the trip to me as a "'What the fuck?' type of moment."

McCarthy defended his right to keep in touch with the former president and pushed back on the idea that Trump should be a political pariah. That loyalty alone should have been enough for McCarthy to earn Trump's endorsement, but it wasn't. Nearly two months after the House Republican leader visited Mar-a-Lago, Trump—still frustrated his effort to overturn the election had failed—told me that he hadn't decided whether he would support McCarthy's bid for Speaker if Republicans won back the House.

It'd be more than a year before Trump finally got around to backing the man who'd stood by him during his darkest hour, calling the Republican leader a "tireless advocate for the people of Bakersfield and the Central Valley" in a Truth Social post on June 4, 2022.[2] But speaking with the conservative radio host Wayne Allyn Root later that month, Trump made clear his support for McCarthy was limited.

"No, I endorsed *him* in *his race*," he interjected when Root suggested he was backing him for Speaker of the House. "But I haven't endorsed anybody for Speaker."

Trump's support for McCarthy in California's Twentieth Congressional District—where McCarthy faced no real opposition—was politically meaningless, and not the speakership endorsement McCarthy coveted. But the former president was determined to dangle that in front of him awhile longer, forcing the Republican leader to prove his loyalty over and over again.

So as McCarthy jetted across the country campaigning for Republican House candidates—helping raise nearly $500 million in the process[3]—he was also trying to prove himself worthy of the speakership in the eyes of the former president. He was in regular communication with Trump, often seeking his advice and visiting him at his golf club in Bedminster, New Jersey, and never saying anything critical about him in public.

McCarthy, though, had been silent on Trump's continued effort to discredit, and even overturn, the 2020 election. So, on June 9, 2022, I went to the Republican leader's weekly press conference on Capitol Hill and asked him a question that, remarkably, he had not yet directly answered.

"Can you just clarify something?" I began. "Do you believe that Joe Biden was the legitimate victor of the 2020 election? And do you believe that Donald Trump is just flat wrong when he says the election was stolen?"

"Look, we've answered this question a long time [ago]," McCarthy replied. "Joe Biden is the president. I think you can [see] that there's a lot of problems still with the election process."

To illustrate his point about "problems with the election process," he brought up a recent news story about a former congressman and Democratic operative who had pleaded guilty to bribing election supervisors in Philadelphia from 2014 through 2018. The case was unfortunate, as was a separate instance—which McCarthy didn't bring up—involving a North Carolina Republican operative charged with election fraud in 2019. But neither occurrence had anything to do with Donald Trump or his claims about the 2020 election.

"That wasn't my question," I shot back. "We know Joe Biden is the president. He lives at the White House. My question is: Was it legitimate? Is [Trump] wrong when he says the election was stolen? It is a very simple question."

"You know, Jonathan, we've talked about this a long time," McCarthy said. "I've already answered that question."

Knowing full well that he hadn't, I asked again: "What was the answer?"

McCarthy had had enough. "We'll move on now," he said, pointing to another reporter. "Thank you very much."

"So, you won't answer that?" I said, trying one last time. "I just want to know: Is he wrong when he says the election was stolen?"

"Thank you for your time," McCarthy responded.

Behind closed doors, McCarthy had no problem acknowledging

that Biden was the true winner of the election. He quietly told friends and colleagues that the claims of massive fraud were "crazy" and that Trump knew he had lost and would eventually concede. On at least one occasion, McCarthy put his true feelings in writing, sending a text message to Fox News host Maria Bartiromo on November 17, 2020, that read, "I don't believe there was a mass cheat." But that text message only became public because hosts like Bartiromo continued pushing the bogus claims anyway, resulting in a high-profile defamation lawsuit by Dominion Voting Systems against Fox News. McCarthy was a regular guest on these shows and never pushed back on the absurd theories—publicly.

In private, McCarthy didn't just acknowledge that Trump's rhetoric was wrong—he argued it was dangerous. In 2022, Jonathan Martin and Alexander Burns of *The New York Times* reported on a private House GOP leadership phone call from January 10, 2021, in which McCarthy said he was planning to tell Trump he should resign as president. McCarthy denied the report, insisting he never said anything of the sort. In response to the denial, the *Times* published an audio recording of the conversation. McCarthy had said precisely— word for word—what Martin and Burns reported he had said.[4]

McCarthy was able to weather that storm. Trump later said he "didn't like the call" but appreciated how McCarthy had quickly re-embraced him once he "found out the facts."[5] Another transgression, however—like admitting to a reporter in a televised press conference that Trump's claims of a stolen election were bunk—could have angered Trump and likely caused him to withhold his endorsement.

Trump finally endorsed McCarthy for Speaker on November 8, 2022, hours before polls closed on Election Day. But by the time ballots were counted that night, Trump's support wasn't exactly the golden ticket McCarthy had been hoping for. After the GOP's disastrous midterm performance—a poor showing many Republicans blamed on Trump—the former president's influence was, at least temporarily, diminished. He was essentially a nonfactor in the Republican leadership elections that followed. Trump had encouraged Senator Rick Scott of Florida to mount a challenge to Senate Republican leader Mitch McConnell, for example, and publicly endorsed him in the race. It didn't matter: McConnell trounced Scott, 37 votes to 10. Trump technically stayed out of the competitive House Republican whip race between Representatives Tom Emmer, Jim Banks, and Drew Ferguson, but just about everyone around him—including Donald Trump Jr.—was aggressively pushing Banks. It didn't matter: Emmer—the only one of the three who did not support Trump's effort to overturn the 2020 election—defeated Banks in a runoff, 115 votes to 106.

The surest sign of Trump's weakness, however, was his inability to deter challenges to his handpicked candidate for Speaker of the House. Although McCarthy was the overwhelming favorite for the position, Representative Andy Biggs of Arizona, a far-right close Trump ally who helped lead the congressional effort to overturn the 2020 election, decided to mount a bid of his own, claiming the country wanted a "different direction."[6] His challenge was easily brushed back when the GOP conference gathered for internal elections on November 15—188 House Republicans voted for McCarthy, 31 voted for Biggs, and 5 voted for someone else—but it revealed the severity of McCarthy's predicament. He needed only 112 votes (a majority of Republicans in the House) to be elected *Republican leader*, but he'd need 218 votes (a majority of the full House) to be elected Speaker in early January.

A small but dedicated group of lawmakers was determined to stop him. With the GOP holding a razor-thin, five-seat majority after the party's midterm flop, McCarthy could afford only four Republican defectors. A group of five—Biggs, Matt Gaetz of Florida, Ralph Norman of South Carolina, Matt Rosendale of Montana, and Bob Good of Virginia—declared themselves "Never Kevin," and the standoff had begun. Asked by *Axios* reporters Alayna Treene and Andrew Solender whether he could foresee *any* scenario where he didn't oppose McCarthy, Biggs shook his head: "I could be dead I guess."[7]

Gaetz—the colorful, pro-Trump firebrand—anticipated the group of McCarthy objectors would end up even bigger. "There are definitely more than five members of Congress who would rather be waterboarded by Liz Cheney than vote Kevin McCarthy for Speaker of the House," he told right-wing commentator Charlie Kirk. "And I'm one of them."[8]

Waterboarding aside, Gaetz was right that the anti-McCarthy faction *was* significantly larger than five. When the House convened on January 3 to begin the proceedings, nineteen Republicans voted against McCarthy—fifteen more than he could afford to lose. Adding to McCarthy's humiliation, he not only failed to win a majority—he actually came in second place. Representative Hakeem Jeffries of New York—the Democrats' nominee for Speaker—secured more support than he did, though neither had enough to be elected.

The Republican renegades opposed McCarthy for a variety of reasons, ranging from his close ties with donors and lobbyists, to his lack of ideological convictions, to his view of how the House should operate. Gaetz's opposition, in particular, seemed to be driven by a personal beef: Another leaked phone call revealed McCarthy had privately trashed the Florida Republican for his behavior surrounding January 6.[9]

But whatever the reason for the various lawmakers' resistance to McCarthy, Trump's endorsement—which he had made again in mid-December[10]—wasn't enough to get them to fall in line. After two more rounds of voting failed to put McCarthy over the top, the House agreed to adjourn until the next day. As the House reconvened the following afternoon, Trump decided to weigh in again.

"Some really good conversations took place last night, and it's now time for all of our GREAT Republican House Members to VOTE FOR KEVIN," he wrote on Truth Social as the second day of voting began. "CLOSE THE DEAL, TAKE THE VICTORY, & WATCH CRAZY NANCY PELOSI FLY BACK HOME TO A VERY BROKEN CALIFORNIA."[11]

"REPUBLICANS, DO NOT TURN A GREAT TRIUMPH INTO A GIANT & EMBARRASSING DEFEAT," he added. "IT'S TIME TO CELEBRATE, YOU DESERVE IT. Kevin McCarthy will do a good job, and maybe even a GREAT JOB—JUST WATCH!"[12]

Trump's increasingly frantic pleas—the random capitalization in those quotes is Trump's, not mine—did nothing to sway the holdouts. Gaetz even seemed to mock the former president's efforts. "Supporting McCarthy is the worst Human Resources decision President Trump has ever made," he tweeted. "Sad!"[13]

Electing a House Speaker had long been a mere formality, a routine that takes place every two years and almost always without a glitch. The party in power nominates its consensus choice for the role, the votes are cast, and the House moves on with its business. Occasionally a few members of the majority cast a protest vote, but that hadn't mattered for decades. In fact, it had been one hundred years since the majority party's nominee for Speaker had lost a single round of voting. In 1923, the Massachusetts Republican Frederick Huntington Gillett required nine rounds of voting before securing enough support to win.

Electing a Speaker is the new Congress's first order of business. Nothing else can be done until someone wins a majority of all those voting and is elected Speaker of the House. No members can be sworn in, no committees can be formed, and no bills can be introduced. All the House can do is keep voting—ballot after ballot—until someone finally wins an outright majority. Crucially, that means no rules can be implemented to govern the House chamber and that had major implications for the TV coverage of the McCarthy drama. Typically, House proceedings are covered by stationary and robotic cameras operated by the House Recording Studio that are strictly limited in what they can show—only zooming in on whoever is speaking or showing a static wide view of the entire chamber. For major special events, such as a State of the Union address, the TV networks can request permission from the Speaker of the House to place additional network cameras in galleries above the floor. A request had been made to the previous Speaker, Nancy Pelosi, shortly before the end of the previous Congress to have three network cameras operating inside the House chamber for the start of the newly elected Congress. With no Speaker to grant or deny permission beyond that, the cameras simply stayed for the whole proceeding and were not limited by any rules on what they could shoot. The cameras, which were operated by C-SPAN on behalf of all the television networks, were free to show the drama in exquisite detail, zooming in to capture all the vivid interpersonal dynamics playing out on the House floor.

C-SPAN producers and camera operators took full advantage of their freedom to operate. The proceedings were a television spectacle unlike anything in the history of Congress, capturing McCarthy's despondent reactions to his fellow Republicans betraying him again and again and the real drama between votes. At one key moment, viewers could see a GOP congressman lunging at Gaetz and being restrained. Viewers tuned in for days on end, as groups of lawmakers huddled and negotiated in the back of the chamber. Early on in the process, George Santos—a newly elected congressman who had recently been exposed for fabricating his own life story and would later be indicted on multiple counts of fraud, money laundering, and theft of public funds—hovered awkwardly off to the side, shunned by his colleagues. But by the third day of voting, Santos could be seen sitting and chatting with GOP lawmakers of all stripes, a smile glued to his face. With a majority this narrow, no Republican—not even a serial liar—could be shunned for long.

The prime-time drama caught the attention of the former president, who was soaking up every minute of coverage from his perch in Mar-a-Lago. The must-see television spectacle briefly revived an idea Trump had dismissed long ago: that *he* could become Speaker of the House, the only congressional leadership post you can be elected to even if you are not a member of Congress. "He saw the power of television," a close Trump advisor told me. "[He saw] how galvanizing it was, how mesmerizing it was—everybody was watching it, right? That's when Trump realizes it's the biggest reality show in America. He could sit up there like *The Celebrity Apprentice*. It'd be *The Apprentice* with him with a big-ass gavel."

The idea that Trump should be elected Speaker of the House had been circulating for nearly two years at that point. As far as I can tell, it originated with a Trump supporter and online activist who went by the name "@DC_Draino" and posted the idea on Twitter less than an hour after Joe Biden took the oath of office and officially became president.[14] "Ok this is a crazy idea, but hear me out," he wrote on January 20, 2021. "Trump runs for Congress in Florida in '22. Red Wave and R's control. Trump elected Speaker of the House. Boom, now he controls a branch of the Federal Gov't again and can impeach Kamala. Best part? He can still run for POTUS in '24."[15]

Steve Bannon was so intrigued by the proposal he invited Rogan O'Handley—the man behind "@DC_Draino"—on his *War Room* podcast the next day to discuss it. "It's so brilliant on so many levels," Bannon gushed. "We don't need to wait until 2024 to have a presidential election. This nationalizes the midterm elections. This gives [Republicans] a unifying message."[16]

Over the coming months, the idea took hold with more of Trump's fans, as Bannon continued to promote it. "Donald Trump will take over, at least on an interim basis, as Speaker of the House to take the gavel from Nancy Pelosi and then to gavel in the impeachment panel to impeach Joe Biden," he said on *The John Fredericks Show* in early June, adding an important clarification. "You do not have to be a member of Congress to be Speaker."[17]

Around the same time, conservative radio host Wayne Allyn Root discussed the plan with Trump himself. "I'm hoping you'll run in 2024, but why not run in 2022 for the United States Congress?" he asked the former president. "Lead us to a dramatic landslide victory. Take the House by 50 seats. Then you become the Speaker of the House, lead the impeachment of Biden and start criminal investigations against Biden. You'll wipe him out for this last two years."

"That's so interesting," Trump replied. "You know, it's very interesting."[18]

Trump wasn't actually interested. He considered the role to be beneath him. Why would he want to leave Palm Beach to spend his days in Congress? The only time anybody paid attention to what was going on in the House, he figured, was during the State of the Union address—and even then, all eyes are on the president, not the Speaker. "It never got any traction," a Trump advisor said of the idea. "He had literally no interest."

But with the nation's attention focused on the McCarthy drama on the House floor, Trump began to have second thoughts. And when, on the seventh ballot, Gaetz stood up and announced his vote for Speaker—"Donald John Trump"—the former president was mildly amused. Until, that is, he saw the final vote tally being broadcast on all the news networks:

> 212 votes for Hakeem Jeffries
> 201 votes for Kevin McCarthy
> 19 votes for Byron Donalds*
> 1 vote for Donald Trump

Gaetz called Trump after the balloting concluded, congratulating him on becoming the first former president since John Quincy

---

* After initially parking their protest votes with Representative Andy Biggs, McCarthy's detractors moved on to Representative Jim Jordan of Ohio in rounds two and three, before settling on a mix of Representative Byron Donalds—a forty-four-year-old Republican from Florida who had just been elected to his second term in the House—and Representative Kevin Hern of Oklahoma for the remainder of the process.

Adams to receive a vote for Speaker. But Trump wasn't pleased—he was embarrassed. When the House clerk read off the vote totals at the end of the round—"the Honorable Donald J. Trump of Florida has received one"—laughter could be heard in the House chamber. Democratic lawmakers and progressive commentators were mercilessly mocking his lackluster support. The ridicule only grew louder when Gaetz pulled the same stunt in the next round and the result was the same. "One vote," tweeted Don Lemon, who was then a CNN anchor. "That's it. That's all #Trump got for speaker of the House. #onevote."[19]

Gaetz eventually realized his stunt was upsetting the former president and switched his vote to Representative Kevin Hern of Oklahoma for the next two rounds of balloting. But during that time, Trump, still stewing, told at least two people the *real* problem was that Gaetz had not formally nominated him for Speaker. If Republicans realized he was a real candidate for Speaker, Trump thought, they would have overwhelmingly voted for him.

Word of Trump's thinking quickly reached Gaetz, and the Florida Republican acted accordingly.

"For what purpose does the gentleman from Florida rise?" the House clerk asked Gaetz before the eleventh round of balloting kicked off.

"To place a name in nomination for the position of Speaker of the House," he replied.

And with that, Trump was officially nominated as a candidate for Speaker. One Republican close to both Gaetz and Trump later told me Gaetz ran the idea by the former president and got his approval before making the move. Another said Trump had proactively asked Gaetz to do it. Either way, the former president's name was formally placed in contention—with Trump's blessing.

With that all sorted out, Gaetz had a speech to give. "My friends, when Donald Trump was president, taxes were cut, regulations were slashed, energy was abundant, wages were rising, capital was returning from overseas to fund the dreams and ambitions of our fellow Americans, and the economy was roaring," Gaetz began. As he spoke, the murmuring and heckling—mostly from Democrats— grew so loud the clerk had to bring down her gavel and demand the House be in order. But Gaetz kept going: "I nominate President Trump because we must make our country great again. And he can start by making the House of Representatives great again." When Gaetz finished his speech, Representative Lauren Boebert of Colorado was the only person in the entire chamber to applaud.

The result was exactly the same. Donald Trump received just one vote—from Matt Gaetz—for Speaker of the House. And once again, the cable networks rubbed it in, plastering a measly "1" next to Trump's name as commentators mocked the former president's pathetic vote total.

That was the final straw. "Once CNN and MSNBC started mocking him, that he had the lowest vote count in history," a Trump confidant—who was in touch with the former president throughout the process—told me, "all of a sudden, he was like, 'Get me out of there!'"

At that point, an infuriated Trump just wanted to get McCarthy elected and put an end to the humiliation—his party's, but, more importantly, his own. On the next round of balloting the following day—the second anniversary of the January 6 riots—fourteen of the remaining anti-McCarthy lawmakers gave in and tossed their support to the Californian from Bakersfield. Between votes, McCarthy had been making more and more concessions—promising to put some of those who had opposed him on the powerful House Rules Committee, pledging to give rank-and-file members more control, even changing the House rules to make it easier for him to be tossed out as Speaker—in order to bring people over to his side. But he was still short of the votes he needed.

The seven remaining Republican holdouts—Matt Gaetz, Lauren Boebert, Andy Biggs, Eli Crane, Bob Good, Matt Rosendale, and Andy Harris—were among Donald Trump's staunchest supporters in Congress. Yet none of them seemed to care Trump was demanding they flip their vote. During the fourteenth round of balloting, the former president was on the phone with Representative Marjorie Taylor Greene, and—as captured in an iconic photograph taken by Chip Somodevilla for Getty Images—she tried to hand the phone to Rosendale. The Montana Republican brushed her off. "It was completely out of line," Rosendale later said. "To try to insert me into a conversation while I was involved in a historic, rapidly changing vote—that was out of line."[20]

The final tally on that fourteenth ballot was 216 votes for McCarthy and 212 votes for Hakeem Jeffries, with two lawmakers—Gaetz and Boebert—voting "present" and lowering the threshold McCarthy needed to hit. But he was still one vote short.

McCarthy—visibly deflated in a scene that played out on live television—walked over to Gaetz and accused him of breaking a promise to finally vote for him, but Gaetz reminded him he'd only promised to vote "present." This was a guy who had said he'd rather be waterboarded by Liz Cheney than vote McCarthy—"present" was the best his fellow Republicans were going to get.

McCarthy turned away, his shoulders hunched, and slowly walked back to his seat in the chamber. His dream of becoming Speaker, it seemed, had slipped away once again. But as Republicans moved to adjourn for the evening—it was nearly midnight—Biggs, Crane, Good, and Rosendale agreed to do what Gaetz and Boebert had done: vote "present." McCarthy would finally prevail on the fifteenth ballot with 216 votes.

Trump was quick to take credit. "The Fake News Media was, believe it or not, very gracious in their reporting that I greatly helped Kevin McCarthy attain the position of Speaker of the House," he posted on Truth Social. "Thank you, I did our Country a big favor!"[21]

But ask any of the holdouts, and they'd tell you their change of heart was theirs alone. "President Trump had no influence on the votes, myself or any of my colleagues," Good told ABC News's Will Steakin. "Saturday morning, it became clear that it was inevitable that Mr. McCarthy was going to become speaker, and I saw no reason to prolong that through the weekend."[22]

Norman, who voted against McCarthy until the twelfth round, told ABC News that Trump "didn't have anything" to do with his about-face. "In fact, I disagreed with him getting involved," he said. "This is a House function. We elect the speaker."[23]

Months later, one of the holdouts crudely described why he'd decided to finally step out of the way. McCarthy, the Republican member of Congress told me, had given in to so many of the lawmakers' demands that he was effectively "our bitch."

McCarthy had indeed made so many concessions during the voting process that he had little left to offer the bloc opposing him. But in the final hours of voting, they came to him with a new request: Promise to release all the video footage recorded by Capitol Police surveillance cameras during the January 6 riots.

None of the lawmakers had even thought to ask McCarthy for this until that evening—the Capitol Police had already given plenty of footage to the January 6 Committee, but they'd resisted turning it all over because it could expose security measures throughout the complex. So where did this eleventh-hour request come from?

According to one of the anti-McCarthy holdouts involved with the negotiations, the idea for the request came directly from Tucker Carlson, a longtime McCarthy critic who regularly used his Fox News show to brand the Californian as a weak and unprincipled Republican.

"If Kevin McCarthy wants to be the Speaker, he is going to have to do things he would never do otherwise," Carlson said on his show after the first day of balloting. "First, release the January 6 files. Not *some* of the January 6 files and video—all of it.

"Release them to the public directly, so that the rest of us can finally know what actually happened on January 6, 2021," Carlson said of the surveillance tapes. "It's been two years. It's long overdue. It's our right as Americans to know, and McCarthy could tell us."[24]

The anti-McCarthy holdouts saw Carlson's monologue and, according to one of them, took the demand to McCarthy the following day.

McCarthy quickly agreed to the request, and when it came time to make good on his promise, he released the tapes directly and exclusively to Tucker Carlson. The host and his production team then selectively edited the material, airing just minutes of the footage—out of the tens of thousands of hours provided—to suggest the pro-Trump rioters that day were actually well-behaved tourists who were being unfairly maligned. "They were peaceful. They were orderly and meek," Carlson said on his show as he played a clip of a small group of Trump supporters in the hallway outside the Speaker's office.

"These were not insurrectionists. They were sightseers."[25] Not included in the segment were shots of the rioters attacking police officers and shattering windows as they broke into the building and ransacked it.

Carlson's selective and deceptive use of the surveillance video predictably received enormous backlash and forced elected Republicans—most of whom never wanted to discuss January 6 again—to rehash the whole saga once more. "It's definitely stupid to keep talking about this," GOP representative Dan Crenshaw of Texas said. "So, what is the purpose of continuing to bring it up, unless you're trying to feed Democrat narratives even further?"[26] Carlson would be fired by Fox News less than two months later for unrelated reasons.

But the damage was done. Although McCarthy likely agreed with Crenshaw's analysis, he believed he had no choice. In order to secure the job, he made concessions that would not only limit his own power as Speaker but also further hamstring the Republican Party's ability to appeal to voters outside its already shrinking base.

"Now It's the Tallest"

Donald Trump's building "40 Wall Street actually *was* the second-tallest building in downtown Manhattan," he told a New Jersey television station on September 11, 2001. "And now it's the tallest."

What had changed? Earlier in the day, New York's two tallest buildings—skyline-defining landmarks visible from virtually everywhere in the city—were struck by jumbo jets hijacked by terrorists armed with box cutters. As black smoke poured out of the upper floors, firefighters, police officers, and paramedics rushed in to attempt to rescue the thousands of people trapped inside. The city stopped and stared, transfixed by the inferno, as final calls were made to family and friends by people who knew they were going to die. Bodies could be seen falling through the sky—desperate people jumping out of shattered windows when the heat and the smoke became too intense. Just over an hour after the planes struck, the Twin Towers came crashing down. Dust and debris coated the city. The stench of death and destruction was impossible to escape.

As the September 11 attacks horrified the nation and the world, Trump called into WWOR-TV in Secaucus, New Jersey, and was introduced as a prominent New Yorker who had seen what had happened.

"Well, I have a window that looks directly at the World Trade Center and I saw this huge explosion," Trump said, marveling that the two buildings that dominated the view from his office windows were now gone. "I really couldn't even believe it."

It was when one of WWOR's analysts, Alan Marcus, asked him about whether his building on Wall Street had sustained any damage that Trump offered up his bizarre boast that because terrorists had taken down the Twin Towers, he now owned the tallest building in lower Manhattan. "I think it was an all-of-a-sudden epiphany for him," Rolland Smith, one of Marcus's co-anchors, remembered years later. "He seemed to just blurt it out."[1]

It was a wildly inappropriate thing to say. It was also not true. There was a building taller than Trump's at 70 Pine Street—just a block away from his Wall Street property. "I didn't like his line about having the biggest building in downtown," Marcus, a longtime Trump consultant and friend, later said. "But that's just how he talked. By Donald's standards, he was probably very good. He was trying to behave."[2]

As first responders searched for survivors in the rubble, and family members started receiving the worst news of their lives, Trump also talked in the interview about how "disappointed" he was "they closed the stock exchange."

"You want to just say, 'The hell with it, you're going forward, nothing's going to change,'" he said. "But of course at some point, you had no choice."

Because Trump made these comments just hours after the attack, you might think he didn't yet have a full grasp on the severity of what had happened. Maybe he would've exhibited more empathy had he known just how many people had lost their lives earlier that day. Nope. That day, Trump initially thought 9/11 was eight to ten times more deadly than it actually was, and still his immediate reaction was to talk about the stock market and his building's new ranking among the city's tallest skyscrapers.

"This was probably worse than Pearl Harbor, many more people are dead," he told the WWOR anchors. "They have no idea, but I have somebody that was down there who witnessed at least ten people jumping out of the building from 70 and 80 stories up in the air. I mean, you probably have 25,000 or 30,000 is the number I've heard, but I think it would be much more than that."

Trump's memories of the attack shifted over the years, eventually including strange and implausible details like personally witnessing people jumping to their death from his perch at Trump Tower, four miles north of the World Trade Center. In remarks at the Pentagon on September 11, 2019, he told the assembled families of victims that, although early reports said the explosion was due to a boiler or kitchen fire at Windows on the World, he immediately realized those reports were false. "I knew that boilers aren't at the top of a building," he proudly added.

In that same speech, Trump claimed he had helped in the rescue efforts. "Soon after, I went down to Ground Zero with men who worked for me to try to help in any little way that we could," he said. "We were not alone. So many others were scattered around trying to do the same."

To date, there is no evidence Trump did any such thing. If he had, "there would be a record of it," said Richard Alles, a New York City Fire Department battalion chief who was on the scene within twenty minutes of the attacks. "Everybody worked under direct supervision of the police and fire department and the joint commander for emergency services. Is there a chance he was ever down there by himself and I didn't know it? It's possible, but I know of no one who ever witnessed him there."[3]

No one witnessed him at Ground Zero on September 11, 2021, either, on the twentieth anniversary of the attacks. George Bush marked the anniversary by honoring the fallen at the site of a third plane's crash in Shanksville, Pennsylvania. Bill Clinton, Barack Obama, and Joe Biden paid tribute to the victims at a ceremony on the site where the Twin Towers once stood. Trump wasn't there. He spent the day criticizing President Biden on social media and making a short stop at a police precinct and firehouse nine blocks from Trump Tower in Manhattan, where he also criticized Biden and complained about crime in New York.[4] At the police precinct, Trump only briefly referenced September 11, but he did thank the assembled police officers for endorsing his previous presidential campaign and claimed, "I must have gotten close to 100 percent of the vote."[5]

CHAPTER ELEVEN

THE BEGINNING OF THE END

On the morning of December 14, 2022, @realDonaldTrump's Truth Social followers were met with a post designed to stop them in their tracks. "I will be making a MAJOR ANNOUNCEMENT tomorrow," the former president wrote. "AMERICA NEEDS A SUPERHERO!" A fifteen-second video accompanying the message featured Trump—buff like Superman—ripping off his business suit to reveal a fitted red shirt with a "T" emblazoned on the chest. Laser beams shot out of his eyes as orchestral music swelled.[1]

The announcement—posted almost exactly one month after Trump kicked off his third presidential bid—sparked immediate speculation from fans and reporters alike. Had he decided who his running mate would be? Was he prepared to make a new endorsement in the upcoming Republican speakership fight? Did he and his advisors have a new strategy to push back against the newly appointed special counsel investigating him?

Nope.

"My official Donald Trump Digital Trading Card collection is here!" he declared the following day. "Collect all of your favorite Trump Digital Trading Cards, very much like a baseball card, but hopefully much more exciting. Go to collecttrumpcards.com/ & GET YOUR CARDS NOW!"[2]

The "MAJOR ANNOUNCEMENT" had nothing to do with his campaign—or anything of substance, really. Trump was hawking non-fungible tokens (NFTs).

NFTs—digital images with unique identifiers to certify ownership and create artificial scarcity—had been all the rage about a year and a half earlier, with celebrities and other wealthy individuals spending millions of dollars' worth of cryptocurrencies like Bitcoin or Ethereum on digital "art" to use as their profile picture on social media. It was a silly fad at the time—but even sillier in December 2022. Just weeks earlier the entire industry had tanked after one of the largest cryptocurrency exchanges—Sam Bankman-Fried's FTX—was revealed to be a massive fraud. In January 2022, FTX had been valued at more than $30 billion. Less than a year later, it was bankrupt and Bankman-Fried was under house arrest.

But that didn't stop Trump from trying to get in on the action. For the low, low price of $99, his supporters could receive limited-edition cards featuring "amazing ART" of the former president's "Life & Career."* One showed him rocking out with an electric guitar in front of a stadium full of people. Another depicted him dressed in colonial garb, sailing across the Delaware just like George Washington. There

---

*According to the Trump NFT website, anybody who bought forty-seven of the "cards"—a mere $4,653—would be invited to an "extraordinary dinner" at Mar-a-Lago, where they'd meet the former president and form memories they "will talk about forever."

was Astronaut Trump, Cowboy Trump, NASCAR Trump, and Boxer Trump. Perhaps the least realistic illustration of the man—who dodged the Vietnam War with alleged bone spurs—was as a fighter pilot. Customers weren't allowed to pick out which card they wanted; they forked over the cash and a randomly generated NFT was delivered to their digital "wallet."

The gambit was reminiscent of Trump's many pre–White House ventures like Trump Steaks, Trump Vodka, and Trump Water. The former president had no ownership stake or controlling interest in the NFTs. He just licensed his name, image, and likeness to the company behind them—for a fee. But at least the people who bought Trump Steaks or Trump Vodka bought something tangible. With these "trading cards," buyers didn't even receive physical cards—just digital-only illustrations depicting Donald Trump doing things he had never done before. Proving the old adage, attributed to P. T. Barnum, that there's a sucker born every minute, Trump actually made money on the scheme. On his 2022 financial disclosure form—a requirement of running for president—he reported taking in between $100,001 and $1 million in income from selling the "cards."[3] In July 2023, Trump filed a more detailed disclosure with the Office of Government Ethics that showed he had taken in between $250,000 and $500,000 worth of cryptocurrency from the venture.

This money wasn't going toward Trump's 2024 campaign—it was going into Trump's own pocket. And the tacky profiteering turned off even some of the former president's most ardent defenders, increasingly concerned his heart wasn't in the race to the White House. "He's one of the greatest presidents in history, but I've got to tell you, whoever [encouraged Trump to sell NFTs] ought to be fired—today," Steve Bannon said on his *War Room* podcast. "I can't do this anymore."[4]

Far-right influencer Anthime Gionet, aka "Baked Alaska"—who was awaiting sentencing for his role in the January 6 attack on the Capitol—was even more downtrodden: "I can't believe I'm going to jail for an nft salesman 😔."[5]

Such tawdry showmanship was entirely expected from Trump, but also extraordinarily bizarre from somebody trying to get elected president. The launch of a White House bid is typically accompanied by a flurry of activity—one-on-one interviews, trips to Iowa and New Hampshire and other early primary states, big policy speeches, fundraisers, flashy political ads—but Donald Trump's third campaign had been off to a decidedly slower start.

The morning after Trump's big Mar-a-Lago announcement, he played a round of golf at a neighboring Trump property in Florida. A day later, he did it again. The pattern repeated itself several times over the coming weeks. Trump would emerge from his winter home in Palm Beach to go down the road to a neighboring Trump property for a round of golf and then return home. In fact, for a solid sixty-three days after he announced his quest to retake the White House, the only time Donald Trump left Mar-a-Lago was to take a short ride to one of his other Florida properties to play eighteen holes.

It's not that Trump didn't have anything going on. He was, after all, the former president of the United States and the only major declared candidate for president in the next election (not even President Biden had said at that point whether he would run again). Exactly one week after Trump's November 15 campaign launch, for example, he invited one of the biggest celebrities in the world, rapper and fashion designer Kanye West, or Ye, as he now called himself, to dinner at Mar-a-Lago. The two men hadn't seen each other since October 2018—when West visited then President Trump in the Oval Office—Both men had seen their stars fall significantly in the intervening four years. Trump, of course, had lost his reelection bid and failed in his desperate attempt to stay in power. West, meanwhile, had rebranded as a born-again Christian, only to unravel while going through a bitter and very public breakup with wife Kim Kardashian.

The rapper had been open about his bipolar diagnosis for years, but by fall 2022, his erratic behavior had grown increasingly hateful. He lashed out at "Jewish record labels" and the "Jewish media mafia," and in remarks to Fox News host Tucker Carlson that didn't make it to air, he described Hanukkah as a holiday that "comes with some financial engineering."[6] His social media accounts were restricted in early October after he tweeted—in an apparent reference to the Pentagon's military alert system—that he's "a bit sleepy tonight but when I wake up I'm going death con 3 [sic] on JEWISH PEOPLE." By the time West broke bread with Trump at Mar-a-Lago, he had become so toxic that he was dropped by nearly all of his corporate sponsors, and his net worth had reportedly plummeted from $2 billion to $400 million—essentially overnight.[7]

Remarkably, West managed to bring along a guest even more controversial than himself: Nick Fuentes, a twenty-four-year-old white supremacist and Holocaust denier who had built a significant far-right audience online. The three men and a former Trump advisor named Karen Giorno dined at Trump's usual table on the club's patio, set off with a velvet rope but fully in view of the other diners at the club. Fuentes later described a scene almost exactly like the one I had witnessed when I met with Trump at Mar-a-Lago in March 2021.

"We saw everybody in the dining room get up and start applauding," he told NBC News. "And then the president entered."[8]

West posted a video recapping the dinner on Twitter the following day, claiming Trump was "really impressed with Nick Fuentes." Giorno, who was sitting right there at the table with Trump, confirmed that account, noting Fuentes had told the former president that he is much better unscripted and that advisors do him a disservice when they try to rein in his natural political instincts. It was apparently exactly what Trump wanted to hear. At one point in the evening, according to Giorno, Trump turned to West and, gesturing to Fuentes, said, "I really like this guy. He gets me."

News of the dinner put Trump in the spotlight again for all the wrong reasons, reminding even his supporters how poor his judgment could often be. David Friedman, Trump's onetime ambassador to Israel, was particularly scathing. "To my friend Donald Trump, you are better than this," he tweeted. "Even a social visit from an antisemite like Kanye West and human scum like Nick Fuentes is unacceptable. I urge you to throw those bums out, disavow them and relegate them to the dustbin of history where they belong."[9]

Trump, however, did no such thing. "Kanye West called me up, and he wanted to know if I could meet him because he has a lot of problems," Trump would later tell Olivia Nuzzi of *New York Magazine*, claiming he didn't know who Nick Fuentes was before West brought him to dinner. "It was a very quick meal, it went very fast. It was pleasant. There was nothing said of any great import."[10]

Even if he truly didn't know of Fuentes before West brought him to Mar-a-Lago, he certainly did after the controversy erupted. But still, Trump wouldn't explicitly condemn the young white supremacist or his views. A comment from Milo Yiannopoulos, a far-right provocateur who claimed to be behind Fuentes's presence at the dinner, may explain why. "I wanted to show Trump the kind of talent that he's missing out on by allowing his terrible handlers to dictate who he can and can't hang out with," he later told NBC News. "I also wanted to send a message to Trump that he has systematically repeatedly neglected, ignored, abused the people who love him the most, the people who put him in office, and that kind of behavior comes back to bite you in the end."[11]

The entire saga reminded me of a similar controversy that had erupted six years earlier, when Trump first ran for the Republican presidential nomination. David Duke, the neo-Nazi and Ku Klux Klan leader, had endorsed Trump, telling listeners of his radio show that voting against him was essentially "treason to your heritage."[12] When first asked about the comments, Trump seemed more bothered by the question than by Duke's support. "I didn't even know he endorsed me," Trump said. "David Duke endorsed me? Okay, all right. I disavow, okay?" But in a CNN interview two days later, Trump seemed to backtrack. "I know nothing about David Duke. I know nothing about white supremacists," he said when asked if he would denounce Duke's abhorrent views. "You're asking me a question that I'm supposed to be talking about people that I know nothing about.

"You wouldn't want me to condemn a group that I know nothing about," he added. "I would have to look."[13]

Despite the bluster, Trump clearly knew who David Duke was—he'd forcefully condemned him and labeled him a racist decades earlier.[14] But for whatever reason, he wouldn't do it again now that he was the frontrunner for the GOP presidential nomination—and Trump's refusal to renounce the notorious white supremacist horrified Reince Priebus, who was then the chairman of the Republican

National Committee. Priebus reached out to former New Jersey governor Chris Christie, who had just endorsed Trump, and pleaded for him to intervene.

"Priebus was freaking out that Trump had not yet put out a statement pushing back on the endorsement," Christie told me. "He had been trying to reach Trump, and Trump would not take his calls."

Christie himself was eventually able to reach him on the phone, but Trump let him know he was very busy. "Let's work on a statement to put out right now,'" Christie said.

"I'll do it later," Trump replied. "I'm about to play golf."

Christie was adamant. "This is pretty simple, let's do it now," he told him. "Just say you have no interest in his endorsement. The longer this waits, the worse it gets."

"I'll do it," Trump conceded. "But remember, Chris, those people vote too."

Although Trump got in his eighteen holes, he eventually got around to making a clear statement disavowing Duke's endorsement. But by the time he launched his 2024 campaign, Trump no longer had advisors like Christie or Priebus. There was nobody around to push him to denounce Fuentes or West. And he never did.

Dining with two avowed antisemites was just the first of several decisions Trump made after announcing his presidential campaign that would have sunk any other Republican candidate. The following week, he opened up an entirely new controversy by calling for the termination of the US Constitution.

Once again, the issue was Trump's false claims of voter fraud and his still persistent belief, more than two years later, that the 2020 election should be nullified and Joe Biden removed from the White House. The immediate cause of Trump's outburst was newly revealed details about Twitter's decision to temporarily restrict the sharing of a *New York Post* story about a laptop belonging to Joe Biden's son Hunter shortly before the 2020 election. The internal documents released by Elon Musk, Twitter's new owner, did not show the government had forced Twitter to take any specific actions, but Trump and some of his allies portrayed the revelations as smoking-gun evidence the social media platform had somehow been in cahoots with the Biden campaign.

"So, with the revelation of MASSIVE & WIDESPREAD FRAUD & DECEPTION in working closely with Big Tech Companies, the DNC, & the Democrat Party, do you throw the Presidential Election Results of 2020 OUT and declare the RIGHTFUL WINNER, or do you have a NEW ELECTION?" Trump asked in a December 3 post on Truth Social. "A Massive Fraud of this type and magnitude allows for the termination of all rules, regulations, and articles, even those found in the Constitution. Our great 'Founders' did not want, and would not condone, False & Fraudulent Elections!"[15]

The statement was nuts—even for Trump. Especially the sentence calling for "the termination of all rules, regulations, and articles, even those found in the Constitution."

The GOP reaction followed a familiar pattern, with a handful of Republicans criticizing Trump's statement while the vast majority kept their thoughts to themselves. Representative Mike Turner of Ohio said he disagreed "vehemently" with Trump,[16] as did Senate leader Mitch McConnell. "Anyone seeking the presidency who thinks that the Constitution could somehow be suspended or not followed," McConnell said, "would have a very hard time being sworn in as president of the United States."[17]

Criticizing a politician calling for the termination of the Constitution shouldn't have required much political courage, but most Republicans, including future Speaker of the House Kevin McCarthy, said nothing about Trump's statement. One particularly painful-to-watch non-reaction came from Representative David Joyce of Ohio. When my ABC News colleague George Stephanopoulos asked him whether Trump's comment was disqualifying, Joyce dodged the question four times. "You can't come out against someone who's for suspending the Constitution?" an incredulous Stephanopoulos asked. "Well, he says a lot of things," Joyce finally said. "But that doesn't mean that it's ever going to happen."[18]

Trump eventually tried to walk back his remark by pretending he never said it in the first place. But even as he denied his own words, he refused to give up on the idea that his 2020 election loss could—and should—still be undone: "Steps must be immediately taken to RIGHT THE WRONG."[19]

It had now been nearly one month since he announced his presidential campaign and Trump had still not left the confines of a Trump property to go anywhere but another Trump property—or engage in a campaign event of any kind. But there were campaign-related events coming to him at Mar-a-Lago. On December 6, three days after his call to terminate the Constitution and two weeks after his dinner with Kanye West, Trump hosted a fundraiser featuring a prominent proponent of the QAnon conspiracy theory, which is fringe even for MAGA-world. Adherents contend there is a secret government source feeding followers information through cryptic messages about dastardly deeds happening within the government, which the source alleges is run by a cabal of pedophiles and other miscreants. A number of QAnon adherents were among those who broke into the Capitol on January 6, and the FBI has repeatedly warned that the movement is dangerous and may inspire its followers to be violent.

The fundraiser at Mar-a-Lago was for a "documentary" on sex trafficking that featured some of the movement's core theories. One of the event's organizers was a woman named Liz Crokin, who had gained notoriety for pushing "Pizzagate," an imagined QAnon conspiracy, which preposterously alleged Hillary Clinton was helping to operate a child sex-trafficking ring out of the basement of a Washington, DC, pizza shop. The restaurant's owners received death threats— as did several of its employees—and in December 2016 a man drove from North Carolina to "investigate" the situation, firing a rifle into the shop in an attempt to break in.[20]

The Pizzagate theory was considered so crazy—and potentially dangerous—that Michael Flynn Jr., the son of Trump's first national security advisor, was fired from the Trump transition team in 2016 after he promoted it on social media.[21] But Trump had grown more divorced from reality and more welcoming of his supporters' most extreme views since then. In August 2020, while he was still president, he declined to criticize QAnon, saying, "I don't know much about the movement, other than I understand they like me very much, which I appreciate." After leaving the White House, he had no problem fully embracing the movement. "You are incredible people, you are doing unbelievable work," Trump told the crowd at Mar-a-Lago in a video of his remarks posted by Crokin. "We just appreciate you being here, and we hope you're going to be back." Later, Crokin—who snagged a picture with Trump—boasted on social media that she had discussed "Pizzagate" at the event.

When he wasn't golfing, dining with antisemites, or welcoming Q-Anon adherents to his club, candidate Trump kept himself busy with another hobby—filing a blizzard of lawsuits in state and federal courts against his enemies, real and perceived. These lawsuits are too numerous to fully detail in one chapter, but here is a sampling of the people Trump sued after he left the White House: CNN (for using the term "the Big Lie" to describe his false claims of election fraud), Bob Woodward (for releasing an audiobook of his Trump interviews), New York attorney general Letitia James (for successfully investigating allegations of fraud against the Trump Organization), *The New York Times* (for reporting on his tax returns), and Hillary Clinton and thirty other individuals (for "an unthinkable plot" to tie Trump to Russia).

The legal filings are riddled with errors, false allegations, and shoddy legal reasoning, but they deserve more attention than they have received. Not because they have any merit—they don't—but because the lawsuits themselves represent an abuse of the legal system by the former president, who systematically wasted the resources of courts around the country and used them to harass his critics and saddle them with legal bills. The legal filings also provide another look at Trump's priorities as he launched his third presidential campaign.

One week after he welcomed QAnon adherents to Mar-a-Lago, Trump filed a defamation lawsuit that had dubious legal merit, to say the least, against the nineteen members of the Pulitzer Prize board. Trump's suit followed two letters he had sent the Pulitzer board in

2022 demanding that prizes given to *The Washington Post* and *The New York Times* in 2018—for their coverage of Russia's well-documented efforts to interfere in the 2016 presidential election and Special Counsel Robert Mueller's subsequent investigation of Trump and his associates—be revoked. The Pulitzer Center acted on the request, conducting multiple reviews of the articles submitted by the two publications. But the probes, according to the Pulitzer Center, found "no passages or headlines, contentions or assertions in any of the winning submissions were discredited by facts that emerged subsequent to the conferral of the prizes."[22]

Trump's lawsuit was absurd for a number of reasons, including where it was filed: Okeechobee County, Florida—a rural county in central Florida with about forty thousand residents that voted overwhelmingly for Trump in 2020. Trump didn't reside there, and neither did the Pulitzer Center nor any of its board members. So why Okeechobee? Because, his lawyers contended, the organization had posted its July 2022 statement defending its awardees online, where "third parties" in Okeechobee County (and anywhere else with internet access) could read it. Or maybe it was just a conservative county where Trump believed he could find a judge to go along with his harassment of the Pulitzer board for honoring articles he did not like.

The substance of the suit was just as ridiculous as the venue. Most of the thirty-page filing focuses on *New York Times* and *Washington Post* reporting that, the suit alleges, contributed to a "hoax [that] reverberated through the echo chambers of social media" and triggered "a completely-debunked witch hunt of astounding proportion." Awarding the Pulitzer Prize to such journalism, the suit argued, was "intended to stoke feelings of hatred, distrust, and discouragement" toward Trump.[23]

Judges around the country routinely swatted down Trump lawsuits just like this one, but on January 19, 2023, Trump and one of his lawyers received a particularly stunning rebuke—and a fine of nearly $1 million—for the lawsuit he filed against Hillary Clinton and thirty others for allegedly conspiring to defame him. Judge Donald M. Middlebrooks of the Southern District of Florida, who was nominated to his post by President Bill Clinton and unanimously confirmed by a Republican-controlled Senate, issued a blistering takedown of Trump's misuse of the courts. "This case should never have been brought," he wrote. "Its inadequacy as a legal claim was evident from the start. No reasonable lawyer would have filed it."

Those were the first three sentences of Judge Middlebrooks's forty-six-page order. He went on to detail a number of false claims and factual inaccuracies in Trump's lawsuit, and, although he found fault with Trump's lead lawyer on the case, Alina Habba, he made clear the primary responsibility for the case lay with the former president himself. "Mr. Trump is a prolific and sophisticated litigant who is repeatedly using the courts to seek revenge on political adversaries," Middlebrooks wrote. "He is the mastermind of strategic abuse of the judicial process, and he cannot be seen as a litigant blindly following the advice of a lawyer."[24]

Middlebrooks put the Hillary Clinton lawsuit in the context of several other equally frivolous suits Trump had recently filed, arguing his serial abuse of the system was more than a nuisance: it threatened the law itself. "A continuing pattern of misuse of the courts by Mr. Trump and his lawyers undermines the rule of law, portrays judges as partisans, and diverts resources from those who have suffered actual legal harm," he wrote.

Trump's extensive legal bills—both for the multiple criminal investigations he was facing and for the multitude of frivolous law-suits he was filing—were effectively being paid for by his rank-and-file supporters and the small-dollar donations that they were constantly being asked to give in emails and text messages sent by Trump's various political organizations. The Republican National Committee had been paying some of his legal bills, but that had stopped when Trump announced his presidential campaign. By its own long-standing rules, the RNC had to remain neutral in the 2024 Republican presidential primary and could not, therefore, provide financial resources to a candidate for the party's nomination.

The self-described billionaire and former president long had found creative ways to get money out of his working-class supporters—and not just through NFTs. Emails obtained by the January 6 Committee reveal that just days after the 2020 election, for example, Trump asked Dan Scavino, one of his top advisors, to trademark the term "Rigged Election!"—a request Scavino immediately passed on to Jared Kushner. They didn't succeed in getting the phrase trademarked, but Trump's political organization, combined with the RNC, did manage to raise some $250 million between Election Day 2020 and January 6, 2021, from donations generated almost entirely by frantic appeals to Trump voters that the election was being stolen and their donations could help stop it. But according to the January 6 Committee's report, a significant portion of those funds was not spent on legal work but rather diverted to various Trump-affiliated organizations and entities.[25]

The next time Trump would come close to matching the "Stop the Steal" fundraising boom was after he was indicted by Manhattan district attorney Alvin Bragg and again when he was hit with indictments from Special Counsel Jack Smith—proving that playing victim not only came naturally to Trump, but it was also quite profitable.

———

As Trump's campaign got underway, one person he frequently talked to over the phone was the controversial right-wing commentator Tucker Carlson. I had heard about these calls—and that they had increased in frequency after Carlson was fired by Fox News in late April 2023. Although I hadn't talked to him in years, I'd known Carlson for nearly three decades—and I wanted to learn about his conversations with the former president. So, I picked up the phone and called him, reaching him at his home in Maine. The person who told me about their frequent conversations suggested to me that Trump reached out to Carlson so often because he was increasingly lonely in Mar-a-Lago, surrounded only by a small and ever-tightening circle of aides and political advisors. Carlson told me there may be something to that. The way he saw it, Trump's entourage was filled with unimpressive people who, for the most part, didn't really agree with him on much of anything, but who thought they earned some kind of special status by being around the former president. When I suggested that was because Trump had already burned through so many staffers over the years, Carlson wasn't convinced.

"You could get—I don't know—like, legit true believers who actually agreed with your program," Carlson said. "So why wouldn't you get, I don't know, every fucking, you know, get the Proud Boys to hang out, or whatever. But it's this weird social-climbing thing around him, which is just revolting."

Carlson told me his conversations with Trump became more frequent and routine after Russia invaded Ukraine in February 2022, and that they focused primarily on the war and foreign policy. According to Carlson, Trump wanted to talk to someone who shared his opposition to US military aide to Ukraine. "The real reason he calls me is because he knows that I'm sympathetic to his basic program," Carlson told me. "I hate the war in Ukraine more than anything, and I think it's fucking insane. And he's like the only person who agrees with me on that." Carlson said Trump is "more radical" in his opposition to US support for Ukraine than he lets on in public. And given Trump's record as president—and his longstanding refusal to criticize Vladimir Putin about anything—it's not surprising that he doesn't think the United States should be standing up to Russian aggression now.

But those first few months of Trump's 2024 campaign—the Mar-a-Lago meetings with extremists, the frivolous lawsuits, the efforts to squeeze money out of his supporters—laid bare the central truth about Trump's third White House bid: He wasn't running to fulfill a policy agenda. He was running to promote himself, settle scores, and raise cash.

The lack of a policy agenda was nothing new for Trump. Outside of a few recurring themes—build the wall, impose tariffs on America's trading partners, perhaps, and being tougher on NATO than Russia— Trump has had only one consistent belief, which he uttered during a press conference in June 2019: "Ultimately, I'm always right."[26]

As president, he demanded Senate Republicans abolish the legislative filibuster—which effectively requires 60 of 100 votes to pass a bill rather than a simple majority—because it was holding up the GOP's push to repeal Obamacare. In 2021—when Joe Biden was in the White House—he loved the filibuster again, arguing it would be "catastrophic for the Republican Party" if it was removed.[27] In 2019,

Trump called the raising the debt ceiling a "sacred element of our country" and lambasted Democrats for trying to use it as a bargaining chip.[28] Four years later, he posted on Truth Social that "REPUBLICANS SHOULD NOT MAKE A DEAL ON THE DEBT CEILING UNLESS THEY GET EVERYTHING THEY WANT." Asked during a CNN town hall why he did a complete 180 on the issue, Trump had a simple response: "Because now I'm not president."[29]

Even where Trump does have strong policy beliefs, he rarely has a plan to enact them. As former Trump attorney general Bill Barr said in a speech to the City Club of Cleveland in May 2023, "If you believe in his policies, what he's advertising as his policies, he's the last person who could actually execute them and achieve them."

"He does not have the discipline. He does not have the ability for strategic thinking and linear thinking or setting priorities or how to get things done in the system," Barr continued. "It's a horror show, you know, when he's left to his own devices. And so you may want his policies, but Trump will not deliver Trump policies. He will deliver chaos and, if anything, lead to a backlash that will set his policies much further back than they otherwise would be."[30]

Barr was actually being generous there. Trump's "policies"—outside those few through lines on immigration and trade—are whatever the people around Trump can get him to do by appealing to his ego and his desire to win.

One of the genuine accomplishments of the Trump administration, for example, was the Abraham Accords, which established diplomatic relations between Israel and two of its Arab neighbors: the United Arab Emirates and Bahrain. It truly was a groundbreaking agreement, but also one that Trump had nothing to do with brokering. In fact, according to a source involved with the negotiations, when he was briefed on the deal shortly before it was announced, the question he had was about the name. "Why isn't it called the Trump Accords?" he asked, prompting a nervous laugh in the room. He was joking, right?

Trump supporters used to tout criminal justice reform as an example of Trump's ability to get a big bipartisan achievement. He did in fact sign into law the First Step Act in 2018, which cut federal sentences on several crimes and aimed to improve conditions at federal prisons. As part of the reform push, Trump also made a high-profile pardon of a sixty-three-year-old woman named Alice Johnson who had been in a federal prison in Alabama for twenty-two years, serving a life sentence for a nonviolent drug conviction.

Reality-TV star Kim Kardashian, who often used her fame to champion the causes of people who had been wrongly or excessively imprisoned, personally came to see Trump in the White House in May 2018 to appeal for the pardon. The pardon earned Trump positive coverage and was evidence, some of his supporters said, of his deep commitment to criminal justice reform. In 2020, the Trump campaign even spent more than $10 million running a commercial during the Super Bowl about it. "Thanks to President Trump people like Alice are getting a second chance," a narrator read. "Politicians talk about criminal justice reform. President Trump got it done. Thousands of families are being reunited."

In an interview with Bret Baier on Fox News in June 2023, Trump again touted his pardon of Alice Johnson. Baier reminded Trump he had recently announced a plan to impose the death penalty for drug dealers.

"But she'd be killed under your plan," Baier pointed out.

"Huh?" Trump said.

"As a drug dealer," Baier explained.

"No, no. No. Under my, oh, under that? Uhh, it would depend on the severity," Trump said.

"She's technically a former drug dealer," Baier observed. "She had a multimillion-dollar cocaine ring."

"Any drug dealer," Trump replied.

"So even Alice Johnson?" asked Baier.

"She can't do it, okay? By the way, if that was there, she wouldn't be killed, it would start as of now," Trump insisted.

The exchange was painful to watch and showed that Trump had no understanding either of his rationale for pardoning Alice Johnson or of his new plan to execute all drug dealers.

During the final days of the Trump presidency, Kim Kardashian pushed for more pardons and commutations. A source familiar with the conversations tells me Trump listened to her requests and demanded a straight-up quid pro quo. He would grant the commutations, he told Kardashian, if she leveraged her celebrity connections to get football stars who were friends of hers to come visit him at the White House.

Trump was clearly stung by the refusal of Bill Belichick, head coach of the New England Patriots, to visit him at the White House days earlier. Trump had long considered Belichick a friend and supporter, and had offered him a Presidential Medal of Freedom—the federal government's highest civilian honor. After January 6, however, Belichick announced he would not come to the White House to receive the award. He was "flattered" by the offer, he said in a statement, but was turning it down because of "the tragic events" of the week prior. "Above all," he said, "I am an American citizen with great reverence for our nation's values, freedom and democracy."[31]

Apparently, Trump wanted to show up Belichick by getting somebody else from the NFL to come see him at the White House.

Kardashian actually tried to do what Trump demanded, seeing it as a small price to pay to get justice for people she believed were serving unjust sentences. But all the players she approached declined. Trump had become too toxic. In the final two weeks of his presidency, nobody wanted to be anywhere near him.

Months after Trump left the White House, Kardashian had a new cause—saving the life of Julius Jones, a forty-one-year-old man on death row in Oklahoma who had been convicted of murder in a 1999 carjacking. Jones's advocates had successfully petitioned the Oklahoma pardon and parole board to recommend clemency based on new evidence they said proved his innocence, but under Oklahoma law, the commutation had to be approved by the state's governor, Republican Kevin Stitt.

Kardashian appealed directly to Stitt to stop Jones's execution. The governor, though, was worried about the political blowback of stopping the execution of a convicted murderer. He urged Kardashian to get Trump to endorse the commutation too, which would give him all the political cover he needed.

Kardashian, eager to save the man's life, reached out to Trump's team at Mar-a-Lago and quickly received a call back from Trump.

Hell no, the former president told her. He wouldn't do it.

"You voted for Biden and now you come asking me for a favor?" Trump told her. Kardashian has never publicly said who she voted for in 2020, but after Biden was projected the winner, she posted a tweet of Biden and Vice President–elect Kamala Harris along with three blue hearts. That was apparently enough for Trump. He didn't want to hear anything about the merits of Julius Jones's case. After a few more choice words, the line went dead. Trump had hung up on her.

Ultimately, Governor Stitt decided at the eleventh hour to commute the sentence as recommended by the parole board. Fortunately for Julius Jones, his life didn't depend on the goodness of Donald Trump's heart.

Despite the absurdly unconventional and farcical start to his campaign, by the summer of 2023 Trump was the clear frontrunner for the GOP presidential nomination. Poll after poll showed Trump with a decisive lead, with most of his Republican challengers in single digits.

Trump was facing serious legal peril at the time, but none of the revelations eroded his status as the Republican favorite. In fact, they seemed only to cement his status as the leader of the GOP. In one typical poll, a whopping 61 percent of likely Republican primary voters said the first special counsel indictment didn't alter their view of Trump, and 14 percent said it made them like him more. Just 7 percent said the charges changed their opinion of Trump for the worse.[32]

By the time Special Counsel Jack Smith announced his first indictment of Trump, Bannon told me he believed the Republican primary was over. "Of the Keebler elves," Bannon, dismissively referring to Trump's primary opponents, asked me in late May, "who could step up and actually control this movement? Or get its respect? Or lead it?"

Although plenty of Republican leaders and strategists privately acknowledged Trump was too polarizing and toxic to ever win a general election again (even Bannon himself had expressed doubts), few believed his bond with Republican primary voters could be severed. In that context, at least, most thought that he was still Teflon Don, and that no indictment, conviction, or embarrassing misstep would keep him from winning another Republican presidential nomination.

It seemed to me that Trump's lofty poll numbers were less a sign of his continued strength than of his Republican rivals' unwillingness to exploit his many weaknesses. But by early June, that was starting to change. "He hasn't won a damn thing since 2016," Christie—who endorsed Trump's first presidential bid and loyally supported him through the 2020 election—said in a CNN town hall. "Three-time loser: 2018, we lost the House; 2020, we lost the White House. We lost the United States Senate a couple of weeks later in 2021. And in 2022, we lost two more governorships, another Senate seat, and barely took the House of Representatives when Joe Biden had the most incompetent first two years I've ever seen in my life. Loser. Loser. Loser."[33]

At first, Christie stood more or less alone in his willingness to take Trump on directly—and he reveled in his rivals' cowardice. "I don't understand the other candidates who won't even mention his name," he said. "How do you beat someone if you won't talk about them?"

Eventually, however, others started to join in—though likely because of Trump's newfound vulnerability more than any moral epiphanies of their own. Nikki Haley—Trump's former ambassador to the United Nations—started to criticize him on his tepid support for Ukraine as it defended itself from the Russian invasion.[34] Tim Scott eventually got around to acknowledging that the Trump documents indictment was a "serious case with serious allegations."[35] Ron DeSantis began knocking Trump from the right, criticizing the former president for his inability to complete a wall along the southern border during his presidency, unwillingness to support strict abortion restrictions, and refusal to fire Dr. Anthony Fauci early in the COVID-19 pandemic. "This is a different guy than 2015, 2016," DeSantis told right-wing commentator Ben Shapiro.[36]

Whether the collective weight of these attacks—and the four separate sets of indictments he now faces—will prove enough to sink Trump in the primary is yet to be determined, but the amount of political baggage Trump is carrying is unprecedented in American history. The question is whether Republican voters will grow tired of all the drama—and all the losing.

It won't be the political courage of Republican leaders that brings Trump down. By summer 2023, the limits on their willingness to challenge Trump was as painfully obvious as ever. In an interview with CNBC on June 27, Republican Speaker of the House Kevin McCarthy was asked if he thought Trump could beat Biden and "Is it good for the Republican Party if Donald Trump is the nominee?"

"Can he win that election? Yeah, he can win that election," McCarthy answered. "The question is, is he the strongest candidate to win the election. I don't know that answer."

McCarthy wasn't saying anything remotely controversial—and he certainly wasn't suddenly taking on Trump. But the mere suggestion that Trump might—*might*—not be the strongest Republican candidate against Joe Biden in 2024 infuriated Trump and people around him. As Steve Bannon texted me about McCarthy shortly after the interview, "I'm on a jihad against that worthless fuck now."

And sure, enough, McCarthy backtracked, almost immediately. As soon as he got wind of the backlash, McCarthy called Trump. At first, Trump wouldn't take the call. Then in a hastily arranged interview with Breitbart News, the right-wing news outlet cofounded by

Bannon, McCarthy declared that Trump was "stronger today than he was in 2016" and would be the "strongest political opponent" against Biden—taking back what he had just said. His momentary flash of candor lasted less than a couple hours. And after the public groveling, Trump took McCarthy's call.

Launching his longshot presidential campaign in Iowa on June 7, Mike Pence—Trump's embattled former vice president—made a devastating case against his former running mate and his actions on January 6, 2021. "The American people deserve to know on that fateful day, President Trump also demanded I choose between him and our Constitution," he said. "Now voters will be faced with the same choice. I chose the Constitution, and I always will."

The most remarkable aspect of Pence's comments was how long it took him to make them. He had previously defended his decision to defy Trump's orders on January 6, but his criticism of the former president had been remarkably muted—even after the pro-Trump mob had called for his execution, and even after Trump had rationalized that mob's murderous chants ("Well, the people were very angry," Trump had told me more than a year earlier.).

So why did Pence finally decide to take Trump on directly? "It's time," he told CBS News's Robert Costa. "It's time."[37]

CHAPTER TWELVE

DEFENDANT #1,090

S itting aboard his private jet en route to his golf club in Bedminster, New Jersey, on June 13, 2023, Donald Trump was too dejected to eat. "Disgusting," he said aloud, pushing away the food an aide had ordered for him before the flight took off. McDonald's burgers and fries apparently don't taste nearly as good when they're cold.

Cold Big Macs, however, were the least of Trump's worries: He was officially in the fight of his life. Hours earlier, on the thirteenth floor of the Wilkie D. Ferguson Jr. US Courthouse in downtown Miami, the former president had pleaded not guilty to thirty-seven federal charges brought by the Department of Justice and Special Counsel Jack Smith—all related to Trump's alleged retention of classified material and obstruction of the government's efforts to get it back.

The stakes could not have been higher. Adding up the maximum sentences on all thirty-seven counts, Trump figured the special counsel was threatening him with hundreds of years behind bars. That's typically not how judges mete out punishments, but Trump was turning seventy-seven years old the next day. A conviction on just one of the counts brought against him could be effectively a life sentence—and Smith's case was strong. The way some of those closest to the former president saw it, Trump's 2024 campaign was now more than a race to retake the White House; it was a race to keep him out of prison. Perhaps the only way Trump could ensure his freedom, they figured, was to get elected president and either call off the prosecution (if the legal proceedings were still underway) or attempt to pardon himself (if he had already been convicted).

"We must all be STRONG and DEFEAT the Communists, Marxists, and Radical Left Lunatics that are systematically destroying our Country," the former president posted on Truth Social as he traveled to Miami for his Tuesday arraignment.[1] Before his appearance in court, he had derided Smith, a career prosecutor, as "deranged" and a "thug," arguing that both the special counsel and his wife—documentary filmmaker Katy Chevigny—were "Trump Haters."[2]

Smith appeared at the arraignment in person—an unusual move for a special counsel—giving Trump the opportunity for a face-to-face encounter with the man he had vilified so often in interviews, on social media, and in speeches. Smith sat in the first row behind the prosecution's table, right across the aisle and just ten feet or so from Trump. For about ten minutes, the defendants and their assembled legal teams sat in silence waiting for the judge to appear. Trump didn't say anything to Smith. In fact, he never even turned in his direction. According to Rachel Scott, my ABC News colleague who was in the courtroom, Smith frequently looked over at Trump but could see only the side of his head—Trump seemed to be trying to avoid making eye contact.

A similar scene had played out when Trump was arraigned on charges brought by Manhattan district attorney Alvin Bragg two months earlier. Although Trump had loudly and viciously attacked the prosecutor and judge in the hours and days before that indictment, he demurred when given a chance to confront them in person. As I noted in Chapter One, Trump had spoken just ten words during his arraignment in New York City, softly offering one- and two-word answers to the judge he had so harshly criticized before stepping into his courtroom. In Miami, he left it to his lawyer to enter his not guilty plea and to answer all the judge's questions.

That doesn't mean Trump was silent in the courtroom. Although there is no record of him speaking in the official transcript, he was quite talkative as he sat between his two lawyers, Todd Blanche and Christopher Kise. Shortly after the proceeding got underway, Trump gestured over to the special counsel's team of prosecutors and—still avoiding eye contact with Jack Smith—expressed shock at the showing. "I can't believe there are twenty of them," he told his lawyers. He was exaggerating, but only slightly. Blanche counted and gently corrected his client. "There are thirteen," he whispered back. A few minutes later, Trump started complaining to Blanche about Kise, the lawyer sitting on the other side of him.

On paper, Kise seemed like the most important player on Trump's legal team. He was a former solicitor general of Florida who maintained powerful connections in the state—a serious lawyer with the experience to take on such a high-stakes case. But Trump had grown to despise him.

Earlier in the day, as the former president and his entourage gathered at Trump National Doral golf club before heading over to the courthouse, Trump had attempted to humiliate Kise, loudly proclaiming that the only reason the lawyer was coming to the arraignment was because he wanted to be seen on television. "You just want to come for the media attention," Trump said to Kise, according to a source who was there with Trump and his staff in the club's presidential suite. But in reality, Trump needed Kise there that day. Two of the former president's leading lawyers had resigned four days earlier, and Kise was the only qualified lawyer left on the Trump team who was licensed to practice in Florida.

Trump, however, had come to believe Kise was not confrontational enough with the Justice Department. And he had other reasons for disliking him. Chief among them: Kise had long-standing ties to Florida governor Ron DeSantis, who was then Trump's leading rival for the Republican nomination. Trump had hired Kise in a moment of weakness—shortly after the FBI executed a search of Mar-a-Lago, discovering boxes filled with classified documents Trump had failed to turn over. And aware of Trump's history of failing to pay his lawyers, Kise drove a hard bargain, joining the legal team only after securing a $3 million retainer[3]—the money guaranteed and nonrefundable. As a result, Trump had two reasons he couldn't fire a lawyer he had grown to hate: He needed him, and he had already paid him $3 million.

Once the arraignment was underway, the judge had a question for each Trump lawyer.

"Are both of you here temporarily or permanently?" he asked.

"Permanently, Your Honor," Kise answered. Blanche said the same.

Trump—who at times seemed more irritated by the lawyer sitting next to him than by the charges that could result in a de facto life sentence—didn't like what he heard. "Why the hell is he saying that?" he whispered to Blanche. Blanche quietly explained that the judge needed to hear that the sole Florida lawyer of record was committed to seeing the case through to its conclusion.

After Trump signed his bond paperwork and, through his lawyers, agreed to the various conditions of his release, the proceeding came to an end. And as Trump exited the courtroom, Smith glared at him once again, keeping his eyes locked on the former president until he was out of sight. Trump didn't return the stare, opting instead to glance at the handful of reporters in the rear of the courtroom. Neither man had said a word to the other, but one was clearly in control.

Safely aboard his plane and on his way back to New Jersey, Trump was once again his typical bombastic self. "Can we sue the special counsel?" he shouted at Todd Blanche from across the aisle. "Can we sue [Attorney General] Merrick Garland? We can sue them, right? Why don't we sue them?"

As I detailed in the last chapter, Trump has relentlessly deployed the countersuit throughout his career, suing just about anyone who refused to comply with his version of reality. Blanche knew he needed to shut down the idea, but he'd also worked with Trump long enough to know that shouting "No!" at him from his seat on the plane would almost certainly backfire. Instead, he got up and walked over to the former president's table. "I don't think we can do that," Blanche told him. "He hasn't done anything wrong—at least not yet."

In reality, Blanche—like anyone who'd read the indictment against Trump—was well aware of the legal peril his client was facing. Unsealed the Friday before Trump was arraigned, the forty-four-page document compiled by Smith and his team laid out a damning case against the former president, divulging stunning details about his cavalier handling of some of the nation's most sensitive secrets.[4]

One of the most striking features of Smith's indictment was the photographs he included of the myriad boxes Trump had taken from the White House and worked so hard to keep from investigators. The boxes were stuffed both with highly classified documents and odd ephemera from the Trump presidency, including letters, newspaper clippings, pictures, and seemingly random handwritten notes. In one of the photographs included in the indictment, about three dozen of the boxes are seen stacked on the marble floor of an ornate bathroom with gold fixtures, a crystal chandelier, and a cheap tension-rod shower curtain. In another photo, several dozen boxes—of differing sizes and colors—can be seen spread out on the stage of the Mar-a-Lago ballroom. A third photograph shows a box that had tipped over in a storeroom, spilling its contents—newspapers, copies of photographs, and at least one document marked classified—on the floor.

A member of the Trump legal team who had gone through several of the boxes as part of the court-ordered search for official records told me the process was a bit like an archaeological excavation. The layers of papers in each box represented different periods of time—with the older items at the bottom. There didn't appear to be any sort of organizational method. Items were randomly thrown together, connected only by the time they were placed there. Throughout Trump's time in the White House, his aides would often talk about

Trump's *"Beautiful Mind"* boxes, a reference to the movie where actor Russell Crowe plays a schizophrenic mathematician and code breaker who covers his office in paper clippings to find hidden patterns.

As president, Trump brought his boxes with him virtually everywhere he went. Looking through the photographs in the indictment, I thought back to the countless times I watched Trump's junior staffers walking across the South Lawn of the White House carrying boxes to Marine One minutes before Trump boarded the presidential helicopter. I didn't realize it at the time, but Trump stored many of those boxes in the White House residence, and when he finally left the White House for good, he took them to Mar-a-Lago. As Smith bluntly described in his indictment, Trump had absconded with some of America's most tightly held military secrets—information that would be invaluable to America's enemies:

> The classified documents **TRUMP** stored in his boxes included information regarding defense and weapons capabilities of both the United States and foreign countries; United States nuclear programs; potential vulnerabilities of the United States and its allies to military attack; and plans for possible retaliation in response to a foreign attack.

The next sentence in the indictment makes crystal clear the danger of leaving such material in a bathroom or ballroom at Trump's Palm Beach club:

> The unauthorized disclosure of these classified documents could put at risk the national security of the United States,

foreign relations, the safety of the United States military, and human sources and the continued viability of sensitive intelligence collection methods.

In other words, Trump's retention of his *"Beautiful Mind"* boxes wasn't just a nuisance for the National Archives; it represented a genuine national security risk. To underscore this point, Smith noted in the indictment that Mar-a-Lago was "an active social club" that "hosted events for tens of thousands of members and guests" during the time the boxes were unsecured on the premises. National security experts had expressed concerns throughout Trump's presidency about a possible infiltration of the club by foreign spies, and, in fact, at least two Chinese nationals were arrested for trespassing on the grounds in 2019 and 2020.[5]

Reading through the indictment, four words in particular stood out to me: "United States nuclear programs." Even before he was elected president, Trump's critics warned of the danger posed by such an unstable person having access to the nuclear codes. He lost the power to launch a nuclear attack when his time in office came to an end, of course, but Trump's knowledge of American nuclear secrets didn't vanish upon his leaving the White House grounds.

When Trump's possession of the classified documents first surfaced, he claimed he had a complete and total right to declassify anything, and even suggesting he could have declassified it all "by thinking about it."[6] It's true that US presidents, while in office, have wide latitude to declassify America's secrets. But nuclear secrets are so sensitive that not even a president has the authority to declassify them. As outlined in the Atomic Energy Acts of 1946 and 1954, anything related to the use or development of nuclear weapons is classified by law—no individual, not even a president, can change that.[7]

Trump had a clear obsession with nuclear weapons throughout his presidency, often declaring publicly how much he understood about the science behind the bombs capable of destroying the world. As I wrote in Chapter Five, Trump went off on a tangent during a December 18 Oval Office meeting with his national security team, telling the Pentagon's top leadership, "I know more about nukes than all you people."

I can't speak to Trump's knowledge of the science behind nuclear fusion—he often talked about his uncle John Trump, who was a professor at MIT, as evidence of his expertise—but the nuclear program is one of the very few functions of the federal government that he expressed a genuine interest in.* And it all started the day before he was sworn in as president.

On the eve of his inauguration in 2017, Trump was at Blair House, the townhome near the White House where incoming presidents have traditionally stayed as they wait for the outgoing president to leave 1600 Pennsylvania Avenue. During a period of downtime

---

* It's an obsession Trump has had for a long time. In a 1990 interview with *Playboy* magazine, a forty-three-year-old Donald Trump said this about the issue: "I've always thought about the issue of nuclear war; it's a very important element in my thought process. It's the ultimate, the ultimate catastrophe, the biggest problem this world has, and nobody's focusing on the nuts and bolts of it. It's a little like sickness. People don't believe they're going to get sick until they do. Nobody wants to talk about it. I believe the greatest of all stupidities is people's believing it will never happen, because everybody knows how destructive it will be, so nobody uses weapons. What bullshit." (Glenn Plaskin, *Playboy*, March 1, 1990.)

before his inauguration, Trump was secretly taken out the back door of Blair House by his Secret Service detail and through a closed court-yard to a nearby federal building. Once there, they entered a secure room known as a SCIF, or secure compartmentalized information fa-cility, where the most sensitive classified information can be reviewed without fear of external surveillance. This little trip was not mentioned on Trump's public schedule and has never before been reported.

Inside the secure room, Trump was met by several people, includ-ing four uniformed military officers. These were the individuals who would serve in the White House Military Office as Trump's military aides. At the time, there was a total of five—each representing one of the military services (Army, Air Force, Navy, Marines, and Coast Guard).* Only four were present for this meeting with Trump be-cause the fifth was currently on duty with President Barack Obama.

The military aides are mid-level officers (usually at the rank of major or lieutenant colonel) who travel with the president carrying the so-called nuclear football, which can be used to launch a nuclear strike. The purpose of the meeting was to give Trump a briefing on the responsibilities of his military aides and the operational details of the nuclear football. During the course of his presidency, Trump was famously impatient and uninterested during briefings, often skipping them entirely. But on this occasion, he paid very close attention, ask-ing questions and expressing a clear fascination with the device that would accompany him wherever he went over the next four years. The knowledge he learned there in that secure room would have been as sensitive and highly classified as any document he took with him to Mar-a-Lago.

---

* After the creation of the Space Force in 2019, there were six military aides.

The first public confirmation of Trump's indictment didn't come from the special counsel's office, or the Department of Justice, or even from Trump's lawyers—it came from the former president's Truth Social account. "The corrupt Biden Administration has informed my attorneys that I have been Indicted, seemingly over the Boxes Hoax," he wrote on Truth Social just before 8 P.M. on June 8. "I never thought it possible that such a thing could happen to a former President of the United States, who received far more votes than any sitting President in the History of our Country, and is currently leading, by far, all Candidates, both Democrat and Republican, in Polls of the 2024 Presidential Election. I AM AN INNOCENT MAN!"[8]

Strategically, it was a smart move. By publicizing the indictment nearly twenty-four hours before the DOJ unveiled the details of its investigation, Trump goaded dozens of Republicans to rally to his defense in a way they may not have if they knew the actual allegations against him. Within minutes of Trump's Thursday night statement, Representative Jim Banks claimed in a tweet, "Democrats are throwing away 247 years of American democracy over a records case."[9] Senator Marco Rubio accused the Biden administration of "ripping our country apart and shredding public faith in the institutions that hold our republic together" in order to "protect their power and destroy those who threaten it."[10] House Speaker Kevin McCarthy promised to stand with Trump against such a "grave injustice" and vowed to "hold this brazen weaponization of power accountable."[11]

By the time the full scope of Trump's cartoonish scheme was exposed the following afternoon—military secrets being kept next to a toilet, aides texting each other "oh no oh no" after they saw some of the boxes tipped over in a storage room, a tape recording of Trump showing a classified military map to a Mar-a-Lago visitor and openly acknowledging he hadn't declassified it—many GOP lawmakers had already boxed themselves into defending him.

"There's no allegation that he sold [classified information] to a foreign power or that it was trafficked to somebody else or that anybody got access to it," Rubio, the top Republican on the Senate Intelligence Committee, told CBS News days after the indictment was released.[12] In 2016, Rubio was harshly critical of Hillary Clinton's use of a private email server when she was secretary of state, arguing that it "left sensitive and classified national security information vulnerable to theft and exploitation by America's enemies" and "sent the worst message to the millions of hard-working federal employees who hold security clearances and are expected to go to great lengths to secure sensitive government information."[13] Seven years later, as long as Trump wasn't actively selling classified material to America's enemies, Rubio wasn't too concerned.

Kevin McCarthy's post hoc rationalization was even more suspect. Asked about the location where some of Trump's boxes were stored, the Speaker of the House deflected by pointing to the revelation—still under investigation by a separate special counsel—that classified documents were discovered in Joe Biden's garage. "I don't know, is it a good picture to have boxes in a garage that opens up all the time?" he responded. "A bathroom door locks." Yes, bathroom doors do lock—but generally from the inside.

Not every Republican came away looking so foolish. "We don't get our news from Trump's Truth Social account," Chris Christie—a recent entrant into the GOP presidential race—said when Trump first announced he'd been charged. "Let's see what the facts are when any possible indictment is released."[14] After it was released, Christie didn't hold back.

"There are people in my own party who are blaming DOJ," he said during a CNN town hall. "How about blame him? He did it. He took documents he wasn't supposed to take. He kept them when they asked for them back. They got a grand jury subpoena. He refused to comply. They raided his home finally because he refused to comply. All those things were brought on himself, as was this indictment."[15]

Trump's former attorney general Bill Barr was even harsher. "If even half of [the indictment] is true then he's toast," Barr told Fox News. "Yes, he's been a victim in the past. Yes his adversaries have obsessively pursued him with phony claims, and I've been at his side defending against them when he is a victim, but this is much different. He's not a victim here. He was totally wrong that he had the right to have those documents. Those documents are among the most sensitive secrets that the country has."[16]

Reading the indictment and watching the public reaction from Republican leaders, one individual who had served at a high level in the Trump White House pulled out his computer and wrote down his thoughts. A few days later he shared what he had written with me.

"He lacks any shred of human decency, humility or caring," the former White House official wrote of the man he had served for more than a year. "He is morally bankrupt, breathtakingly dishonest, lethally incompetent, and stunningly ignorant of virtually anything related to governing, history, geography, human events or world affairs. He is a traitor and a malignancy in our nation and represents a clear and present danger to our democracy and the rule of law."

Those words were written by a person who had served Trump in a critical role in the West Wing. This person was not a high-profile public figure and has not openly criticized Trump. The individual shared his thoughts with me, but has chosen to remain anonymous—in large part to shield himself and, especially, his family from the vengeance Trump and his allies have directed at others who have turned on Trump.

On the evening of Sunday, July 16, 2023, Donald Trump's legal situation took a sharp turn for the worse. Special Counsel Jack Smith sent him a target letter, informing the former president he would likely face criminal charges related to the January 6 investigation. The letter caught Trump by surprise and enraged him. His lawyers had been telling him for months that they believed Smith would not seek another indictment and would instead conclude this part of his investigation with a final report. Trump summoned several of his legal advisors to Bedminster, New Jersey, the following morning—including Todd Blanche (who was already leading Trump's defense against the previous indictments he had received in New York and Florida), John Lauro (a new Trump attorney who had just agreed to join the team the night before), and Boris Epshteyn (who would soon come to be referred to as "Co-Conspirator 6" by the special counsel). The lawyers raised, and then rejected, the possibility of asking for a meeting to try to change Smith's mind about an indictment. The consensus among Trump and his advisors was that such a meeting would be a waste of time. As one Trump advisor put it, "Fuck them. There's no way they're going to change their minds."

A few days later, however, the special counsel reached out and asked if they wanted a meeting and Trump and his lawyers decided to do it after all. "If they were inviting us," the advisor explained, "we figured we should meet with them and then we could say that at least we tried."

So on July 27, Trump lawyers John Lauro and Todd Blanche traveled to Washington, DC, for what was supposed to be a secret meeting with Special Counsel Jack Smith. To keep from being seen, the lawyers had arranged to drive straight into the garage beneath the Department of Justice annex building, where the special counsel's office is located. Once inside the garage, they were quickly escorted into an elevator and up to a conference room, walking through a hallway that was lined with seven-foot-tall dividers to prevent anybody inside the building, even the special counsel's staff, from seeing the Trump team's arrival.

Inside the conference room, the Trump lawyers were greeted by Jack Smith and two of his lead prosecutors—Joseph "J. P." Cooney and Raymond Hulser, both longtime DOJ lawyers with experience prosecuting public corruption cases. Cooney, in fact, had prosecuted Trump loyalists Steve Bannon and Roger Stone, both of whom had been convicted and later pardoned by President Trump. After some short pleasantries, Smith invited the Trump lawyers to sit at the conference table and offered them some water to drink.

Trump lawyer John Lauro came prepared with a lengthy presentation making the case against a January 6 indictment of the former president. Sitting across the table from Smith and his prosecutors, Lauro spoke virtually uninterrupted for nearly an hour. He argued that there was nothing illegal about what Trump did and that he was simply trying to contest an election he believed he won. Trump was exercising his rights under the First Amendment, Lauro insisted, and following the advice of lawyers along the way. Lauro also pointed out that Trump had already faced an impeachment trial over January 6 and an extensive investigation by the House January 6 Committee. Through it all, he argued, the public's view of Trump's actions hadn't changed. An indictment of the former president on this issue wouldn't change public opinion either, and would only further divide the country. As Lauro spoke, the prosecutors took notes, but they said nothing.

Smith waited until Lauro was done speaking and then, without commenting on what he just heard, he bid the Trump lawyers farewell. According to sources with direct knowledge of the meeting, Smith did not ask a single question. And aside from the pleasantries at the start of the meeting (including the offer of a glass of water) and the goodbye at the end, neither Smith nor the two prosecutors said anything at all. Though Smith did listen carefully, Lauro's one-hour presentation didn't change his mind; but it did give the special counsel a detailed outline of how Trump's legal team would defend the former president against charges related to January 6.

Jack Smith wasn't quiet for long. About four hours after the former president's lawyers left his office, he hit Trump with serious new felony charges. These weren't January 6–related charges—those would come soon enough—but a superseding indictment accusing Trump of attempting to destroy evidence in the classified documents case. The new indictment was devastating—and Smith had given the Trump lawyers no hint it was coming. Trump was charged with attempting to destroy surveillance video from Mar-a-Lago—just hours after it was subpoenaed by federal authorities. The alleged criminal acts were as shockingly brazen as they were stunningly incompetent. The special counsel alleged that Trump ordered two of his employees—personal assistant Walt Nauta and Carlos De Oliveira, the property manager at Mar-a-Lago—to carry out the deed. Not only did Nauta and De Oliveira fail to erase the footage, their actions were captured on video by the very surveillance cameras that shot the footage Trump was allegedly trying to destroy.

The indictment documented the entire escapade in vivid, and almost comical, detail. Nauta, for example, hastily changed his travel plans to fly to Palm Beach, Florida, after Trump received the subpoena. Once he arrived at Mar-a-Lago, he grabbed a flashlight and walked with De Oliveira "through the tunnel where the Storage Room was located, and observed and pointed out surveillance cameras." According to the indictment, De Oliveira pulled aside the club's information technology director, Yuscil Taveras (identified in the indictment as "Trump Employee Number Four"), and walked with him through another tunnel to a small "audio closet" where they could speak privately. De Oliveira allegedly told Taveras that "the boss" wanted the server containing the video deleted; Taveras responded by saying he was not sure how to erase the server—or if he had the authority to do so. At any rate, Taveras didn't do what "the boss" wanted. Instead, the failed cover-up served only to add additional criminal counts against Trump and two of his employees—and to give the clear impression Trump was trying to hide something.

To make sure De Oliveira remained loyal after the indictment, "the boss" agreed to get him a lawyer and pay his legal bills, as he had done with so many other witnesses and potential co-defendants. At his arraignment, the Mar-a-Lago property manager appeared in the courtroom in Fort Pierce, Florida, with Trump-approved lawyer Donnie Murrell. But when it came time for De Oliveira to enter his plea, Murrell had to ask for a short delay because he had not filed the necessary paperwork to represent De Oliveira. What was the problem? According to two Trump legal sources, Murrell had not yet received the agreed-upon $300,000 retainer from the Trump Organization. He wasn't going to go forward until the wire transfer landed in his bank account. Trump lawyers have learned a lesson over the years about the need to get paid up front. Ultimately, the arraignment was rescheduled for the following week.

The superseding indictment was soon old news. Jack Smith had a much bigger hammer to drop. On August 1, 2023, Donald J. Trump became the 1,090th person to face federal charges in connection with the January 6 attack on the US Capitol.

Many of the previous 1,089 defendants had sought leniency in court, saying they had gone to the Capitol on January 6 because the president of the United States had told them to go there and urged them to fight like hell. At a sentencing hearing on December 1, 2021, Judge Amy Berman Jackson responded directly to a rioter who said he was just doing what Trump wanted him to do. "There may be others who bear greater responsibility and should be held accountable," she said. "But this is not their day in court. It's yours."

Two-and-a-half years after that fateful day, the man whom many of the rioters said was ultimately responsible for the carnage seemed on his way to finally being held accountable.

Coming after Trump had already faced criminal charges in New York and Florida, the news of the charges in Washington may have seemed to many like just another indictment. But this one was different. Not because he faces a maximum sentence of 55 years in prison— the maximum in the classified documents case is higher—but because Trump now stands accused of betraying the very oath of office he hopes to take once again. The charges include defrauding the United States and depriving Americans of their right to have their votes count—a right central to the meaning of democracy.

Smith's indictment showed there was a reason the prosecutors had been taking notes when Trump lawyers John Lauro and Todd Blanche had visited the special counsel's office five days earlier. On page two of the indictment, Smith preempted Lauro's argument that Trump had been merely exercising his First Amendment rights. "The Defendant had a right, like every American, to speak publicly about the election," Smith wrote, "and even to claim, falsely, that there had been outcome-determinative fraud during the election and that he had won." He wasn't indicting Trump for his words; Smith was indicting the former president because he tried to overturn the presidential election by attempting to nullify the votes of millions of Americans.

Republican Senate leader Mitch McConnell had foreshadowed the criminal case against Trump with the speech he gave after Trump was acquitted in his second impeachment trial on February 13, 2021. "He didn't get away with anything—yet," McConnell said. "We have a criminal justice system in this country. We have civil litigation and former presidents are not immune from being accountable by either one." Underscoring the need to hold Trump accountable, McConnell said then, "President Trump is practically and morally responsible for provoking the events of the day. No question about it."

Perhaps the biggest question raised by Jack Smith's indictment is this: What took so long? McConnell told the world Trump hadn't gotten away with anything—yet. But that was two-and-a-half years ago. The Republican frontrunner now has a road map for getting away with it all—win the upcoming election and delay the trial until after the inauguration.

CONCLUSION

Years from now, when the last of Donald Trump's presidential records are released, future historians will discover some highly unconventional official White House documents. Amid the White House visitor logs, transcripts of phone calls with foreign leaders, and signed executive orders, they will find papers torn up by the president himself—some of them neatly ripped lengthwise into three or four long pieces, others torn into smaller one- or two-inch squares. These remnants of the Trump era will be a strange reminder of how Trump operated—his disregard for history and for the law. The law—in this case, the Presidential Records Act of 1978—says that official presidential records are the property of the American people, not of any individual, not even a president. Trump destroyed some of them; others he took home to Mar-a-Lago as if they were personal souvenirs of his time as commander in chief. Fortunately for future historians—and current criminal investigators—many of the documents he attempted to pilfer were returned, and many of those he tried to destroy were gathered, taped back together, and preserved by government employees attempting to comply with a law their boss had no intention of following.

One of the more unusual documents now under seal at the National Archives is a paper napkin from Air Force One. The napkin, the existence of which has never been made public, is hardly a state secret, but it reveals much more than the words written on it by Donald Trump with a black Sharpie: "MITT ROMNEY IS A TOTAL LOSER." We don't know the exact context for this presidential musing—or even the date it was retrieved—or why Trump chose to scrawl those words on a napkin. Did he write it after Romney became the only Republican to vote to convict him in his first impeachment trial? Or when Romney became one of seven Republicans to vote to convict him in the *second* impeachment trial? Or maybe it was after Romney and his wife, Ann, congratulated Joe Biden and Kamala Harris on winning the 2020 election. "We know both of them as people of good will and admirable character," Senator Romney said in a statement issued minutes after Biden and Harris were projected the winners of the election. "We pray that God may bless them in the days and years ahead."

Trump had called Romney a loser many times, but the context of the words scrawled on the napkin—*total loser*—were different than those he blurted out on Twitter or in speeches. The napkin was a private note, likely one Trump wrote to himself, and an indication Trump had Romney on his mind, and perhaps a reflection of his unhealthy obsession with the man who won the Republican nomination four years before Trump did. Of course, the note wasn't entirely wrong—Romney, like Trump, was a loser. Both men had lost a presidential election. But, unlike Trump, Romney took his loss with grace and dignity. He did what Trump would never do. He congratulated his opponent—Barack Obama—and put the country above himself, offering words of support to the man who had defeated him. As it turned out, Romney's defeat wasn't the end of his political career. Elected to the Senate in the midst of the Trump era, he became the conscience of a party that all too often appeared as if it didn't want a conscience, standing up to Trump consistently and forcefully when most of the party's elected leaders either enabled and placated him or stood by silently as he treated the Constitution the way he treated those documents taped back together by the National Archives.*

When I wrote *Betrayal*, in the immediate aftermath of January 6, the horror of what had happened, and how close Trump came to plunging the country into an even greater crisis, was still raw. I had long felt a reverence for the place I saw plundered on that day. I first visited Washington, DC, when I was eleven years old and was in awe as I went inside the Capitol building and had a chance to sit in the visitors' galleries of the House and Senate. I looked down at the seats in the House and the desks in the Senate and thought of the great debates that had played out there long before I was born. I marveled at how the members of Congress I was able to watch were sent to those chambers to represent people all across the country. I eventually had the chance to work in the Capitol building as a reporter—to ask questions of the powerful and to see history unfold.

---

* The "MITT ROMNEY IS A TOTAL LOSER" napkin took a circuitous journey to the National Archives, including a detour to Mar-a-Lago along with the classified documents that would lead to the special counsel investigation led by Jack Smith and the first federal indictment of a former president of the United States. The napkin was among the items packed into fifteen boxes of White House materials Trump returned to the National Archives on January 22, 2022. According to a source who has reviewed the contents of those boxes, the napkin is now in an acid-neutral, pH-balanced envelope at the National Archives.

I was at the Capitol when it was evacuated on September 11, 2001. The heroes of United Airlines Flight 93 broke into the cockpit and brought down a plane that was likely headed for the majestic Capitol dome, saving countless lives as they ended their own in Shanksville, Pennsylvania. One of those passengers, Todd Beamer, was heard saying "Let's roll" as he helped lead the charge on the cockpit door to take out the hijackers. I was there on Capitol Hill late that night, when members of Congress from both parties briefly returned and assembled on the steps outside the building. After a few short speeches and a moment of silence, the congressional leaders started to walk away. The building was still closed, but their moment of defiance wasn't over. A few members toward the rear of the assembled group of about two hundred members of Congress started singing "God Bless America." Soon they were all singing. Reporters are trained to be skeptical—as an old *Chicago Tribune* editor put it, "Chum, if your mother says she loves you, check on it"*—but I had to hold back tears as I watched those politicians sing that song. I had never felt more proud of my country, or more privileged to be on the grounds of the US Capitol. Sure, there were politicians who were corrupt—scandals that I covered and uncovered—and there were others who were cravenly cynical and seemed more dedicated to their party than their country. But in the darkness that night, the Capitol felt to me like sacred ground.

On September 12, Congress did in fact reconvene and I was back

---

* According to the website Quote Investigator, the quote first appeared in the *Chicago Tribune* on March 30, 1970, and was attributed to an editor named Arnold A. Dornfeld. Dornfeld, however, said it originated with his colleague Edward H. Eulenberg. An obituary for Eulenberg in 1988, however, offers a slightly different and harsher version of the phrase: "If your mother tells you she loves you, kick her smartly in the shins and make her prove it."

at work. "I felt like my eyes were about to tear up when I walked into the Capitol this morning," I wrote in my journal the next day. "The enormity of what has happened is just now sinking in. I'm haunted by the images of those planes crashing into the Twin Towers, haunted by the images of those so desperate they jumped from 100 stories just minutes before those mighty symbols crashed to the earth. I look at the Capitol dome, the single most powerful symbol of American democracy, and wonder, what if? What if that plane that crashed in Pennsylvania instead crashed squarely into the Capitol dome?"

Not long after September 11, I met Todd Beamer's widow, Lisa, inside the Capitol building and sat with her in the visitors' gallery of a mostly empty House chamber. For what seemed like several minutes, neither of us said anything as we looked down on the House floor, a place that might have been reduced to rubble if not for the sacrifice those passengers made on Flight 93. "Your husband saved this place," I whispered to her. "And he saved my life too." It was hard to contemplate her pain and sacrifice. She was the mother of two young boys and was five months pregnant with a baby girl when her husband died in the wreckage of that flight on the field in Shanksville, Pennsylvania.

As a young reporter, I was particularly fascinated by the desks assembled on the floor of the Senate. They all have a documented history, a detailed record of which senators had used each desk going back to the renovation of the Capitol after the British attacked the building in 1814.[1] For several years, Senate Republican leader Mitch McConnell sat at the desk once used by Henry Clay, "the Great Compromiser," who did his part to keep together a nation heading toward

Civil War. McConnell, a master of Senate procedure, is known for using his power and cunning to shape the Supreme Court, but he also used it to pass a Senate resolution in 1999 to mandate that Clay's desk always be assigned to the senior senator from Kentucky—securing for himself one of only three desks whose assignment is mandated by a Senate resolution.* In 2006, McConnell was elected Republican Senate leader and decided he wanted a different desk—the one used by Republican leaders since Robert Taft, known as "Mr. Republican," had it in the 1940s. But first McConnell had to draft and pass an amendment to his earlier resolution to allow the senior senator from Kentucky to assign Henry Clay's desk to the junior senator from Kentucky if the senior senator is elected party leader.

As a young reporter, I remember watching the debate over authorizing the first Iraq War in 1991. I can almost still hear the booming voice of Senator Ted Kennedy speaking out against the resolution as tourists in the gallery immediately above strained to look down to see where the thunderous voice was coming from. Kennedy was at the far end of the Senate floor, right next to the side door. He was one of the most senior members of the Senate and could have had a spot up front where most of the other senior senators positioned their desks. But Kennedy chose to be in the rear of the chamber so that as he spoke he would be facing his colleagues and never have his back to

---

* A 1974 Senate resolution by New Hampshire senator Norris Cotton mandates that Daniel Webster's old desk be assigned to the senior senator from New Hampshire, despite the fact that Webster, who was born in New Hampshire, actually was a senator from Massachusetts. A 1995 resolution by Senator Thad Cochran of Mississippi mandates that Jefferson Davis's old desk go to the senior senator from Mississippi. It's hard to imagine why a senator would want to use this desk; Davis was a Mississippi senator, but he was also, of course, the president of the Confederacy.

any senator (there was also the added benefit of being next to the door, so he could quietly slip in and out of the chamber with little notice). Ted Kennedy's desk was the same one used by his older brother John F. Kennedy.

When I was covering the impeachment trial of Bill Clinton in 1999, I read *Profiles in Courage*, the 1956 Pulitzer Prize–winning book the young senator John F. Kennedy wrote along with his future White House speechwriter Ted Sorensen. I was drawn to the book because one of the chapters seemed directly relevant to the story I was then covering—a "profile in courage" of a Republican senator who defied his party in the 1868 impeachment trial of President Andrew Johnson. But there is another chapter, an especially dramatic and important story of political courage, that is far more relevant to the story I am writing now. It's about Sam Houston, the former governor of Tennessee, battlefield hero, and founding father of Texas independence. He was the first president of the Independent Republic of Texas, the first senator from the state of Texas, and, as Kennedy put it, "one of the most independent, unique, popular, forceful and dramatic individuals ever to enter the Senate chamber." Houston put all of that on the line beginning with a vote he took in the Senate in 1854 against what would become the Kansas-Nebraska Act. To Houston's fellow Democrats, it was a must-pass bill, a test of Southern unity and survival. Houston saw the bill for what it was—a way to reopen the issue of expanding slavery that would set America on a path to civil war. Not a single Senate Democrat joined him in voting against it. The backlash was ferocious. He faced calls for his resignation—and worse. "Nothing can justify this treachery," declared one Texas newspaper. "Nor can anything now save the traitor from the deep damnation which such treason shall merit." The Texas state legislature, which had elected Sam Houston to serve in the Senate in the first place, voted to condemn him by a vote of 73–3. "It was," Houston later said, "the most unpopular vote I ever gave, but the wisest and most patriotic."[2]

The vote seemed to doom the political career of one of the most storied and celebrated leaders in the South. Three years later, he ran for governor and lost in a landslide. A year after that, he lost his Senate seat. Sam Houston was now an old man—an "old fogey" he said, devoted "to those primitive principles upon which our government was founded"—but his fight was not over. As an ex-senator, ex-president of the Republic of Texas, and a pariah in the Democratic Party, he ran again for governor in 1859—this time as an independent. With no party organization and not a single major newspaper supporting him, he campaigned against secession and the reopening of the slave trade in Texas and, miraculously, he won. His stand against Southern calls for secession was so forceful, Houston received a few votes at the 1860 Republican convention to be Abraham Lincoln's vice president, unsolicited votes that served to motivate his enemies. When the Southern states seceded after Lincoln's inauguration and formed the Confederate States of America, Governor Houston traveled around his state to make what had become a very unpopular case for Texas to remain in the Union. While he was campaigning in the city of Waco, a bomb exploded behind the hotel he was staying in—an unsuccessful attempt to either kill or intimidate him. He survived the bombing, but he lost the battle. And when Texas officially seceded from the Union and joined the Confederacy, Houston was once again defeated, removed from office after he refused to take the oath to the new Confederate state of Texas. Sam Houston was far from perfect, but at the end of his life, he stood up

to the madness of his own party—and the madness of his own constituents. Despite the steep personal price he paid, his place in history
was secure—and it started with a vote, an act of political courage,
made inside the Senate chamber.*

As I watched the attack on the Capitol unfold on January 6, I felt
angry that people were defiling a place I considered sacred. I feared
that the history and the principles the building represented were being destroyed right before my eyes. One of the images that particularly pained me was the sight of the rioters inside the Senate chamber,
rummaging through those antique desks while a guy with face paint
and a headdress made of coyote fur and buffalo horns—the so-called
QAnon Shaman—took a seat in the presiding officer's chair and
penned a threatening note to Mike Pence: "It's only a matter of time,
justice is coming."

I was angry and afraid by what I saw and further horrified by what
I learned months later about the threat our nation faced from the
man who was sworn to protect it. But as I finished *Betrayal*, I felt a
degree of optimism. Trump left office after failing spectacularly in
each and every effort he made to prevent Joe Biden from becoming
president. He failed in part because ordinary people did what in ordinary times would be ordinary things. But in the context of what
was happening, their actions were extraordinary, even heroic. Vice
President Pence, who I saw right there on the Capitol steps on September 11 singing "God Bless America" as a freshman member of
Congress, presided over the counting of the electoral votes, refusing
Trump's demand that he single-handedly overturn the election.

---

* The current Senate chamber opened in 1859, the year Senator Houston left the Senate.
Most of his term was spent in what is now known as the Old Senate Chamber, which is
located just down the hall from where the Senate now convenes.

Trump appointees at the Department of Justice refused his illegal demands and threatened to resign en masse if he appointed an acting attorney general who would help him subvert the Constitution. The Supreme Court refused to go along—including the three justices nominated by Trump. Local Republican politicians who had fully supported Trump defied his demands to overturn the elections in their states. Some key people inside Trump's White House held the line, quietly assisting the transition to a Biden presidency even as the man they served was trying to stop it from happening. The system held because there were Republicans in positions high and low who acted as Americans, not as blind servants of a party or of a president. That was genuinely heartening, but there was still the unmistakable truth that Trump came close to succeeding. While there were notable profiles in courage, there were all too many profiles in cowardice and profiles in malevolence. Trump's betrayal showed just how vulnerable our democracy is and how much it depends on people who are in positions of responsibility to act responsibly. As I wrote in the very last sentence of *Betrayal*, "The continued survival of our republic may depend, in part, on the willingness of those who promoted Trump's lies and those who remained silent to acknowledge they were wrong, that it was a terrible mistake to put one man's ego above the truths we should all hold to be self-evident."

Nearly three years later, that clearly hasn't happened. Even among those who were shocked and saddened by what happened on January 6, the memories of the attack on the Capitol and what it represented have begun to fade. All too many people have begun to forget how desperately and madly Donald Trump tried to cling to power and what he was willing to do to avoid being branded a loser. As of this writing, Trump is the overwhelming frontrunner to be, once again, the Republican nominee for president. Precious few of those who promoted his lies have recanted, and even fewer who remained silent in the face of what he did have acknowledged their mistake or have chosen to speak out now.

Trump has mounted his comeback with behavior even more outrageous than what the world witnessed when he was president. Whatever guardrails may have existed before are gone—he no longer has people of stature around him who are willing to defy his demands and to protect the nation from his most destructive instincts. But it's more than that. It's not just that people like James Mattis and Bill Barr and Pat Cipollone are gone. It's that his destructive instincts are even more destructive than they were in January 2021. While he is beginning to be held to account by the criminal justice system for what he did, so far, Trump has gotten away with it. Not only has he not yet paid a price for his betrayal of our democracy, he's been rewarded for his defiance. He continues to be treated as the leader of the party that nominated Abraham Lincoln. As this book documents, Trump is more detached from reality than ever and more willing to trash the norms and customs that our system of government needs to survive as a working democracy. On January 6, he refused to condemn those who attacked the Capitol. By the time he announced his 2024 presidential campaign, Trump was speaking of the January 6 rioters as heroes, even playing video of the riot at his first campaign rally.

That's an awful set of facts. It's hard to be optimistic about the state of American democracy when Trump and the lies he has told have taken root so deeply. He may lose yet another presidential election, but the damage he has done and his assault on decency and democracy will haunt our politics long after he is gone. Yet even as I write those grim words, I believe there is reason to be optimistic—or at least hopeful. If John F. Kennedy and Ted Sorensen were alive today, they would be able to write a worthy, even inspiring, addendum to *Profiles in Courage* about the Republicans who were willing to sacrifice their careers and, more, to hold Trump accountable and to try to keep him from ever being in position to do the kind of damage he did after the 2020 election.

Rusty Bowers, for example, is a profile in courage. The Republican Speaker of the Arizona State House of Representatives, Bowers refused the demands of Donald Trump and his attorney Rudy Giuliani to nullify Biden's victory in Arizona. When he asked for evidence of election fraud, Giuliani told him, "We've got lots of theories, we just don't have any evidence." Bowers rejected their scheme, telling them, "You are asking me to do something against my oath, and I will not break my oath." Giuliani's reply: "Aren't we all Republicans here? I would think we'd get a better reception."[3]

Like so many Republicans who refused to go along with Trump's efforts to overturn the election, Bowers was bombarded with taunts and death threats; Trump supporters gathered in front of his house blasting hateful words at his home from loudspeakers while his daughter Kacey was inside and so gravely ill she would die less than two months later. Despite the threats to his family and his career, Bowers told his story to the January 6 Committee and continued to fight efforts of fellow Republicans in the state legislature to decertify Biden's election victory—efforts that continued nearly two years after the 2020 election. Bowers was rewarded for his courage with a resounding defeat in a Republican primary in 2022—a long and storied career in Arizona Republican politics upended because he did what was right instead of what his president demanded. I spoke to Bowers on the floor of the Arizona House not long after he lost the primary. He said the party leadership in his state had been taken over by "a cabal of like-minded thugs. I mean, their whole methodology seems to be—and I'm talking about the party leadership—we're going to beat you into submission. It's our way or walk the plank."

He may have walked the plank, but had no regrets for what he did or the price he paid for doing it. A deeply religious man, Rusty Bowers left his lofty position in the Arizona statehouse with no doubt he had done the right thing.

The new *Profiles in Courage* would prominently feature the ten House Republicans who voted to impeach Donald Trump for his actions on January 6. Ten is a pathetically small number, especially considering the vote took place just seven days after the Trump-inspired mob attacked the Capitol. If Trump's actions didn't constitute "high crimes and misdemeanors," what does? But the Impeachment Ten represented a fairly wide range of the Republican Party, both ideologically and geographically. They didn't have much in common before their votes to impeach, but they will be forever tied together in the history of the Trump era—and by the private group text chain that they set up after the vote and, as of this writing, that all ten of them still use to communicate with one another.

Of the ten, Representative Tom Rice's vote to impeach was the most surprising. He came from a solidly Republican district in South Carolina that voted for Donald Trump by a nearly 20-point margin in both 2016 and 2020. He was among the most conservative members of the House and for four years had been one of the most reliably pro-Trump votes in Congress. He told no one of his intention to vote yes on impeachment, not even his own staff. He cast his vote on the

House floor and then quickly left to walk back to his office. On the way there, he received a call from Republican whip Steve Scalise telling him he needed to come back to the House chamber.

"Why do I need to come back?" Rice asked.

"Because you made a mistake in your vote," Scalise replied. "You voted yes."

"That wasn't a mistake," Rice answered.[4]

Rice was first elected to Congress in 2012 and had been easily re-elected ever since. In 2020, Rice won by an even bigger margin—nearly 24 points—than Trump did in his district. His impeachment vote, however, was a political death sentence. In a familiar pattern, Trump relentlessly attacked him and campaigned for his opponent in the Republican primary. Rice got pummeled, losing by nearly 27 points against an opponent who ran almost entirely on a single issue: Rice's vote to impeach Donald Trump.

Just days before the primary election, I went to see Rice in South Carolina. He was unhappy about the prospect of losing his seat in Congress, but had absolutely no regrets.

"I did it then," he told me of his vote to impeach. "And I would do it again tomorrow."

Rice was a reliably pro-Trump supporter right up to the end. He actually supported Trump's efforts to challenge the election results and voted on January 6 to reject Biden's electoral votes in states Trump was contesting. He voted to impeach the president he supported because he believed his failure to act once the Capitol came under attack was a betrayal of his oath of office—a dereliction of duty. He called the vote in favor of impeaching Trump "the conservative vote."

"When he watched the Capitol, the People's House, being sacked, when he watched the Capitol Police officers being beaten for three or four hours and he lifted not one finger or did one thing to stop it—I was livid then and I'm livid today about it," Rice told me.

When Trump came to his South Carolina district to campaign against him, the former president called Rice "a disaster" and a "total fool" who is "respected by no one."

"If I am a 'disaster' and a 'total fool' and I voted with him 169 times out of 184, what does that make him?"[5] Rice said when I asked him to respond to Trump.

Among the Impeachment Ten, no one paid a steeper political price than Liz Cheney. Cheney held the third-highest ranking position in the House Republican leadership and was likely on the path to be a future Speaker of the House. Before January 6, she pleaded with her Republican colleagues not to vote to throw out any of Biden's electoral votes. All fifty states had certified their election results as required by the Constitution. Rejecting any state's certified electoral votes, she argued, would amount to disenfranchising millions of voters and would put Congress in the position of choosing the president in defiance of the Constitution.

The day before the impeachment vote, she announced her decision with force and moral clarity.

"The President of the United States summoned this mob, assembled the mob, and lit the flame of this attack. Everything that followed was his doing. None of this would have happened without the President," she said in a statement the day before the vote. "There has never been a greater betrayal by a President of the United States of his office and his oath to the Constitution."

———

Cheney's vote to impeach was only the beginning of her stand against Trump. After Trump left office, she pushed hard to establish a bipartisan commission to establish the truth of what happened—and of Trump's multifaceted effort to prevent a peaceful transfer of power to the true winner of the election. On May 12, 2021, Cheney was thrown out of Republican leadership and exiled from the Republican Party. Her replacement was Elise Stefanik, a thirty-six-year-old congresswoman from New York. Stefanik had once been seen as a thoughtful and moderate young star in the party, but by the time she took down Liz Cheney, she had become as blindly subservient to Trump as any Republican in the House. And once in leadership, she remained totally committed to Trump, going so far as to endorse his 2024 presidential campaign even before Trump announced he was going to run again. "I am proud to endorse Donald J. Trump for President in 2024," she said days before he announced his campaign and long before any of her fellow Republican leaders offered their endorsements. "It's very clear President Trump is the leader of the Republican Party."

While some in politics do the right thing and stand for principle despite the risk to their own careers, others do the opposite. Stefanik has said that she got her start in politics by running a study group at Harvard's Institute of Politics with Ted Sorensen, the man who helped JFK write *Profiles in Courage*. "That to me was just an amazing experience," she said of her time with Sorensen. "After that, I was hooked." Sorensen was no longer alive by the time Stefanik did her part to banish Liz Cheney from the Republican Party for taking a principled stand. It's not hard to imagine who he would have seen as courageous and who he would have seen as craven.

Free of her party obligations, Cheney became the vice chairman and the driving force of the House select committee on January 6. She kept the committee's work—through more than a thousand witness interviews and a dozen hearings—focused on proving the words she wrote in the statement announcing her vote to impeach Donald Trump: "There has never been a greater betrayal by a President of the United States of his office and his oath to the Constitution."

For Cheney, taking the principled stance was political suicide. Of all fifty states, no state voted more decisively for Donald Trump than Wyoming, the state she represented in Congress. Trump won Wyoming in 2020 with just over 70 percent of the vote, less than 27 percent going to Joe Biden. Liz Cheney had been decisively reelected that year, too. But after her impeachment vote and her leadership of the January 6 Committee, she faced the wrath of Trump and his many die-hard supporters in her state. She received only 28 percent of the vote in the 2022 Republican primary, getting defeated in a landslide by Trump's chosen candidate.

History will vindicate Liz Cheney and the rest of the Impeachment Ten, just as it will vindicate Mitt Romney and the others who took their stand in the Senate and Rusty Bowers and the others across the country who stood their ground. Most of them—almost all of them—not only acted courageously but also paid a high price for doing so. Of the Impeachment Ten, all but two were gone after the next election, after either being defeated or deciding not to run in the face of near-certain defeat. Today, as of this writing, many of those who acted courageously are treated as pariahs in Trump's party for what they did. To borrow an analogy from another Kennedy, the question is whether each of those acts of courage amounts to a small ripple of hope, and whether those ripples can create a wave big enough to sweep away the madness that has infected our politics. But although history will vindicate those who sacrificed greatly to do the right thing, the question is what happens now. Given Trump's proven track record of losing, the Republican Party does not have time to wait for history's vindication. America may not be able to wait either.

ACKNOWLEDGMENTS

Every morning, my email inbox is bombarded with newsletters from various news organizations teeing up the day's big political events. In the months before I started working on this book, there was one newsletter that stood out among all the others—a publication called the *Morning Dispatch*, which summarized key news developments in a way that also managed to make sense of our confounding, and often maddening, times. As I started working on this book, I reached out to the writer of the *Morning Dispatch*, and, although we had never previously met, he agreed to work with me on *Tired of Winning* as a researcher. Declan became a true collaborator and friend in the process (even though he is a tortured Cubs fan).

Douglas Kennedy guided me throughout this project—from the initial idea to the final edits. He encouraged my good ideas and talked me out of my bad ones. I have no idea where I would be if I had never met Douglas, but I do know this: I wouldn't be writing this book. Thank you, DK.

ACKNOWLEDGMENTS

I have many brilliant and generous colleagues at ABC News who have helped me navigate the challenges of reporting in the Trump era, both for ABC and for the three books I have written over the past five years. Nobody has done a better job of covering Donald Trump's legal saga than Katherine Faulders. She is determined, tireless, and deeply sourced. I am grateful for Katherine's input on this book—and the work she does every day at ABC.

A troika of my ABC colleagues—Chris Donovan, Rick Klein, and Claire Brinberg—read every chapter of this book as it was written, providing feedback, encouragement, and constructive criticism along the way. Ben Siegel and Will Steakin also offered important feedback and suggestions. Justin Fishel offered ideas as well as some comic relief. Alex Mallin has done a brilliant job covering the prosecution of the January 6 rioters and offered invaluable insight along the way. Jordyn Phelps, Devin Dwyer, and Jonathan Greenberger have helped me navigate this strange era in America. So has John Santucci, who has tirelessly covered all things Trump since the announcement of the first campaign in 2015. I am especially grateful to Kim Godwin for supporting my work from the day she became president of ABC News. I am indebted to too many ABC colleagues to name, but I'll name a few anyway: Emily Cohen, Maggy Patrick, Rachel Scott, Kerry Smith, Gabe Ferris, Allie Pecorin, Jenn Metz, Marc Burstein, Almin Karamehmedovic, Aaron Katersky, Pierre Thomas, Averi Harper, Mary Bruce, Mason Leib, Pete Austin, Mariam Khan, George Sanchez, Simone Swink, Andrea Owen, Audrey Taylor, Luke Barr, Jack Date, Ben Siu, Karen Travers, Ben Gittleson, Jon Garcia, Olivia Rubin, Lucien Bruggeman, Van Scott, Katie DenDaas, Stacia Deshishku, Derek Medina, Khadijah Sharif-Drinkard, and Josh Margolin.

ACKNOWLEDGMENTS

Anthony Perrone made the audio version of this book possible, as he did with *Betrayal* and *Front Row at the Trump Show*. Thank you, Anthony! It's been great to be on this journey with David Muir, covering so many of the major developments as they happened, live on ABC.

At ABC's *This Week*, I work with a team of journalists on what I believe is the best political show on network television. As we worked on the show together, Dax Tejera encouraged me to write this book. He read and gave me feedback on my initial book proposal. Tragically, Dax died on December 23, 2022. I thought often about him as I wrote this book. I miss you, Dax.

Meg Mistry and Quinn Scanlan have photo credits in this book— but their photography is secondary to their journalism. I worked with Meg and Quinn on major interviews for *This Week* that helped provide perspective for this book as well. As my great co-anchors Martha Raddatz and George Stephanopoulos know, we have a brilliant and dedicated team: Kendall Heath, Mitch Alva, Julia Cherner, Perita Carpenter, Mae Joo, Tina Yin, Eric Fayeulle, Michael Allen, Chris Boccia, and our new team leader, Brooke Brower.

Thank you to Barbara Fedida for being such a good friend for nearly twenty years. Tom Shine has retired from ABC News, but not from helping me out. Thank you for edits, Tom! After leaving ABC News, my former boss James Goldston went to work for the January 6 Committee—I am grateful for all he did to make sure America and the world could see the truth about the attack on American democracy.

Alan Berger, for the third straight book, read every chapter shortly after it was written, giving me near-instant feedback and prodding me to keep going whenever my pace slowed.

ACKNOWLEDGMENTS

I met Mike Allen one day in Iowa in 1999—and Mike Feldman a year or two before that. They both paved the way for this book in ways they don't realize. Frank Luntz helped me explore the ideas in this book, sharing his deeply held concerns for the future of the country and for the Republican Party. Don Rockwell and Mary Ann Gonser once again offered ideas and edits; Don also taught me to understand and appreciate both left and right (specifically, Left- and Right-Bank Bordeaux). Mark Laufman read and offered edits on some of these pages. Franco Nuchese, Yousef Al Otaiba, Wendell Allsbrook, John Rogers, and Todd Harris provided me with crucial distractions when I needed them the most. Harry Truman said, "You want a friend in Washington? Get a dog." I do have a great dog (Brooklyn!) but I am also blessed with true friends outside of Washington who have helped me keep it all in perspective—Paul and Karen Freitas, Dave Almy, Richard Dawson, Maria Loi, Pete Madej, Brian Brown, Paul Jensen, Renae Schrier, and Todd Surdez. Scott Alexander carefully read an early draft, frequently calling me with comments and suggestions. A lifelong Republican, he urged me to tell the stories of Republicans who stood up to Trump. Regarding Mike Pence, Scott told me, "He betrayed Trump when it mattered most and history will celebrate that."

Thank you to my editor, for the third time, John Parsley, and the mighty team at Dutton, including Amanda Walker, Sarah Thegeby, Ella Kurki, and Stephanie Cooper. None of these books would have happened without David Larabell. Thank you to fact checker Ben Kalin for paying attention to every detail.

As with most things in my life, this was a family project. Audrey Shaff, my incredible mother, read through and edited every page. As

ACKNOWLEDGMENTS

I said in the dedication to *Betrayal*, she is the kindest person on the planet. She also never fails to make my writing cleaner and better. My brother Allan (the legendary Worldrider) is a mentor like no other. My brother Jim taught me a lot about the world over the years and wanted to be mentioned here. I look forward to Aiden writing a book someday, or maybe playing for the Red Sox. My nephew Robert played a big role in *Betrayal* and his input on that book improved this one too. My incredibly talented father-in-law, Sal Catalano, inspired me with his wisdom, his work ethic—and his mind-blowing artwork. Thank you, MaryAnn, for the unwavering support.

Emily and Anna made their mark on all three of my Trump books. All those "take your daughters to work" days have really paid off.

And, finally, the most important acknowledgment of all: Maria. On every chapter and every fragment of a chapter, Maria was the very first person to read what I had written. Some of those first drafts were really rough. Beginning with *The Right to Bear Arms* all those years ago, Maria has now helped me write four books—cleaning up those messy early drafts and putting up with me along the way.

NOTES

INTRODUCTION

1. Donald Trump interview with the author, March 18, 2021.
2. Aaron Couch and Emmet McDermott, "Donald Trump Campaign Offered Actors $50 to Cheer for Him at Presidential Announcement," *The Hollywood Reporter*, June 17, 2015.
3. Michelle Lee, "Fact Check: Has Trump declared bankruptcy four or six times?," *Washington Post*, September 26, 2016.
4. Jon Campbell, "VIDEO: 15 Donald Trump 'wins' in 50 seconds," *Democrat & Chronicle*, April 12, 2016.
5. Michael D'Antonio, *The Truth About Trump* (New York: St. Martin's, 2016).

CHAPTER ONE: "COME RETRIBUTION"

1. "McVeigh's Apr. 26 Letter to Fox News," *Fox News*, April 26, 2001.
2. Jonathan Karl, *The Right to Bear Arms* (New York: HarperCollins, 1995).
3. Paul Weber, "Trump Rally Falls During Anniversary of Waco's Dark Past," Associated Press, March 25, 2023.
4. @RobertDownen_, Twitter, March 25, 2023.
5. @realDonaldTrump, Truth Social, May 5, 2023.
6. Brian Kilmeade, *Fox & Friends*, Fox News, March 27, 2023.
7. William Rashbaum, Ben Protess, Jonah Bromwich, and Hurubie Meko, "Manhattan Prosecutors Begin Presenting Trump Case to Grand Jury," *New York Times*, January 30, 2023.
8. @realDonaldTrump, Truth Social, March 18, 2023.
9. @realDonaldTrump, Truth Social, March 18, 2023.
10. @realDonaldTrump, Truth Social, March 24, 2023.

NOTES

11. Jonathan Dienst, Dareh Gregorian, and Laura Jarrett, "Bragg, DA Probing Trump, Received Death Threat Letter with White Powder," NBC News, March 24, 2023.
12. Sophia Cai, "Trump Suggests DA 'Dropped' Stormy Case," *Axios*, March 25, 2023.
13. Erica Orden, "Manhattan Trump Grand Jury Set to Break for a Month," *Politico*, March 29, 2023.
14. @realDonaldTrump, Truth Social, March 29, 2023.
15. Asawin Suebsaeng and Tim Dickinson, "Trump's Campaign Is Already Hawking Merch with a Fake Mugshot," *Rolling Stone*, April 4, 2023.
16. Hugo Lowell, "Trump Wants to Be Handcuffed for Court Appearance in Stormy Daniels Case, Sources Say," *The Guardian*, March 22, 2023.
17. @realDonaldTrump, Truth Social, April 4, 2023.
18. "Trump Explains His Arraignment to Tucker Carlson," Fox News, April 11, 2023.
19. Michael Isikoff, "Trump's Tale of Crying Manhattan Court Employees Was 'Absolute BS,' Law Enforcement Source Says," Yahoo! News, April 12, 2023.
20. Jonah Bromwich, "Trump Pleaded Not Guilty, Then Sat Quietly as Lawyers Sparred," *New York Times*, April 4, 2023.
21. @realDonaldTrump, Truth Social, April 5, 2023.
22. @DonaldTrumpJr, Twitter, April 7, 2023.
23. Jonah E. Bromwich, "Trump Criminal Trial Scheduled for March 2024," *New York Times*, March 23, 2023.
24. William A. Tidwell, James O. Hall, and David Winfred Gaddy, *Come Retribution: The Confederate Secret Service and the Assassination of Lincoln* (Oxford: University Press of Mississippi, 1988).
25. @realDonaldTrump, Truth Social, August 4, 2023.

CHAPTER TWO: DARK DAYS AT MAR-A-LAGO

1. Sean Spicer, *Radical Nation* (West Palm Beach: Humanix Books, 2021).
2. Jake Tapper, "Former White House Chief of Staff Tells Friends That Trump 'Is the Most Flawed Person' He's Ever Met," CNN, October 16, 2020.
3. Spicer, *Radical Nation*.
4. Gideon Welles, *Diary of Gideon Welles: Secretary of the Navy Under Lincoln and Johnson*, vol. 3 (Boston: Houghton Mifflin, 1911).
5. @realDonaldTrump, Twitter, January 8, 2021.
6. "Permanent Suspension of @realDonaldTrump," Twitter Inc., blog post, January 8, 2021.
7. Jonathan Karl, *Betrayal: The Final Act of the Trump Show* (New York: Dutton, 2021).
8. Karl, *Betrayal*.
9. Will Steakin, "Trump Told RNC Chair He Was Leaving GOP to Create New Party, Says New Book," ABC News, November 8, 2021.
10. *Donald J. Trump for President v. Secretary Commonwealth of Pennsylvania*, 20-3371 (3rd Cir. 2020).
11. Jeff Amy, "Georgia Governor Again Rejects Lawmakers Replacing Electors," Associated Press, December 6, 2020.

12. Rob Crilly, "Trump Travel Pool Reports of January 20, 2021."
13. "Donald Trump x Nelk Boys," *Full Send Podcast*, March 9, 2022.
14. Alexander Burns and Jonathan Martin, "'I've Had It With This Guy': G.O.P. Leaders Privately Blasted Trump After Jan. 6," *New York Times*, April 21, 2022.
15. Andrew Restuccia, "Trump Has Discussed Starting a New Political Party," *Wall Street Journal*, January 19, 2021.

THE GRIM REAPER

1. Olivia Nuzzi, "Inside the Breitbart Embassy, Where Steve Bannon Entertains Elites and Plots His Populist Takeover," *New York Magazine*, November 15, 2017.
2. Michael Wolff, "Ringside with Steve Bannon at Trump Tower as the President-Elect's Strategist Plots 'an Entirely New Political Movement,'" *Hollywood Reporter*, November 18, 2016.
3. Anthony Zurcher, "Trump's 'Brain' Steve Bannon Emerges from the Shadows," BBC, February 24, 2017.
4. David Von Drehle, "Is Steve Bannon the Second Most Powerful Man in the World?," *Time*, February 2, 2017.
5. "Oval Office Cold Open," *Saturday Night Live*, February 5, 2017.
6. Michael Wolff, *Fire and Fury: Inside the Trump White House* (New York: Henry Holt and Co., 2018).
7. @realDonaldTrump, Twitter, January 4, 2018.
8. "Read Trump's Reaction to Steve Bannon's Comments," *New York Times*, January 3, 2018.
9. Mike Allen, "Exclusive: Bannon Apologizes," *Axios*, January 7, 2018.
10. @realDonaldTrump, Twitter, August 2, 2019.
11. Dan Friedman, "Leaked Audio: Before Election Day, Bannon Said Trump Planned to Falsely Claim Victory," *Mother Jones*, July 12, 2022.
12. Hearing on the January 6th Investigation: Hearing Before the Select Committee to Investigate the January 6th Attack on the United States Capitol, House of Representatives, 117th Congress, July 12, 2022 (hereafter cited as January 6 Committee).
13. Wolff, "Ringside with Steve Bannon at Trump Tower."
14. Steve Bannon, "Exclusive Sit Down with President Donald J. Trump," *War Room: Pandemic*, April 29, 2023.

CHAPTER THREE: THE CHOKER

1. Dan Katz, "Text messages reveal Texas Rep. Chip Roy encouraged an overturn of the 2020 election and then warned against it," Texas Public Radio, April 15, 2022.
2. Select Committee to Investigate the January 6th Attack on the United States Capitol, Continued Interview of Robert Engel (March 4 and November 17, 2022).
3. Donald Trump, interview with the author, March 18, 2021.
4. Transcribed interview of Pasquale Anthony "Pat" Cipollone before the January 6 Committee, July 8, 2022.

5. Deposition of General Mark A. Milley before the January 6 Committee, November 17, 2021, transcript, p. 83.
6. https://media-cdn.factba.se/realdonaldtrump-twitter/134690043454024 0897.jpg
7. Eddie Burkhalter, "Tuberville Says He Attended Jan. 5 Fundraiser at Trump's Washington Hotel," Alabama Political Reporter, February 19, 2021.
8. "Mitch McConnell Speech Transcript After Vote to Acquit Trump in 2nd Impeachment Trial," Congressional Record, February 13, 2021.
9. Testimony of Sarah Matthews before the January 6 Committee, July 12, 2022.
10. Testimony of Cassidy Hutchinson before the January 6 Committee, June 28, 2022.
11. Deposition of Judson P. Deere before the January 6 Committee, March 3, 2022.
12. Transcribed interview of Pasquale Anthony "Pat" Cipollone to the January 6 Committee, July 8, 2022.
13. Hope Hicks, interview with the author, October 31, 2022.
14. Testimony of Sarah Matthews before the January 6 Committee, July 21, 2022.
15. US House of Representatives, Final Report of the Select Committee to Investigate the January 6th Attack on the United States Capitol, 117th Congress (Washington, DC: US Government Publishing Office, December 22, 2022), (hereafter cited as Final Report).
16. Deposition of Keith Kellogg Jr. before the January 6 Committee, December 14, 2021.
17. Testimony of Cassidy Hutchinson before the January 6 Committee, June 28, 2022.
18. Testimony of Sarah Matthews before the January 6 Committee, July 12, 2022.
19. Deposition of Nicholas Luna before the January 6 Committee, March 21, 2022.
20. Deposition of John McEntee before the January 6 Committee, March 28, 2022.
21. Transcribed interview of Ivanka Trump before the January 6 Committee, April 5, 2022.
22. @jonkarl, Twitter, January 9, 2021.
23. @PressSec45, Twitter, January 9, 2021.
24. @jonkarl, Twitter, January 9, 2021.
25. *Testimony of Matthew Pottinger before the January 6 Committee, July 21, 2022.

CHAPTER FOUR: THE CRAZY FACTOR

1. @realDonaldTrump, Truth Social, February 21, 2023.
2. Richard Greene, "Is Donald Trump Mentally Ill? 3 Professors of Psychiatry Ask President Obama to Conduct 'a Full Medical and Neuropsychiatric Evaluation,'" Huffington Post, December 17, 2016.
3. "Duty to Warn," conference, Yale School of Medicine, April 20, 2017.
4. "Goldwater Rule," American Psychiatry Association Newsroom.
5. Ross Douthat, "The 25th Amendment Solution for Removing Trump," New York Times, May 16, 2017.
6. @realDonaldTrump, Twitter, September 14, 2019.
7. Chris Wallace interview, Fox News, Sunday, July 19, 2020.

8. Tanya Lewis, "The 'Shared Psychosis' of Donald Trump and His Loyalists: Forensic Psychiatrist Bandy X. Lee Explains the Outgoing President's Pathological Appeal and How to Wean People from It," *Scientific American*, January 11, 2021.

9. Allen Frances, "We Must Not Confuse Trump's Bad Behavior with Mental Illness," *BMJ Opinion*, August 25, 2017.

10. Mick Mulvaney, *A First-Rate Madness: Uncovering the Links Between Leadership and Mental Illness* (New York: Penguin Books, 2012).

11. Jonathan Karl, *Front Row at the Trump Show* (New York: Dutton, 2020).

12. Amanda Macias, "'I Can't Stay Here'—Mick Mulvaney Resigns from Trump Administration, Expects Others to Follow," CNBC, January 7, 2021.

13. @SecElaineChao, Twitter, January 7, 2021.

14. Ingrid Jacques, "Betsy DeVos: Trump's Actions on Jan. 6 Were 'Line in the Sand' That Led to Resignation," *USA Today*, June 22, 2022.

15. Transcribed interview of Mike Pompeo before the January 6 Committee, August 9, 2022.

16. Transcribed interview of General Mark A. Milley before the January 6 Committee, November 17, 2021.

17. Transcribed interview of Steven Mnuchin before the January 6 Committee July 18, 2022.

18. Transcribed interview of Steven Mnuchin before the January 6 Committee, July 18, 2022.

19. Aamer Madhani, "At DC Roast, NH's GOP Governor Skewers Trump as 'Crazy,'" Associated Press, April 3, 2022.

CHAPTER FIVE: TEAM OF SYCOPHANTS

1. @realDonaldTrump, Twitter, June 5, 2018.

2. Michael S. Schmidt and Maggie Haberman, "Trump Humiliated Jeff Sessions After Mueller Appointment," *New York Times*, September 14, 2017.

3. Donald Trump interview with Hill TV, September 19, 2018.

4. Bob Woodward, *Fear: Trump in the White House* (New York: Simon & Schuster, 2018).

5. Maggie Haberman, *Confidence Man* (New York: Penguin Press, 2022).

6. Jeff Sessions, interview with the author, December 21, 2022.

7. Jeff Sessions, interview with the author, December 21, 2022.

8. Jeff Sessions, interview with the author, December 21, 2022.

9. Woodward, *Fear*.

10. Carol E. Lee, Kristen Welker, Stephanie Ruhle, and Dafna Linzer, "Tillerson's Fury at Trump Required an Intervention from Pence," NBC News, October 4, 2017. Notably, Tillerson never denied saying this. When Bob Schieffer asked him about the report in an interview after he left office, Tillerson essentially confirmed the sentiment, saying, "It was challenging for me, coming from the disciplined, highly process-oriented ExxonMobil corporation, to go to work for a man who is pretty undisciplined, doesn't like to read, doesn't read briefing reports, doesn't like to get into the details of a lot of things, but rather just kind of says, 'This is what I believe.'"

11. @realDonaldTrump, Twitter, December 7, 2018.

12. @realDonaldTrump, Twitter, February 13, 2020.

13. Michael S. Schmidt, *Donald Trump v. the United States: Inside the Struggle to Stop a President* (New York: Random House, 2020).

14. Jake Tapper, "Former White House Chief of Staff Tells Friends That Trump 'Is the Most Flawed Person' He's Ever Met," October 16, 2020.

15. Dexter Filkins, "John Bolton on the Warpath," *New Yorker*, April 29, 2019.

16. Zachary Evans, "GOP Rep. Furious After Syria Envoy Boasts His Team Fooled Trump," *National Review*, November 13, 2020.

17. Katie Bo Williams, "Outgoing Syria Envoy Admits Hiding US Troop Numbers; Praises Trump's Mideast Record," *Defense One*, November 12, 2020.

18. Hope Hicks text, quoted in US House of Representatives, *Final Report*.

19. Corey Lewandowski and David Bossie, *Let Trump Be Trump: The Inside Story of His Rise to the Presidency* (New York: Center Street, 2017).

20. Nicholas Fandos, "Hope Hicks Acknowledges She Sometimes Tells White Lies for Trump," *New York Times*, February 27, 2018.

21. Transcribed interview with Hope Hicks before the January 6 Committee, October 25, 2022.

"ONLY ONE"

1. François Clemenceau, "Macron at the JDD: 'My Handshake with Trump Is Not Innocent,'" *Le Journal du Dimanche*, May 27, 2017.

2. Guy Snodgrass, *Holding the Line: Inside Trump's Pentagon with Secretary Snodgrass* (New York: Sentinel, 2019).

3. Jill Lawless, "Trump Calls Trudeau 'Two-Faced' as Palace Gossip Goes Viral," Associated Press, December 4, 2019.

4. Hans von der Burchard, "Merkel Laughs Off Suggestion That She Was Charmed by Trump," *Politico*, August 28, 2020.

CHAPTER SIX: TRUMP'S ESSENTIAL MAN

1. Jonathan D. Karl, "The Man Who Made January 6 Possible," *The Atlantic*, November 9, 2021.

2. "The Conservative Case for Weaponizing the Lawyers (Feat. Andrew Kloster)," *Moment of Truth* podcast, November 21, 2021.

3. Karl, *Betrayal*.

4. Jonathan Swan and Zachary Basu, "Off the Rails: Trump's War with His Generals," *Axios*, May 16, 2021.

5. Deposition of John McEntee before the January 6 Committee, March 28, 2022.

6. Deposition of John McEntee before the January 6 Committee, March 28, 2022, transcript, p. 46.

7. Transcribed interview of Douglas Macgregor before the January 6 Committee, June 7, 2022.

8. Transcribed interview of General Mark A. Milley before the January 6 Committee, November 17, 2021.

9. Deposition of Keith Kellogg Jr. before the January 6 Committee, December 14, 2021.

10. Transcribed interview of Robert O'Brien before the January 6 Committee, August 23, 2022.
11. Deposition of John McEntee before the January 6 Committee, March 28, 2022, transcript.
12. January 6 Committee exhibit #P-R000236 (2021-076).
13. John McEntee note and drafted analysis, National Archives Production, P-R000236-000238, January 6 Committee Final Report and Supporting Materials Collection.
14. John McEntee, "I Was Trump's Aide, Now I Run a Conservative Dating App— He Loved the Idea," *Newsweek*, September 6, 2022.

MARTIAL LAW

1. Solange Reyner, "Michael Flynn to Newsmax TV: Trump Has Options to Secure Integrity of 2020 Election," *Newsmax*, December 17, 2020.
2. Interview of Ryan McCarthy before the January 6 Committee, February 4, 2022.
3. Interview of General James Charles McConville before the January 6 Committee, November 4, 2021.
4. John McEntee note and drafted analysis, National Archives Production, P-R000236-000238, January 6 Committee Final Report and Supporting Materials Collection.
5. Interview of Ryan McCarthy before the January 6 Committee, February 4, 2022.
6. @realDonaldTrump, Twitter, December 19, 2020.

CHAPTER SEVEN: "FIX IT NOW!"

1. Luke Broadwater and Shane Goldmacher, "House Republican Says Trump Asked Him to Illegally 'Rescind' 2020 Election," *New York Times*, March 23, 2022.
2. @RepMoBrooks, Twitter, August 21, 2021.
3. Tina Nguyen and Meredith McGraw, "Trump's Blog Failed, Bigly. His Next Online Venture Won't Be Any Easier," *Politico*, June 2, 2021.
4. @RSBNetwork, Twitter, June 22, 2021.
5. Keith Kloor, "Pirates and Warlords Aside, Michele Ballarin Believes She Can Turn Somalia Around," *Washington Post*, October 4, 2013.
6. Karl, *Betrayal*.
7. Shayan Sardarizadeh, "Why Are QAnon Believers Obsessed With 4 March?," BBC, March 4, 2021.
8. Dianne Marshall, "Trump Ode to the Corporation!," *Marshall Report*, January 20, 2021.
9. Zachary Cohen and Ellie Kaufman, "Nearly 5,000 National Guard Troops to Remain in Washington Through Mid-March Due to Concerns About QAnon Chatter," CNN, February 17, 2021.
10. Cheryl Teh, "MyPillow's Mike Lindell Claims Trump Will 'Be Back in Office in August' in Steve Bannon Podcast Rant," *Business Insider*, March 29, 2021.
11. Cheryl Teh, "MyPillow's Mike Lindell Claims Trump Will 'Be Back in Office in August' in Steve Bannon Podcast Rant."
12. @JennaEllisEsq, Twitter, May 30, 2021.

13. Colby Hall, "Lara Trump Pours Cold Water on Trump's 'Reinstatement' Report: 'Maybe There's Something I Don't Know?'" *Mediaite*, June 3, 2021.

14. Alia Shoaib, "Marjorie Taylor Greene Admits Trump Won't Be Reinstated in the White House in August," *Business Insider*, July 8, 2021.

15. @MaggieNYT, Twitter, June 1, 2021.

16. Will Sommer and Asawin Suebsaeng, "MyPillow Guy Says He 'Probably' Inspired Trump's Idea of an August Restoration," *Daily Beast*, June 3, 2021.

17. Charles C.W. Cooke, "Maggie Haberman Is Right," *National Review*, June 3, 2021.

18. Charles C.W. Cooke, "Maggie Haberman Is Right."

19. Steve Bannon, "The Smoking Howitzer," *War Room: Pandemic*, episode 994, June 2, 2021.

20. Mia Jankowicz, "Mike Lindell Set August 13 as the Date in His Bonkers Theory That Trump Will Be Reinstated as President," *Business Insider*, July 6, 2021.

21. @ErrataRob, Twitter, August 10, 2021.

22. Joseph Clark, "Exclusive: Cyber Expert Says His Team Can't Prove Mike Lindell's Claims That China Hacked Election," *Washington Times*, August 11, 2021.

23. Zachary Petrizzo, "Mike Lindell Moves the 'Reinstatement' Goalposts Again—Now Trump Will Be Back by Thanksgiving," *Salon*, September 23, 2021.

24. Jerod MacDonald-Evoy, "GOP legislators spread debunked claims at Lindell's 'Cyber Symposium,'" *Arizona Mirror*, August 12, 2021.

25. Mike Lindell on the *War Room: Pandemic*, March 29, 2023.

CHAPTER EIGHT: RAZING ARIZONA

1. "Donald Trump Rails on Biden During Wedding Speech at Mar-a-Lago," *TMZ*, March 28, 2021.

2. @MysterySolvent, Twitter, April 30, 2021.

3. Sarah Mimms, "Pro-Trump OAN Reporters Are Blatantly Raising Money for a Bogus Election 'Audit' in Arizona," *BuzzFeed News*, May 18, 2021.

4. Christina Bobb, "Weekly Briefing," One America News, May 2, 2021.

5. Caleb Howe, "Trump Demands State Police or National Guard 'Be Immediately Sent' for Arizona Audit: 'Ducey Will Be Held Fully Responsible,'" *Mediaite*, April 24, 2021.

6. @MysterySolvent, Twitter, April 30, 2021.

7. Arizona State Senate Republican Caucus, "Arizona Senate Hires Auditor to Review 2020 Election in Maricopa County," press release, March 31, 2021.

8. Brad Poole, "Arizona a 'Blue' State Now That Biden Won? Not Likely, Experts Say," *Courthouse News Service*, November 23, 2020.

9. "Joe Biden Will Win Arizona: AG Mark Brnovich," *Your World with Neil Cavuto*, Fox Business, November 11, 2020.

10. Stephen Richer, "The Madness of the Maricopa County Election Audit," *National Review*, May 27, 2021.

11. Nicholas Riccardi, "Experts or 'Grifters'? Little-Known Firm Runs Arizona Audit," Associated Press, May 23, 2021.

NOTES

12. Jeremy Duda, "Election Auditor Wrote 'Election Fraud Facts' Report for GOP Senators Who Tried to Overturn the 2020 Election," *Arizona Mirror*, April 9, 2021.

13. Mary Jo Pitzl, "How the Price Tag of the Arizona Senate's Review of the 2020 Election Grew from $150K to More Than $4M," *Arizona Republic*, February 23, 2022.

14. Garrett Archer, "New Records Show Cyber Ninjas Audit Had $9 Million Price Tag," ABC 15 Arizona, November 1, 2021.

15. Mary Jo Pitzl, "A/C Units, Rent-a-Cops and Legal Fees: Taxpayers Pick Up $425,000 in Audit Costs, with More Coming," *Arizona Republic*, September 3, 2021.

16. Lacey Latch and Mary Jo Pitzl, "Maricopa County Will Spend Millions to Replace Voting Machines Turned Over to the Arizona Senate for Audit," *Arizona Republic*, July 14, 2021.

17. Jonathan Cooper, "Trump Supporters Raise $5.7M for Arizona Election Audit," Associated Press, July 29, 2021.

18. Michael Wines, "Arizona Vote Review Is 'Political Theater' and 'Sham,' G.O.P. Leaders Say," *New York Times*, May 17, 2021.

19. Interview with the author, March 13, 2023.

20. @dennis_welch, Twitter, May 5, 2021.

21. Jonathan Cooper and Bob Christie, "Inside Arizona's Election Audit, GOP Fraud Fantasies Live On," Associated Press, May 10, 2021.

22. "Statement by Donald J. Trump, 45th President of the United States of America," April 23, 2021.

23. Jennifer Morrell, "I Watched the GOP's Arizona Election Audit. It Was Worse Than You Think," *Washington Post*, May 19, 2021.

24. Letter from Principal Deputy Assistant Attorney General Pamela S. Karlan to the Honorable Karen Fann, May 5, 2021.

25. Robert Anglen, "Ex-Lawmaker Who Rallied for 'Stop the Steal' Removed from Arizona Audit," *Arizona Republic*, May 14, 2021.

26. Donald Trump, "Former President Trump Remarks at Turning Point Action Student Action Summit," C-SPAN, July 24, 2021.

27. Jack Healey, Michael Wines, and Nick Corasaniti, "Republican Review of Arizona Vote Fails to Show Stolen Election," *New York Times*, September 24, 2021.

28. Healey, Wines, and Corasaniti, "Republican Review of Arizona Vote Fails to Show Stolen Election."

29. "Statement by Donald J. Trump, 45th President of the United States of America," September 24, 2021.

30. David Gilbert, "QAnon Is Spreading a Fake Version of the Arizona Audit That Says Trump Won," *Vice*, September 29, 2021.

31. Wayne Schutsky, "Pullen: Draft Audit Report Calling for Decertification of Election a Fake," *Arizona Capitol Times*, September 27, 2021.

32. Joe Oltmann and Max McGuire, "Part 2: CyberNinjas CEO Answers Tough Questions About Maricopa Audit," *Conservative Daily Podcast*, October 7, 2021.

33. "Correcting the Record: Maricopa County's In-Depth Analysis of the Senate Inquiry," Maricopa County Elections Department, January 2022.
34. "Statement by Donald J. Trump, 45th President of the United States of America," April 18, 2022.

THE CLUB CHAMP

1. Philip Bump, "Trump's Presidency Ends Where So Much of It Was Spent: A Trump Organization Property," *Washington Post*, January 20, 2021.
2. Donald Trump speech, Charleston, South Carolina, February 19, 2016.
3. Donald Trump speech, Ashburn, Virginia, August 8, 2016.
4. Donald Trump speech, Hickory, North Carolina, March 14, 2016.
5. Philip Bump, "Trump's Presidency Ends Where So Much of It Was Spent: A Trump Organization Property."
6. @realDonaldTrump, Truth Social, January 23, 2023.
7. @realDonaldTrump, Truth Social, January 23, 2023.
8. Rob Crilly, "The Holes in Trump's Golf Win Story: Members of His Club Surprised—but Not Shocked—He Managed to Win Championship Despite Spending the First Day at Diamond's Funeral," *Daily Mail*, January 23, 2023.
9. Rick Reilly, *Commander in Cheat: How Golf Explains Trump* (New York: Hachette Books, 2019).

CHAPTER NINE: THE BIGGEST LOSER

1. Sydney Kalich and Markie Martin, "Trump: My Endorsements Made Ron DeSantis," NewsNation, November 9, 2022.
2. Brittany Gibson, "Voters Appear Ready to Blame Democrats for Economy, Inflation," *Politico*, November 7, 2022.
3. Nathaniel Rakich, "Final Forecast: Republicans Are Favored to Win the House," *FiveThirtyEight*, November 8, 2022.
4. Brooke Singman, "Midterms: Cruz Predicts 'Not Just a Red Wave, but a Red Tsunami' for Republicans on Election Day," Fox News, November 7, 2022.
5. @mschlapp, Twitter, November 8, 2022.
6. @DonaldJTrumpJr, Twitter, November 8, 2022.
7. @realDonaldTrump, Truth Social, November 10, 2022.
8. Jill Colvin, "Trump Faces Blame from GOP as He Moves Forward with WH Bid," Associated Press, November 10, 2022.
9. Interview with the author on *This Week*, ABC News, November 20, 2022.
10. Erin Burnett, "Retiring Senator Partly Blames Trump's Endorsement for 'Epic' Loss in Governor's Race," CNN, November 10, 2022.
11. "Biden Begins Presidency with Positive Ratings; Trump Departs with Lowest-Ever Job Mark," *Pew Research Center*, January 15, 2021.
12. "Bridgewater CEO McCormick on Markets, Politics, and Polarization," The Year Ahead, Bloomberg, January 26, 2021.
13. Alex Leary and Lindsay Wise, "Trump Says McCarthy Relationship Not Damaged," *Wall Street Journal*, April 22, 2022.
14. Tom McGrath, "Podcast: Senate Co-Frontrunner Dave McCormick Opens Up," *PoliticsPA*, podcast, April 3, 2022.

15. 2022 General Primary Statewide Returns, Pennsylvania Department of State, May 17, 2022.
16. Aaron Blake, "Kari Lake's Loss Is the Biggest 2022 Blow to MAGA Yet," *Washington Post*, November 15, 2022.
17. @MarkFinchem, Twitter, January 6, 2021.
18. Ovetta Wiggins and Erin Cox, "Hogan Calls GOP Gubernatorial Nominee Mentally Unstable," *Washington Post*, August 18, 2022.
19. Jim Brunner, "Congressional Candidate Joe Kent Wants to Rewrite History of Jan. 6 Attack," *Seattle Times*, November 4, 2022.
20. "Tracking Congress in the Age of Trump: Jaime Herrera Beutler," *FiveThirtyEight*, January 13, 2021.
21. Andrew Kaczynski, "Trump's Pick to Head Office of Personnel Management Spread 'Satanic' Conspiracy Theory, Called Democrats Party of 'Islam' and 'Gender-Bending,'" CNN, July 22, 2020.
22. Patrick Marley, "Democrats Face Blowback After Boosting Far-Right Michigan Candidate," *Washington Post*, August 3, 2022.
23. Tucker Carlson, "The Candidate: Blake Masters," *Fox Nation*, October 25, 2022.
24. Justin Baragona, "Blake Masters Tells Fox News He Still Believes Trump Won in 2020," *Daily Beast*, October 12, 2022.
25. Alana Goodman, "Camper Recounts Abuse at Warnock Church Camp," *Washington Free Beacon*, December 28, 2020.
26. "Bad Politics, Bad Policies: Election Denial in 2023," States United Democracy Center, April 28, 2023.
27. Nate Cohn, "Trump's Drag on Republicans Quantified: A Five-Point Penalty," *New York Times*, November 16, 2023.
28. Philip Wallach, "We Can Now Quantify Trump's Sabotage of the GOP's House Dreams," *Washington Post*, November 15, 2022.

CHAPTER TEN: SPEAKER TRUMP

1. 169 *Cong. Rec.* H46 (daily ed. January 6, 2023).
2. @realDonaldTrump, Truth Social, June 4, 2022.
3. Jake Sherman, "The McCarthy Machine's 2022 Total: $500 Million," *Punchbowl News*, November 7, 2022.
4. Jonathan Martin, Alexander Burns, and Neil Vigdor, "McCarthy Said Trump Acknowledged 'Some Responsibility' for Jan. 6," *New York Times*, April 22, 2022.
5. Alex Leary and Lindsay Wise, "Trump Says McCarthy Relationship Not Damaged," *Wall Street Journal*, April 22, 2022.
6. Michael Katz, "Rep. Andy Biggs to Newsmax: I'm Challenging McCarthy for Speaker," *Newsmax*, November 14, 2022.
7. Alayna Treene and Andrew Solender, "5 House Conservatives Plan to Vote as Unit on McCarthy's Speaker Bid," *Axios*, December 15, 2022.
8. "Matt Gaetz: I'm NOT Voting McCarthy for House Speaker," *The Charlie Kirk Show*, November 14, 2022.
9. Alexander Burns and Jonathan Martin, "McCarthy Feared G.O.P. Lawmakers Put 'People in Jeopardy' After Jan. 6," *New York Times*, April 26, 2022.

10. Matthew Boyle, "Exclusive—Trump Backs McCarthy for Speaker, Tells Opponents to Stand Down: 'I Think He Deserves the Shot,'" *Breitbart*, December 16, 2022.

11. @realDonaldTrump, Truth Social, January 4, 2023.

12. @realDonaldTrump, Truth Social, January 4, 2023.

13. @mattgaetz, Twitter, January 4, 2023.

14. Madeline Peltz, "House Speaker Trump? A Brief History of the Idea," *Media Matters*, June 8, 2021.

15. @DC_Draino, Twitter, January 20, 2021.

16. Steve Bannon and Rogan O'Handley, *War Room: Pandemic*, January 21, 2023.

17. Madeline Peltz, "House Speaker Trump? A Brief History of the Idea."

18. Joshua Zitser, "Trump on Idea to Run for House Seat in 2022 in a Bid to Become Speaker and Launch an Impeachment Inquiry Against Biden: 'It's Very Interesting,'" *Insider*, June 5, 2021.

19. @donlemon, Twitter, January 5, 2023.

20. Aaron Flint, "Montana Rep Explains Why He Didn't Take Trump's Phone Call," *Montana Talks*, January 10, 2023.

21. @realDonaldTrump, Truth Social, January 7, 2023.

22. Will Steakin, Katherine Faulders, and Lauren Peller, "Some GOP McCarthy Holdouts Scoff at Claims Trump Swayed Speaker Vote Outcome," ABC News, January 13, 2023.

23. Steakin, Faulders, and Peller, "Some GOP McCarthy Holdouts Scoff at Claims Trump Swayed Speaker Vote Outcome," January 13, 2023.

24. *Tucker Carlson Tonight*, Fox News, January 3, 2023.

25. *Tucker Carlson Tonight*, Fox News, March 6, 2023.

26. Sarah Ferris, Olivia Beavers and Kyle Cheney, "House GOP Faces a New Jan. 6 Headache, Courtesy of Tucker Carlson," *Politico*, March 7, 2023.

"NOW IT'S THE TALLEST"

1. Michael Kruse, "What Trump and Clinton Did on 9/11," *Politico*, September 10, 2016.

2. Timothy Bella, "Trump, in Otherwise Somber Interview on 9/11, Couldn't Help Touting One of His Buildings," *Washington Post*, September 11, 2018.

3. Amy Sherman, "Donald Trump Says He Spent a Lot Time with 9/11 Responders. Here Are the Facts," *PolitiFact*, July 30, 2019.

4. Brett Bachman, "'Where Is Trump?' Former President Notably Absent from 9/11 Events," *Salon*, September 11, 2021.

5. Jon Levine, Joe Marino, Larry Celona, and Tina Moore, "Trump Makes Surprise Visit to New York Police and Firefighters on 9/11," *New York Post*, September 11, 2021.

CHAPTER ELEVEN: THE BEGINNING OF THE END

1. @realDonaldTrump, Truth Social, December 14, 2022.

2. @realDonaldTrump, Truth Social, December 15, 2022.

3. Kevin Breuninger, "Trump Made a Bundle of Cash Selling NFTs, Financial Filings Show," CNBC, April 14, 2023.

4. Nikki McCann Ramirez, "'I Can't Watch This': Even Die-Hard Trump Allies Think His NFTs Are Cringe," *Rolling Stone*, December 16, 2022.

5. @bakedalaska, Twitter, December 15, 2022.

6. Anna Merlan, "Watch the Disturbing Kanye Interview Clips That Tucker Carlson Didn't Put on Air," *Vice*, October 11, 2022.

7. Lisette Voytko, "Billionaire No More: Kanye West's Antisemitism Obliterates His Net Worth as Adidas Cuts Ties," *Forbes*, October 25, 2022.

8. Marc Caputo, "The Inside Story of Trump's Explosive Dinner with Ye and Nick Fuentes," NBC News, November 29, 2022.

9. @DavidM_Friedman, Twitter, November 25, 2022.

10. Olivia Nuzzi, "The Final Campaign: Inside Donald Trump's Sad, Lonely, Thirsty, Broken, Basically Pretend Run for Reelection. (Which Isn't to Say He Can't Win.)," *New York Magazine*, December 23, 2022.

11. Caputo, "The Inside Story of Trump's Explosive Dinner with Ye and Nick Fuentes."

12. Andrew Kaczynski, "David Duke Urges His Supporters to Volunteer and Vote for Trump," *BuzzFeed News*, February 25, 2016.

13. Jake Tapper, *State of the Union*, CNN, February 28, 2016.

14. Glenn Kessler, "Donald Trump and David Duke: For the Record," *Washington Post*, March 1, 2016.

15. @realDonaldTrump, Truth Social, December 3, 2022.

16. Margaret Brennan, *Face the Nation*, CBS News, December 4, 2022.

17. Alexander Bolton, "McConnell: Trump Would Have Hard Time Becoming President Given Constitution Comments," *The Hill*, December 6, 2022.

18. Meghan MacPherson, "Trump's Call to Suspend Constitution Not a 2024 Deal-Breaker, Leading House Republican Says," ABC News, December 4, 2022.

19. @realDonaldTrump, Truth Social, December 5, 2022.

20. Olivia Rubin, Will Steakin, and Katherine Faulders, "Trump Hosts Event Featuring QAnon, 'Pizzagate' Conspiracy Theorist at Mar-a-Lago," ABC News, December 7, 2022.

21. Elizabeth Williamson, "Donald Trump Fires a Troll," *New York Times*, December 7, 2016.

22. "A Statement from the Pulitzer Prize Board," Pulitzer Prizes, July 18, 2022.

23. *President Donald J. Trump v. Members of the Pulitzer Prize Board*, Complaint, December 13, 2022.

24. *Donald J. Trump v. Hillary R. Clinton, et al.*, Order on Sanctions, January 19, 2023.

25. US House of Representatives, *Final Report*, p. 770.

26. Caitlin Oprysko, "Trump on Russia Dispute: 'Ultimately I'm Always Right,'" *Politico*, June 12, 2019.

27. "Episode 1: Do You Miss Me Yet? A Tell-All with President Donald J. Trump," *The Truth with Lisa Boothe*, March 22, 2021.

28. Quint Forgey, "Trump Says Debt Ceiling Can't Be a Bargaining Chip. That's Not What He Said in 2012," *Politico*, July 19, 2019.

29. "Transcript of CNN's Town Hall with Former President Donald Trump," CNN, May 10, 2023.

30. Julia Shapero, "Barr: Trump Will Deliver 'Chaos' and 'Horror Show,'" *The Hill*, May 5, 2023.
31. @AdamSchefter, Twitter, January 11, 2021.
32. Anthony Salvanto, Kabir Khanna, Fred Backus, and Jennifer De Pinto, "CBS News Poll: After Trump Indictment, Most See Security Risk, but Republicans See Politics," CBS News, June 11, 2023.
33. Anderson Cooper, "CNN Republican Presidential Town Hall with Chris Christie," CNN, June 12, 2023.
34. Jake Tapper, "CNN Republican Presidential Town Hall with Nikki Haley," CNN, June 4, 2023.
35. Nathaniel Cary, "Tim Scott Calls Trump Indictment 'Serious' but Claims Biden Is Hunting Republicans," *Post and Courier*, June 12, 2023.
36. Ben Shapiro, "DeSantis Blasts Trump's 'Bizarre' Attacks During Shapiro Interview: 'He's Been Attacking Me by Moving Left,'" *Daily Wire*, May 26, 2023.
37. @CostaReports, Twitter, June 7, 2023.

CHAPTER TWELVE: DEFENDANT #1,090

1. @realDonaldTrump, Truth Social, June 12, 2023.
2. @realDonaldTrump, Truth Social, June 13, 2023.
3. Betsy Woodruff Swan, "Trump's Save America Paid $3 Million to Cover Top Lawyer's Legal Work," *Politico*, September 15, 2022.
4. *United States of America v. Donald J. Trump and Waltine Nauta*, June 8, 2023.
5. "Chinese Woman Who Intruded at Mar-a-Lago Sentenced to Six Months," Reuters, February 14, 2020.
6. Olivia Olander, "Trump: I Could Declassify Documents by Thinking About It," *Politico*, September 21, 2022.
7. Graeme Wood, "Not Even the President Can Declassify Nuclear Secrets," *The Atlantic*, August 12, 2022.
8. @realDonaldTrump, Truth Social, June 8, 2023.
9. @RepJimBanks, Twitter, June 8, 2023.
10. @MarcoRubio, Twitter, June 8, 2023.
11. @SpeakerMcCarthy, Twitter, June 8, 2023.
12. Analisa Novak, "Sen. Marco Rubio: Trump's Indictment Is 'Political in Nature,' Will Bring More 'Harm' to the Country," CBS News, June 12, 2023.
13. "Rubio Comments on Hillary Clinton's Mishandling of Classified Information," press release, July 5, 2016.
14. @GovChristie, Twitter, June 8, 2023.
15. "CNN Republican Presidential Town Hall with Chris Christie," CNN, June 12, 2023.
16. Anders Hagstrom, "Bill Barr Says Trump's Indictment Is 'Very Damning' if 'Even Half of It Is True,'" Fox News, June 11, 2023.

CONCLUSION

1. "Senate Chamber Desks, Overview," United States Senate.
2. John F. Kennedy, *Profiles in Courage* (1956).

NOTES

3. Interview with Russell "Rusty" Bowers before the January 6 Committee, June 19, 2022.
4. Tom Rice, interview with the author, June 2022.
5. Benjamin Siegel, Jonathan Karl, and Meghan Mistry, "GOP Rep. Tom Rice Says Impeaching Trump Was 'the Conservative Vote,'" ABC News, June 5, 2022.

INDEX

INDEX

INDEX

INDEX

INDEX

INDEX

ABOUT THE AUTHOR

Jonathan Karl is the chief Washington correspondent for ABC News and co-anchor of *This Week*. The former president of the White House Correspondents' Association, Karl has reported from the White House under four presidents and fourteen press secretaries. He has covered every major beat in Washington, D.C., and has won several of the most prestigious awards in journalism. His previous books *Front Row at the Trump Show* and *Betrayal* were instant *New York Times* bestsellers.